Doing Phonetics

An Introduction to English and General Phonetics

Doing Phonetics

An Introduction to English and General Phonetics

John Stonham
PUKYONG NATIONAL UNIVERSITY

KYUNG MOON Publishers

Doing Phonetics

An Introduction to English and General Phonetics

ISBN 978-89-6105-515-4

KM KYUNG MOON Publishers

174 Wausan-ro Mapo-gu Seoul, Korea
Tel: (82) 2 332 2004
Fax: (82) 2 336 5193

Printed in Korea

Price: ₩ 18,000

For

Eun-Sook

Contents

List of Tables

Preface

This book is the result of my 20 years experience teaching phonetics all over the world, but more specifically, from the past few years teaching in Korea. It is intended to be a general introduction to phonetics for beginning students and has been written specifically with the Korean undergraduate student in mind. Examples are mainly from English, with some from Korean for comparison, depending on the topic being studied. Furthermore, additional clarifications of specific points are provided at various points in the text where I felt that they might be of use or interest.

There are many introductory phonetics textbooks out there, and all of them have their strengths and weaknesses. Some are too advanced, some are too elementary, some are just too long to fit into a single semester. I hope that this book will suit the specific needs of students here in Korea in their study of this interesting but sometimes difficult subject.

I welcome feedback from anyone who notices errors or oversights in the book and I will acknowledge anyone who gives me such feedback. To provide further information concerning errors found in the text, as well as any updates or further information, a website will be established at http://stonham.dyndns.org/phonetics_textbook. This will be updated as new information becomes available.

There are many people I would like to acknowledge at this point. First, I would like to thank all the students who have given me feedback on earlier versions of the manuscript, in particular, Sylvia Minhee Park, who provided detailed comments on an earlier draft of this book and Donghoon Shin and Kyoung-muk You who pointed out several typos. In addition, I would like to thank Mr. Dong Hyun Lee and Ms. Hyo-soon Oh of Kyung Moon Publishing for all their help with bringing this book to completion.

Finally, and most importantly, I thank my wife and research collaborator, Eun-Sook Kim, who has provided support of all kinds, linguistic, academic, and emotional and has put up with all my annoying habits both while writing this book and in all other domains.

John Stonham
Pukyong National University

Abbreviations

asp.	aspirated
ATR	Advanced Tongue Root
BTM	basic tone melody
C	consonant
Ch.	Chapter
cps	cycles per second
dB	decibel
G	glide
Gen	genitive case
Hz	Hertz/cycles per second
imperf.	imperfective aspect
IP	intonational phrase
IPA	International Phonetic Alphabet
L	liquid
m/sec	meters per second
ms	millisecond
N	nasal
Nom	nominative case
O	obstruent
perf.	perfective aspect
pl.	plural
p.p.	past participle

PW	phonological word
R	rhyme
RP	Received Pronunciation
s/sec	second
sg.	singular
V	vowel
vd.	voiced
vl.	voiceless
§	e.g., §14.5.4 = Chapter 14, Section 5, subsection 4
μ	mora
σ	syllable
Φ	foot
→	'becomes'
<	'comes from'

Part I

General Phonetics

Chapter 1

Introduction

1.1 Scope and Format

The format of this book is intended to lead the reader from a general understanding of the basic, surface-level facts of acoustic phonetics, to a more in-depth understanding of the complexities of sound systems. Focus begins with a brief introduction to speech anatomy and physiology, which sets the groundwork for the study of phonetics. We then move on to a discussion of the tools employed in phonetic analysis, including an introduction to the software available for phonetic analysis.

The presentation of acoustic and instrumental phonetics is intended to move gradually from a general exposition of the field in Part I, to a discussion of general phonetic practice in Part II, to a more detailed examination of English phonetics in Part III. The aim is to provide the reader with an appreciation of the complexities of sound systems and the motivation for alternative methods of representation of sounds, the limitations on human speech production, and the nature of various features of sound systems.

After an introduction to the field, we will move on, in Part II, to the examination of the properties of speech sounds in general, beginning with vowels. We then move on to discuss the nature of consonants and, finally, to the examination of prosodic features of language.

Once a basic understanding of the acoustic properties of sounds has been attained, we move on to the study of English sounds in Part III. This begins with a study of English vowels, followed by the obstruents and then the sonorant consonants. There is frequent cross-reference to earlier discussion of sounds. After that, we proceed to the analysis of English stress assignment. We discuss some of the ways to analyze and describe these phenomena, using the tools we have already acquired.

Along the way, additional information is introduced where necessary. The eventual goal will be to understand the nature of phonetics and its use in understanding language sound systems. Throughout the text, exercises are provided in order to allow the students to have some practice in actually *doing* phonetics. It is extremely important for students to gain experience in phonetic analysis by examining data and considering possible analyses. Furthermore, additional readings are suggested at the end of chapters for students to extend or solidify their understanding of the issues discussed in the chapter.

Framed boxes are provided at various points in the text for the discussion of tangential issues and areas of further interest. These may be skipped over or may be employed for special discussion or more detailed study.

1.2 Readership

This book is intended for the beginning phonetics student, either undergraduate or graduate. As such, it assumes only a rudimentary knowledge of linguistics as one might acquire in a general introductory course on the subject. Every effort will be made to avoid introducing concepts which depend on prior knowledge of other areas of linguistics, but this may sometimes prove difficult or impossible. In such cases, I will try to provide the bare minimal amount of information necessary to appreciate the point without going deeply into the allied field. This will necessarily leave the reader with questions and the further readings will be useful here for the interested reader.

By the end of this text students should expect to be able to move on to reading original literature in the different areas of phonetics and to interpreting the various issues in phonetic theory.

Most phonetics textbooks make use of data from many different languages, mostly unknown to the student. While this is often necessary in order to illustrate certain phenomena that do not exist in English, it can be rather intimidating for the student. Where the students are bilingual, in this case in Korean and English, we already have two languages to work with, and so it is ideal for comparing and contrasting phonetic phenomena. The focus will be on data from English and Korean, although there may be a few contexts where another language is better suited to making a point, at which point it will be introduced.

1.3 Software and Equipment

To gain the greatest benefit from the discussion in this book, it will be helpful for the student to obtain some additional tools for the study of phonetics. In this text, I introduce several pieces of accessible and affordable software that are readily available on the Internet. There are many excellent software programs that are useful for performing phonetics-related tasks and the software discussed here is not the only possible choice or even necessarily the best, but it is a good and reliable tool with which a student can learn to do acoustic analysis at a minimum cost. If students learn how to use these, they will be prepared to use other, similar types of software applications. Details of the software to be used are provided in §3.2.2.

Obviously, the student will also need access to a computer. If it is a public computer, it may be more difficult to install software and to listen to sound files, so it is best to gain access to a computer that is readily available. It doesn't have to be an expensive one—a basic model should be sufficient for the tasks in this book. In addition to a computer, headphones and a microphone will be useful at various times for recording and listening to sounds. More discussion of the type of equipment necessary will be provided in §3.2.

1.4 Data Sources

In this textbook, there are a number of exercises involving the use of recorded data. In some cases, the instructor may provide appropriate materials in a suitable format. In other cases, the student may be asked to make recordings for analysis.

An additional, valuable source of data are the various databases and sound archives that are available on the Internet. I will provide references to some of these at various points in the book, but the instructor and the students should also pursue their own investigation of available materials. The Internet is a very useful source of information, but it is also very volatile and sources change constantly. Therefore, the best approach is probably to search for materials using keywords such as 'sound archive,' 'dialect survey,' 'English audio files,' etc.

1.5 Terminology and Notation

In addition to this strategy of employing both English and Korean data to explain phonetic principles, I will also try to provide Korean glosses of terminology upon first sight in the text and a glossary of technical terms at the end of the book to ensure that students become familiar with this terminology.

In a subject like phonetics there are necessarily many notational conventions and an abundance of technical terms for describing issues within the field. However, phonetics is not, and should not be, about terminology or notation, but rather should be concerned with the nature of sound systems, and so every effort has been made to minimize the amount of technical jargon as far as possible. Emphasis will be placed upon understanding the concepts and applying them to new problems in order to train the student in the principles of the subject.

I have provided cross-references throughout the text, indicated by reference to Chapter, as Ch., or Chapter and Section, as §, followed by the number of the chapter, section, subsection, etc., e.g. §15.1.2.3 indicates 'Chapter 15, Section 1, Subsection 2, Subsubsection 3.'

An index is provided at the end of the book so that the reader may refer to the location of terms with which they may be unfamiliar. This will allow the student to refer back to the definition of a concept when meeting it again later in their reading. All references are included in the Bibliography, including those for the **Further Readings** section at the end of each chapter.

1.6 A Special Note on the Transcription of Korean

In transcribing Korean forms, I have used a system which is as close to phonetic transcription as possible, so that students may become accustomed to phonetic transcription as opposed to romanization. This approach has necessitated a few concessions to phonetic accuracy in places. Below I provide a table of the symbols used and their Hangul equivalents.[1]

ㅂ	p	ㅃ	p’	ㅍ	p^h	ㅁ	m
ㄷ	t	ㄸ	t’	ㅌ	t^h	ㄴ	n
ㄱ	k	ㄲ	k’	ㅋ	k^h	ㅇ	Ø/ŋ
ㅈ	c	ㅉ	c’	ㅊ	c^h	ㄹ	l
ㅅ	s	ㅆ	s’	ㅎ	h		
ㅓ	ɔ	ㅏ	a	ㅗ	o	ㅜ	u
ㅡ	ɨ	ㅣ	i	ㅔ	e	ㅐ	æ
ㆍ	ɑ						

More complex structures make use of the same symbols in various combinations. Note that, in some contexts, phonetic representations that are closer to the actual pronunciation have been employed to make the relevant point.

[1] Arae a (ㆍ) is included here because of its use in Middle Korean and in the Cheju dialect. ㅇ has two alternate, context-dependent values: at the beginning of the syllable it is Ø, and at the end of the syllable it is a velar nasal, [ŋ].

1.7 A Final Word

Phonetics is a notoriously difficult subject for students, since it involves rather more reliance on scientific principles and practice than most subjects in the Arts. Nevertheless, I believe, and I have seen through my own experience, that students are able to learn the concepts and techniques of phonetics, as long as they commit themselves to the subject and do the work necessary for developing their understanding. There are also many benefits to be gained from learning the basics of how the human speech system works. Besides a better personal understanding of how humans communicate, there are a number of fields where a knowledge of phonetics is important, some of which are discussed in more detail in Ch. 4 on the applications of phonetics.

Part of the student's commitment to this course is to practice doing the exercises and various tasks assigned by the instructor. Phonetics must be *done*; it cannot be simply read about in a book: you can only learn the subject properly by doing actual analyses of data in order to be able to fully understand the principles underlying this subject.

Chapter 2

Speech Anatomy and Physiology

In order to understand the nature of sound systems, it is important to first understand the apparatus employed to produce and recognize the sounds. In the case of a stereo system or television the components are electronic and mechanical. In the case of human speech production, the same holds true, but the electronics in this case may be better described as *neural*, that is, related to the electrical signals sent by the human brain as instructions to perform various mechanical tasks that involve certain elements of human anatomy and physiology.

In what follows, the emphasis will be placed on only those aspects of human anatomy and physiology that relate directly to speech sounds.

2.1 Speech-related Properties

One question we may wish to ask is how phonetics is related to human anatomy and physiology. What aspects of the human physical make-up are used in producing sounds and speech and how are they employed?

One thing to note is that, for the most part, the sound-generating aspects of human anatomy share the physical system with other functions: air movement in the lungs, shut off valves as protective devices for the lungs, windpipe/*trachea* (기관), and *esophagus* (식도) as channels for the passage of air and nutrients respectively, tongue and teeth for the ingestion of food, etc. Speech can be seen as a secondary system, dependent on anatomy originally intended for more basic functions. Because of this secondary status of the speech apparatus, there are limitations on the kinds of sounds possible due to the anatomical and physiological constraints on the system. Thus, the various kinds of sounds found in languages and the distinctions that can be made, such as voicing, glottalization, aspiration, etc. can all be viewed as due to mechanisms intended to serve other functions.

In what follows we will examine each part of the human sound production system in greater detail.

2.2 Speech Production

The speech or vocal tract, which is responsible for the production of speech sounds, may be divided into three regions, beginning with the source of air movement and moving upwards and outwards: i) the ***subglottal component***, involving all the anatomy and physiology below the *larynx* or *glottis*; ii) the ***laryngeal component***; and iii) the ***supralaryngeal component***, the area above the larynx. In the following, we will examine each of these components in some detail.

2.2.1 The Subglottal Component

The subglottal component consists of those aspects of the anatomical and physiological system responsible for the intake and output of air, i.e., the *diaphragm* (횡격막), lungs and associated musculature. The primary function here is to provide a supply of oxygen as a source of fuel to the bloodstream and eventually the entire body. The lungs act as a bellows (풀무) which draws in fresh, oxygenated air and expels the by-products of the system after processing. The diaphragm, in conjunction with various muscles of the chest and abdomen, provides the mechanical means to expand and contract the lungs.

Figure 2.1 illustrates the gross anatomy of the subglottal region, showing the diaphragm, lungs, trachea and the larynx, the key elements of this region related to speech. The more detailed aspects of this process will not be explored here as they are not relevant to the linguistic description of sound production.

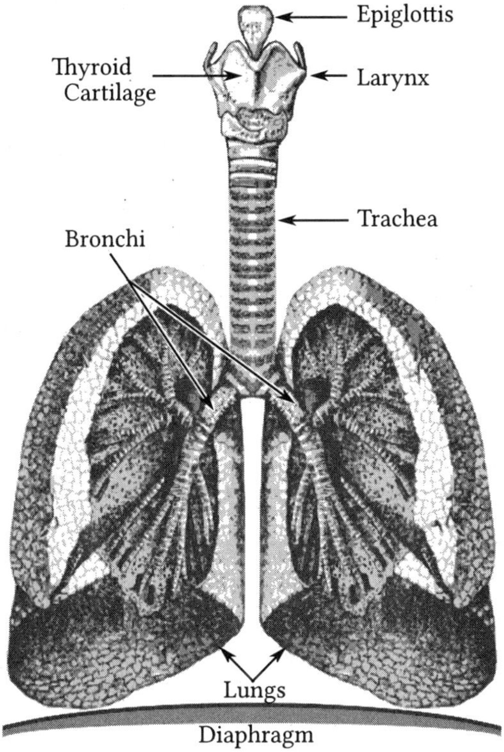

Figure 2.1 The subglottal region (adapted fr. Gray, 1918: 1086)

The diaphragm controls the expansion and contraction of the lungs by using muscular action to raise and lower the diaphragm. Gray (1918: 404) describes the diaphragm as:

> a dome-shaped musculofibrous septum which separates the thoracic from the abdominal cavity, its convex upper surface forming

> the floor of the former, and its concave under surface the roof of the latter. Its peripheral part consists of muscular fibers which take origin from the circumference of the thoracic outlet and converge to be inserted into a central tendon.

Basically, the diaphragm is a large band of tissue shaped like a dome, with muscles attached under the lungs that can raise or lower to push the lungs in or out, resulting in their contraction or expansion, as illustrated in Figs 2.2 and 2.3.

The lungs are connected to the rest of the respiratory system via tubes called *bronchi* (기관지) which are, in turn, connected to the trachea and thereby to the larynx, which controls the flow of air in (inhalation) and out (exhalation) of the respiratory system.[1]

The primary task of the lungs is the exchange of oxygen, accomplished by inhaling oxygenated air from outside, extracting the oxygen, relaying it to the bloodstream, and expelling the by-products of the process, mostly CO_2 (Carbon dioxide) via exhalation.

Air movement is effected by raising and lowering the diaphragm and contracting various chest and abdominal muscles, producing a result much like a *bellows* or *air pump*, as illudstrated in Fig. 2.2 for the inhalation phase and Fig. 2.3 for exhalation.

Naturally, in performing this task, air may be moved in a more or less forceful manner depending on the demands and realized by the amount of force applied by the diaphragm and the contraction of the muscles of the chest. The regulation of this movement of air is accomplished by the use of a certain type of valve, referred to as the larynx, which constitutes the laryngeal component of the system.

2.2.2 The Laryngeal Component

The second component of the vocal tract consists of the larynx and its associated structures. This structure is responsible for the control of airflow between the lungs and the supralaryngeal component.

[1] See *Airstream mechanism* in §6.1.

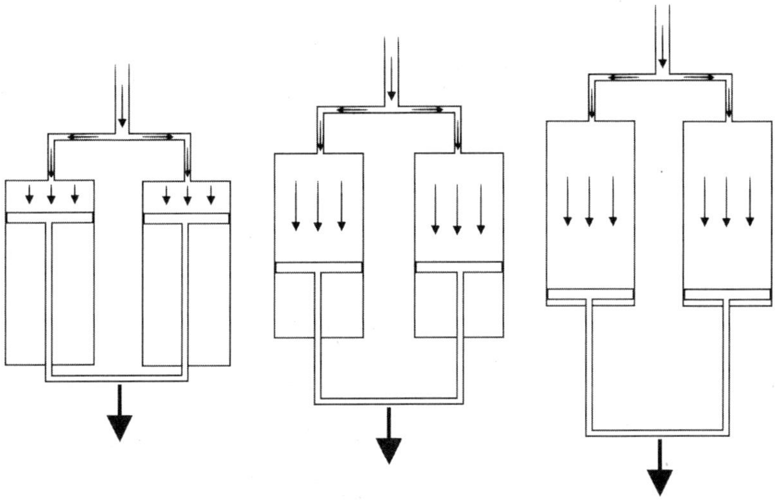

Figure 2.2 Inhalation: lowering the diaphragm

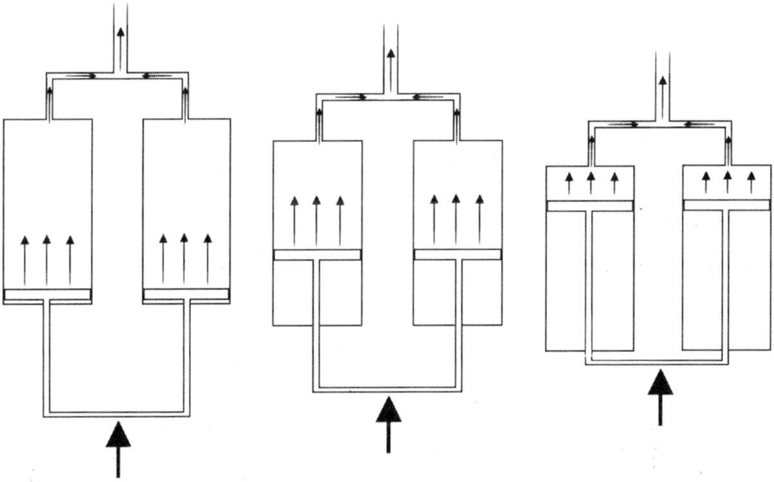

Figure 2.3 Exhalation: raising the diaphragm

2.2.2.1 The Larynx

The larynx, sometimes referred to as the *voice box*, is a structure made up of several distinct cartilages (연골; thyroid, cricoid, arytenoid) connected by muscle and ligaments (인대). The structure actually 'hangs' from the skeleton via the *hyoid* bone (설골), as shown in Fig. 2.4.

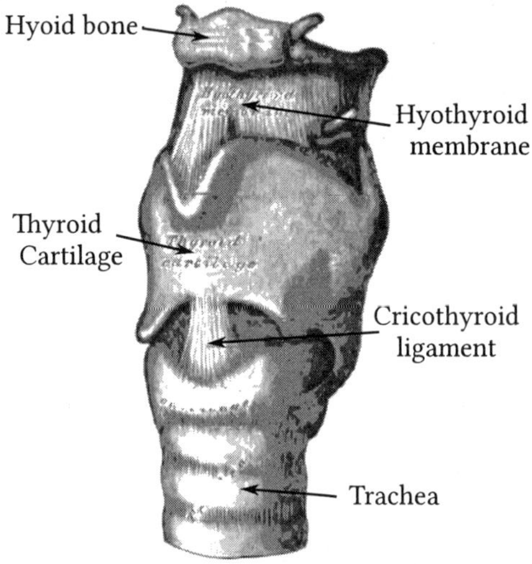

Figure 2.4 The larynx (fr. Gray, 1918:1295)

The internal structure of the larynx will be important for understanding the various processes involved in *phonation*, the process of modifying the quality of sounds by altering the operation of the vocal cords. Fig. 2.5 shows the various parts of the larynx as viewed from above and Fig. 2.6 provides an exploded view of the various cartilages that make up the larynx.

Gender Differences There are gender-based differences in the shape of the larynx, resulting in a greater amount of protrusion of the *Adam's Apple* in the male. This is the result of the more acute (~90°) angle of the male's thyroid cartilage, compared to the more oblique (~120°) angle of the female's, as indicated in Figure 2.7.

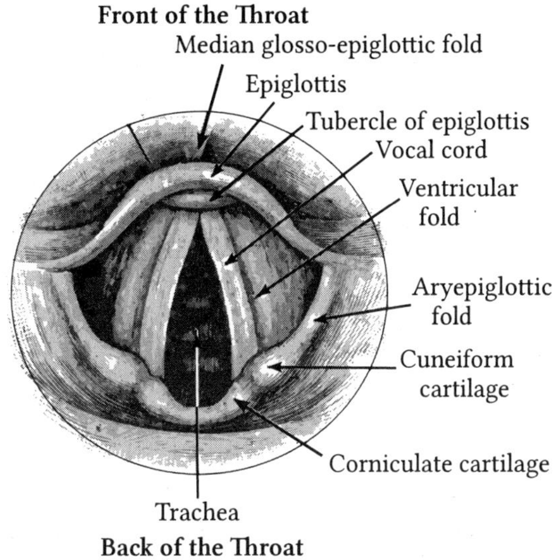

Figure 2.5 The larynx from above (fr. Gray, 1918:1298)

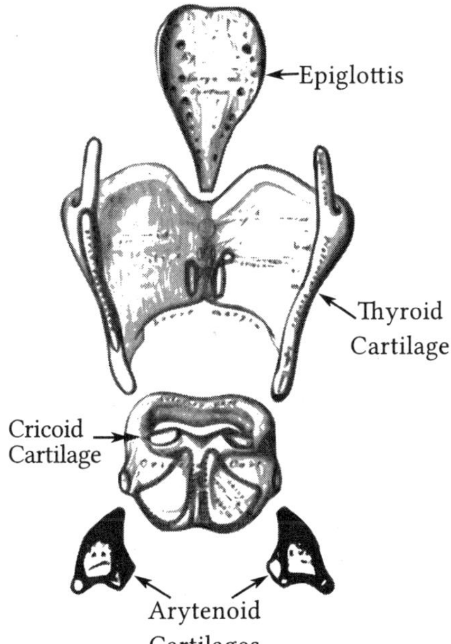

Figure 2.6 The parts of the larynx (fr. Gray, 1918:1076)

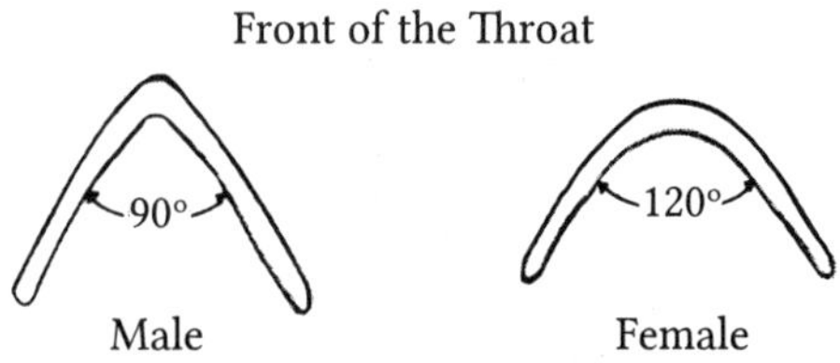

Figure 2.7 Gender differences in the thyroid cartilage

2.2.2.2 Laryngeal Action

The primary task of the cartilages which form the structure of the larynx is to act as a supporting frame for the vocal cords.[2] These vocal cords, sometimes referred to as *vocal folds*, consist of bands of ligamentous (인대의) tissue which can be spread apart ('abducted') or squeezed together ('adducted') by the movement of the arytenoid cartilages, two pyramid-shaped processes attached to the cricoid cartilage (Fig. 2.8).

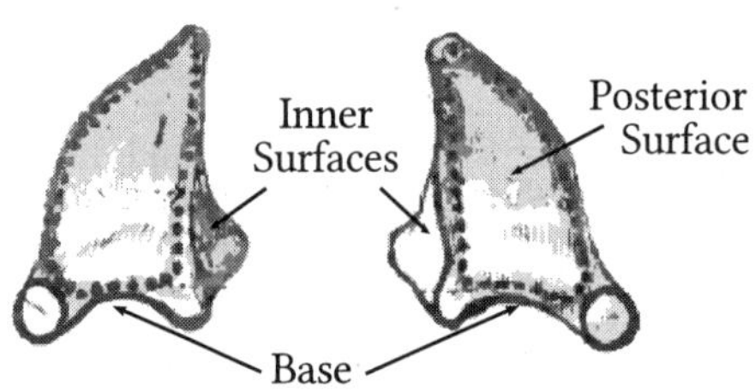

Figure 2.8 The arytenoid cartilages (fr. Gray, 1918:1074)

When these arytenoid cartilages are rotated on their axis, they open or close the vocal cords. Figure 2.9 shows the cords in an open position, permitting the free flow of air associated with respiration. The gap between the vocal cords is referred to as the *glottis* (성문). If the vocal cords are held wide apart and without vibration, the passage of air is easier and the resultant sound will be voiceless.

In Fig. 2.10, the arytenoid cartilages are rotated inward, causing the vocal cords to adduct, cutting off the flow of air. When the vocal cords

---

[2] For a more in-depth discussion of phonation types, refer to §6.2.

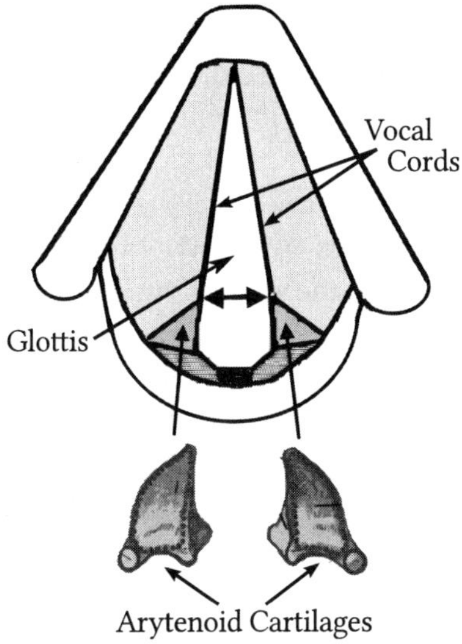

Figure 2.9 Vocal cords in an open position

are brought together in this manner, and the flow of air from the lungs passes over them, then they will vibrate, creating a voiced sound.

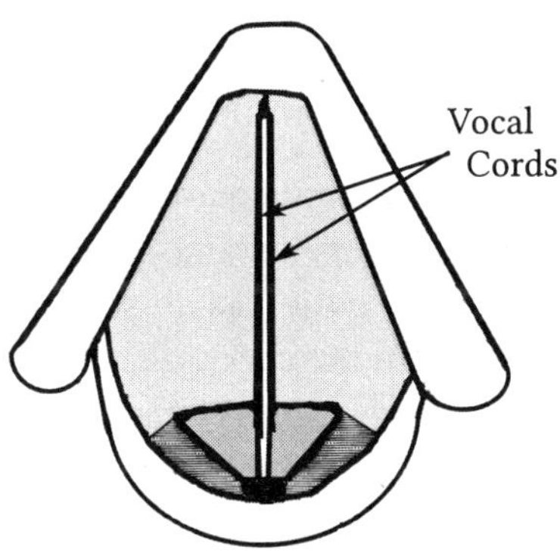

Figure 2.10 Vocal cords in a closed position

In between these two possibilities, there are a number of intermediary stages: a narrow space between the vocal cords, but no vibration, will produce a whisper; if the cords are completely closed, temporarily stopping the flow of air, then the result will be glottalization or glottal closure; if the cords are held open and are allowed to vibrate, as in voicing, then this will produce what is commonly called *breathy voice*; if the cords are moved closer together and kept vibrating, then the result will be laryngealization or *creaky voice.*

These various possibilities are presented in Table 2.1, where **Lax** and **Tight** refer to the tension of the vocal cords and **Open**, **Partly Open**, and **Closed** refer to the gap between the vocal cords. For further discussion of the various manipulations of the vocal cords, see §6.2 on the states of the glottis.

	Lax	**Tight**
Open	Breathy Voice	Voiceless
Partly Open	Voiced	Whisper
Closed	Laryngealization (Creaky Voice)	Glottalization

Table 2.1 States of the vocal cords

2.2.3 The Supralaryngeal Component

The supralaryngeal or supraglottal component consists of those regions of the vocal tract above the larynx, and includes the structures of the pharyngeal, oral, and nasal cavities, as illustrated in Fig. 2.11. These are the areas most responsible for the variation in sounds encountered in the languages of the world.

We will examine each of these regions of the supraglottal component individually in the following sections, focusing on the structures which are relevant to speech.

2.2.3.1 Pharynx

The pharynx (인두) is basically a tube which relays air from the larynx upward and outward to the two other cavities, the oral and the nasal. It

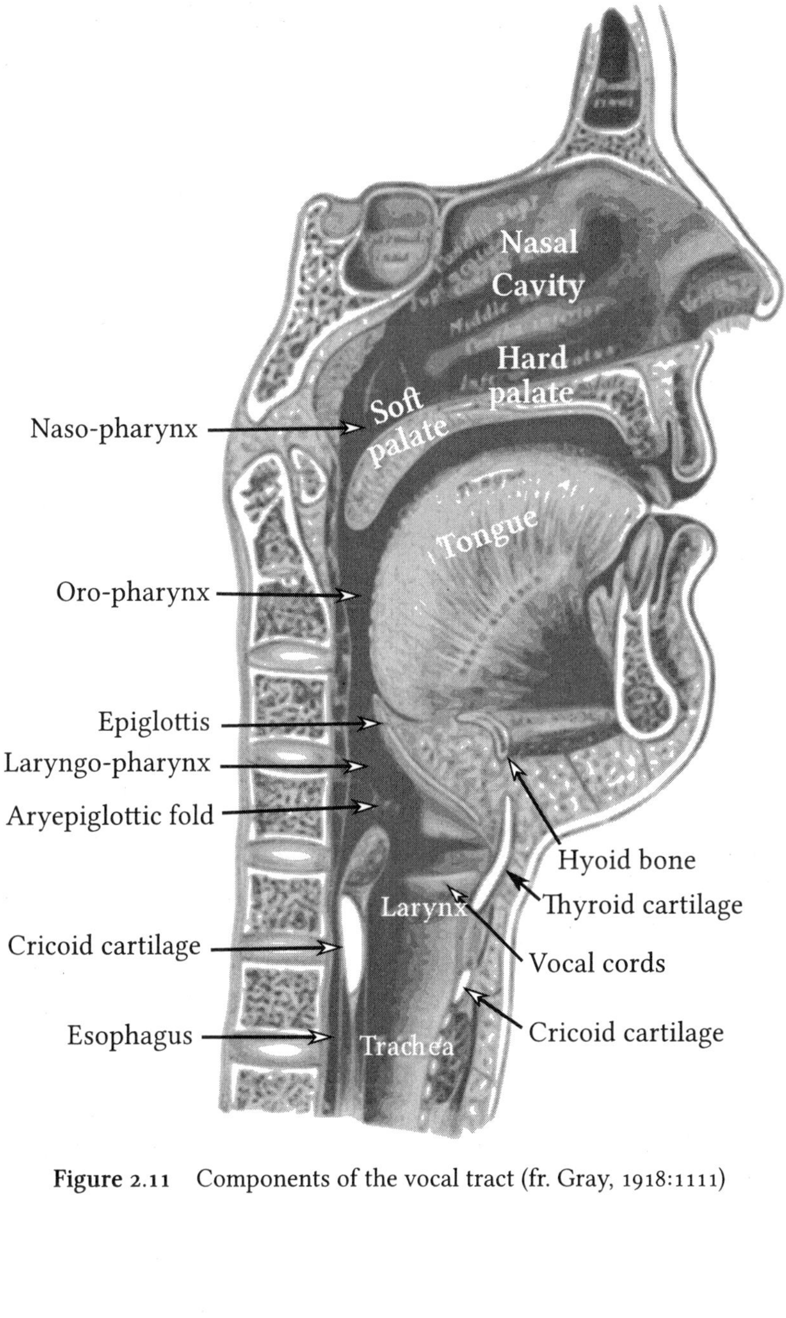

Figure 2.11 Components of the vocal tract (fr. Gray, 1918:1111)

may be divided into three separate parts: i) the ***laryngo-pharynx***, ii) the ***oro-pharynx***, and iii) the ***naso-pharynx***, based on their location in the vocal tract, as shown in Fig. 2.12.

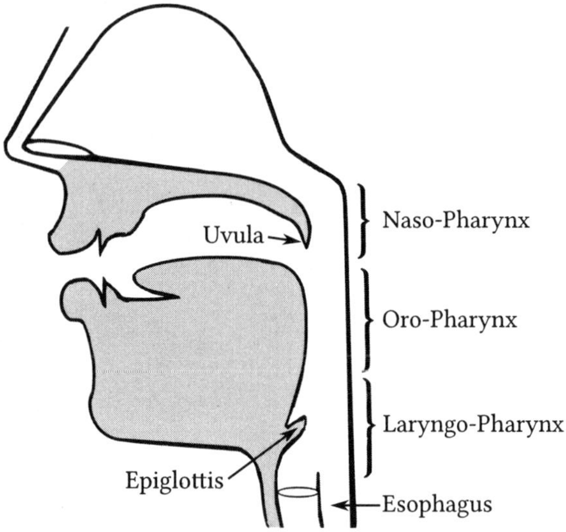

Figure 2.12 The pharynx

The laryngo-pharynx constitutes the lower portion of the pharynx from the larynx to the *epiglottis* (후두개). It also connects the throat to the esophagus, which passes food and liquids to the stomach. One non-linguistic purpose of the epiglottis is to prevent food or liquid from entering the larynx unexpectedly, which could result in choking.

The oro-pharynx occupies the mid position in the pharynx, extending from the *uvula* (목젖) down to the epiglottis. It provides a point of contact for the retraction of the tongue root in certain sounds described as *pharyngeal.*

The naso-pharynx is the upper portion of the pharynx that connects the nasal cavity with the oral cavity and the lower part of the vocal tract via the velo-pharyngeal port (Fig. 2.13). It is in this area that distinctions of oral versus nasal are made.

2.2.3.2 Nasal Cavity

The nasal cavity (비강) is a chamber connected on one end to the pharynx via the velo-pharyngeal port and on the other end to the outside via the nostrils. Air may pass through either the mouth or the nose or both, as illustrated in Figure 2.13. In order for air to pass through the nose, the *velum* must be lowered, thereby opening the velo-pharyngeal port.

Any sound produced by passing air through the nasal cavity will have a certain nasal timbre (비음색) or quality to it, and this may be used as a contrastive linguistic marker. Such sounds are referred to as *nasal* or *nasalized.*

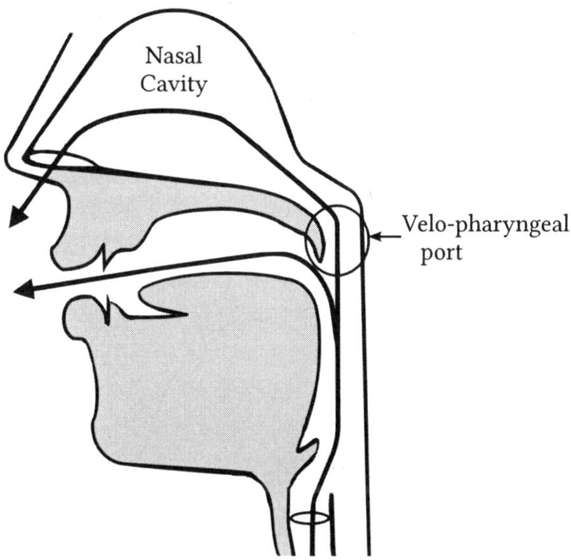

Figure 2.13 The nasal cavity

The process of passing the sound wave through the nasal cavity is referred to as *nasalization* (비음화). Nasalization may affect either consonants or vowels. Other than this process, the nasal cavity plays no role in the linguistic phonetic process.

2.2.3.3 Oral Cavity

If the nasal cavity is sealed off by the raising of the velum, then the air will pass strictly through the oral cavity (구강). Within the oral cavity there are a number of structures, presented in Fig. 2.14, which participate in the production of sounds of various types.

Starting from the pharynx and moving toward the lips, the first structure encountered is the *uvula*. The uvula is the appendage of muscle/flexible tissue/skin which hangs down from the velum at the back of the mouth. It has no clear physiological function, although some believe its function to be to distribute moisture around the pharynx (Back et al., 2004). Phonetically, it may act as a point of contact for the tongue in certain articulatory gestures.

The *soft palate* or *velum* (연구개) is basically a muscle covered in a mucous membrane whose principle function is to close off the nasal cavity at the velo-pharyngeal port (cf. Fig. 2.13). Just as with the uvula, it may also serve as a contact point for the tongue. In front of the velum is the *hard palate* (경구개), also informally referred to as the 'roof of the mouth'. It is the bony area at the top of the oral cavity that separates the nasal and oral cavities and acts as a contact point for the tongue.

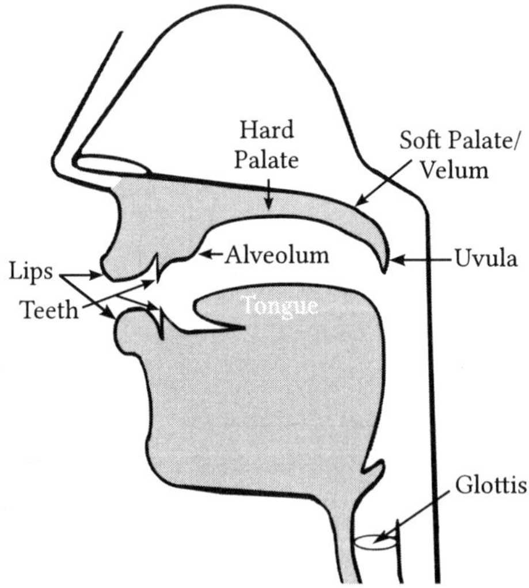

Figure 2.14 The oral cavity

Beyond the hard palate moving forward in the mouth is the *alveolum* or *alveolar ridge* (치경), which is the area above and behind the teeth. Beyond this are the teeth themselves. The physiological function of the teeth is quite straightforward, assisting people in the tearing and mashing of food. Linguistically, dental sounds are made by making contact with the teeth, either with the tongue or with the lower lip.

This brings us to the final structure located in the oral cavity, or perhaps better, at the end of the oral cavity, i.e., the lips. The function of the lips is straightforward and includes the use of labial articulations: sounds made at the front of mouth.

2.2.3.4 The Tongue

The final part of the anatomy to play a role in the sound system is arguably also one of the most important: the tongue. The tongue is basically a mass of muscle which can be constricted and stretched as any other muscle. It consists of several parts: (i) the tip or *apex* of the tongue (설첨; the adjective is *apical*); (ii) the tongue blade, sometimes referred to as the *lamina* (설단; the adjective is *laminal*); (iii) the tongue body (often called the *dorsum*, adjective *dorsal*); and (iv) the root of the tongue (설근; adjective: *radical*). These are illustrated in Fig. 2.15.

The manipulation of the tongue alters the shape of the vocal tract, allowing modification of the airflow, which has a direct effect on the quality of the sound. This results in differences in the sounds produced, as the volume and shape of the vocal tract changes, which is an important factor in producing a wide range of different sounds.

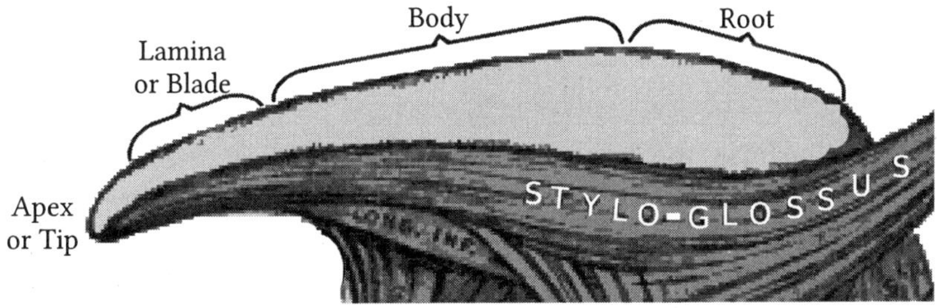

Figure 2.15 The parts of the tongue

2.2.3.5 Active versus Passive Articulators

The combination of tongue with various other parts of the oral cavity has led to a need for a way to categorize the articulators in terms of active versus passive, as demonstrated in Table 2.2. This classification may be employed to fine-tune the description of how a sound is made, e.g., *apico-dental* means 'using the tip of the tongue to touch the teeth.' This may be useful in languages where such differences exist or where one wishes to be precise about the nature of a sound.

Active	Passive
lower lip	upper lip
apex (tongue tip)	teeth
lamina (tongue blade)	alveolar ridge
dorsum (tonguc body)	hard palate
tongue root	velum
etc.	

Table 2.2 Types of articulators

The majority of the articulators are passive, that is, they do not move but simply act as a point of contact for the active articulators.

2.3 Hearing

We now move on to the other end of the speech chain, i.e., the part responsible for receiving and processing the speech signal: the ear and its associated elements.

2.3.1 Anatomy of the Ear

Fig. 2.16 illustrates the basic anatomical structure of the ear, and in particular the parts that are relevant for capturing the acoustic signal. These include the external ear, sometimes referred to as the *pinna*, the eardrum (*tympanic membrane*) (고막), the bone chain of the inner ear, the *cochlea* (달팽이관), and the nerves that pass the signal to the brain.

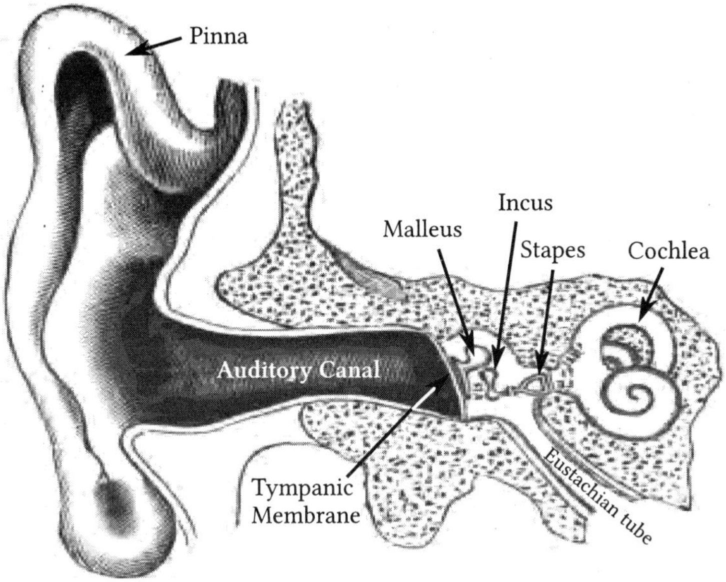

Figure 2.16 The anatomy of the ear (adapt. fr. Hall, 1911:228)

Each one of these elements plays an important role in the hearing process. The external ear is responsible for capturing the sound waves, and more especially for detecting the direction of the signal as it approaches the hearer. The ear canal is responsible for conducting sounds to the eardrum. The resulting vibration is subsequently transferred to a series of bones in the middle ear that relay the signal, from bone to bone and, finally, to the cochlea. The cochlea converts the physical signal from the bones of the ear to an electric signal, and then the connected nerves pass the electric signal to the brain.

How the brain interprets the signal goes beyond what we are studying here, but is clearly a very important aspect of the entire process.

2.3.2 The Hearing Process

The process of hearing involves sound waves traveling from some source to the external ear, which then funnels the sound waves into the ear canal, via the outer ear, until they strike the *tympanic membrane* or eardrum, located at the end of the ear canal. The *auditory canal* relays the acoustic signal or sound wave from outside the ear to the eardrum, much like the striking of a drum causes a series of vibrations of its covering, which produce a particular sound.

When the sound waves contact the ear drum, the vibration they create is then relayed from the tympanic membrane to the *organ of Corti*, part of the cochlea (Fig. 2.17). This organ contains cochlear fluids that process the sound waves, converting them to a signal that can be relayed to the brain.

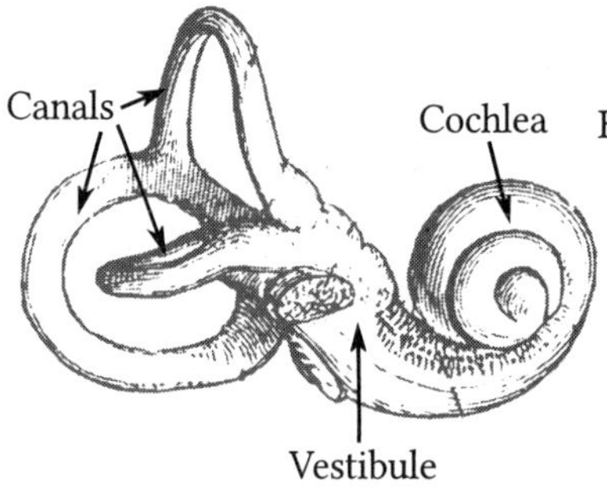

Figure 2.17 The cochlea (fr. Gavarret, 1877: 433)

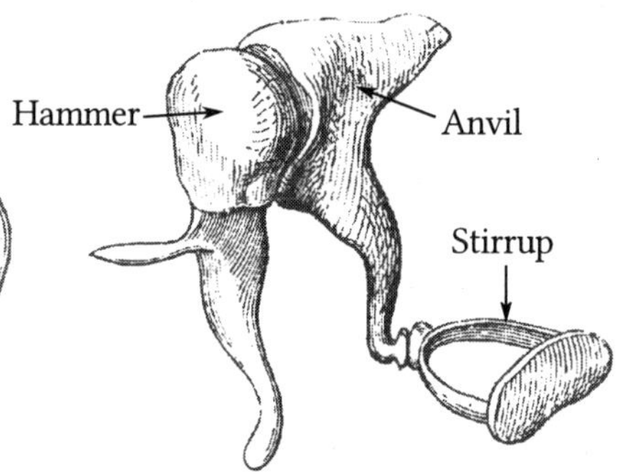

Figure 2.18 Bones of the ear (fr. Gavarret, 1877: 418)

The transfer of sound wave vibrations in Fig. 2.19 is accomplished by a series of bones in the middle ear that relay the vibrations: the *malleus* (hammer; 중이의)망치뼈), which is in contact with the ear drum and which relays the vibrations to the *incus* (anvil; 중이의)모루뼈), just as a blacksmith strikes the anvil with his hammer. The anvil then passes the vibrations to the third bone, the *stapes* (stirrup; 중이의)등자뼈), which looks like the stirrup of a saddle, as illustrated in Fig. 2.18.

The combination of bones acts like a sort of telegraph, relaying the sound to the cochlea, which consists of several canals filled with liquid and a chamber (the cochlea) containing a number of tiny hairs connected to nerves which convert the vibrations into nerve impulses that go to the brain, which then interprets the signal.

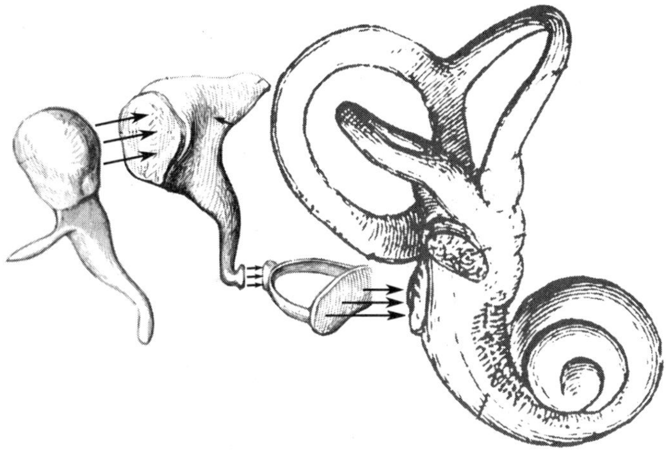

Figure 2.19 Transfer of sound vibrations

2.4 Conclusion

This brings us to the end of our discussion of the anatomy and physiology of the speech mechanism. Now that we have examined the various parts of the anatomy related to speech and how they work together to produce and recognize speech, we move on in the next chapter to the physical realization of the speech sounds produced by this complex system. This is the area of study known as *acoustic phonetics*.

Exercises

1. Make a drawing of the vocal tract and label it for all the parts related to the production of speech.
2. Why is the Adam's Apple more prominent in males?
3. Describe the process of producing a sound from beginning to end.
4. Describe the process of hearing, from beginning to end, including the various elements involved.
5. Why is the task of speech recognition so challenging?

Further Reading

Recommended additional readings for this chapter come from several sources. There are a number of texts, coming mainly from the field of clinical phonetics, that focus on the anatomy and physiology of speech, including Lieberman & Blumstein (1988), Minifie et al. (1973), Perkins & Kent (1991), Seikel et al. (2009), and Zemlin (1997). They all provide excellent illustrations and detailed explanations, although these are sometimes more than the average student of phonetics needs.

For a more general description of the phonetic aspects of speech anatomy and physiology, Clark et al. (2007), Ladefoged & Johnson (2010) and Ogden (2009) are good. Many introductory textbooks in phonetics and phonology also include basic descriptions of the anatomy and physiology of the vocal tract.

Keywords: airstream mechanism, articulator, auditory canal, glottis, larynx, phonation, supralaryngeal component, vocal cords/folds.

Chapter 3

Acoustic Phonetics

Acoustic phonetics is concerned with the physical properties of speech sounds, in particular, how sounds are physically realized and acoustically measured. The facts of physical manifestation are, on one level, quite obvious: to exchange information the speaker produces a sequence of sounds which they assume the hearer will be able to decode in order to obtain the information intended. This signal is received by the hearer who processes the sequence and then may respond with a new signal, and so on. In fact, this exchange of information involves a rather complex set of operations that we will examine in more detail in this chapter.

We begin with a brief look at the physics of sound, how it travels as sound waves and the properties of these sound waves, so that we may better understand the process of analyzing these sound signals.

3.1 The Physics of Sound

In the preceding chapter we examined the different aspects of human anatomy and physiology related to the production and perception of speech. We saw how manipulating the shape of the vocal tract alters the quality of the sound produced. We will now take a brief look at the physical characteristics of sounds and how they travel from the speaker to the hearer. This will help us to understand how sound waves are measured and represented in phonetic analyses.

3.1.1 The Transmission of Sound

Sound is transmitted as vibration produced by the vocal apparatus, traveling in the air or possibly other media (see pg. 34), and received by the eardrum. Without some medium of transmission, the sound vibrations can't travel and therefore sound cannot be transmitted in a vacuum. The speed of sound depends on the medium: for example, sound travels more easily through air than through water.

To understand the transmission of sound, think of a series of balls suspended on strings, often referred to as *Newton's Cradle*,[1] as shown in Fig. 3.1; if you pull back one ball (A) and release it, it strikes the next ball, which does not appear to move but, in fact, conveys energy to the next ball, and so on until the energy is passed to the last ball (B), which moves a similar distance to the original movement of ball (A). Note that it is the energy that has been transmitted, not the original ball (A). It is the same with sound waves, the vibration is transmitted from molecule to molecule until it reaches the eardrum.

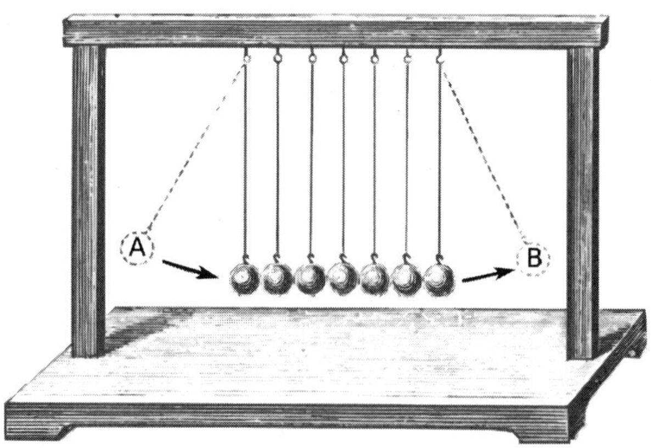

Figure 3.1 Energy relayed via medium (fr. Gavarret (1877:14))

[1] The original Newton's cradle was conceived of more than three hundred years ago by the French physicist, Abbé Mariotte (Mariotte, 1673).

It is also important to note that when sound waves are transmitted, there is an area of pressure in the direction of the sound referred to as an area of *compression* or positive pressure and behind this, an area of partial vacuum (negative pressure), known as *rarefaction*. This is similar to the waves at a beach that come in and go out in a regular, periodic pattern. With sound waves, this creates the positive and negative air pressure of the sound wave.

Sound reaches the ear in the form of a periodic variation in atmospheric pressure, referred to as *sound pressure waves*. The sound is transmitted through the air in the form of compressed waves that move from areas of high pressure to areas of lower pressure. This process is known as *wave propagation*.

The typical form of representation of the sound wave is in the shape of a sine wave, which describes the positive and negative rhythm of the wave in terms of a stretched-out circle of 360°, half of which is above the horizontal line and therefore positive, and half of which is below and negative, as shown in Fig. 3.2, from von Helmholtz & Ellis (tr.) (1912:21).

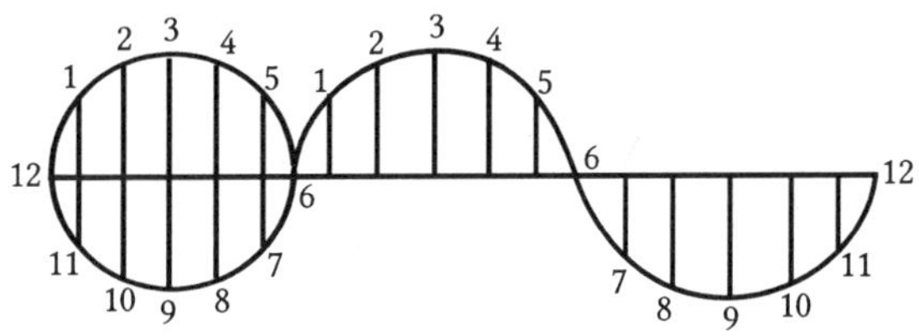

Figure 3.2 A sine wave

Each point on the circle has a corresponding point on the sine wave. These are used to describe the special characteristics of more complex sound waves, formed by combining sine waves of varying shapes.

3.1.2 Waveform Characteristics

A waveform is a graphic representation of a sound's pressure level over time, which enables one to see the propagation of the wave. The main characteristics of waveforms relevant to the study of speech include those listed in (3.1).

(3.1)
- Amplitude
- Frequency
- Velocity
- Wavelength
- Phase

The most fundamental of these characteristics are *amplitude* (진폭) and *frequency* (주파수). The distance above or below the centerline of a waveform represents the *amplitude* of the signal. The greater the distance from the centerline, the more intense the pressure variation (Fig. 3.3). The *peak* is the point at the greatest distance from the centerline in a positive or upward direction. The *trough* is, conversely, the lowest point from the centerline in a negative or downward direction.

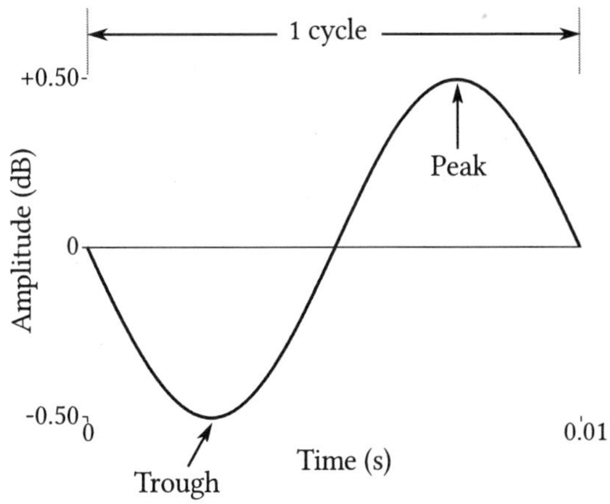

Figure 3.3 Amplitude, time and cycle

The rate at which the sound wave repeats a series of positive and negative amplitudes is known as the frequency of that signal. One completed series, from 0 to the negative *trough* then back to 0 to the positive *peak* and finally back to 0, is known as one *cycle*. The number of cycles that occur over a period of one second is the frequency of the wave and is commonly measured in Hertz (Hz) or cycles per second (cps).

If a waveform shows ten cycles in 0.1 seconds (Fig. 3.4), then there will be 100 cycles in one second and, therefore, the frequency of the signal of that sound wave will be 100Hz.

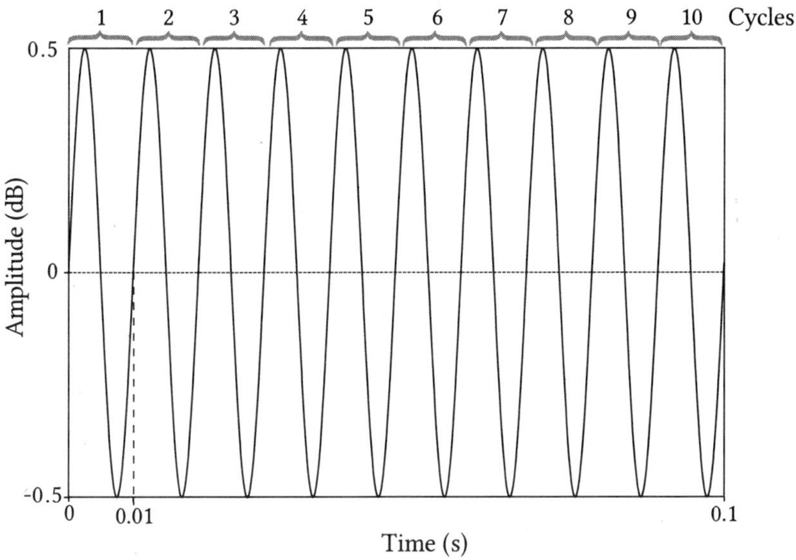

Figure 3.4 Waveform showing 10 cycles in 100 ms.

Velocity refers to the speed at which sound waves travel and this is determined by the *medium* (매체) in which they move. Typically, air is the most common medium for the conveyance of speech, but refer to pg. 34 for values for some other media. The time it takes to complete one cycle is referred to as the *period* of the wave so, for instance, the period of the wave in Fig. 3.4 is 0.01s or 10ms.

The *wavelength* (λ) of a wave is the actual distance in the medium between equidistant points across one cycle, measured in meters, and is equal to the speed (v) measured in m/sec, divided by the frequency (f) in Hz, ($\lambda = \frac{v}{f}$).[2] As can be seen in Fig. 3.5, the measurement may be made at the peak, the trough, the axis or, in fact, at any two points that constitute a single cycle. Note that, while the amplitude (indicated

[2] Other factors, such as *ambient temperature*, may affect the calculation.

by the height of the wave) is the same for the two waves in Fig. 3.5, there are ten cycles in the lower 1000Hz wave and only one cycle in the upper, 100Hz wave. The wavelength is inversely proportionate to the frequency, i.e. shorter wavelengths equate with higher frequencies and longer wavelengths with lower frequencies.

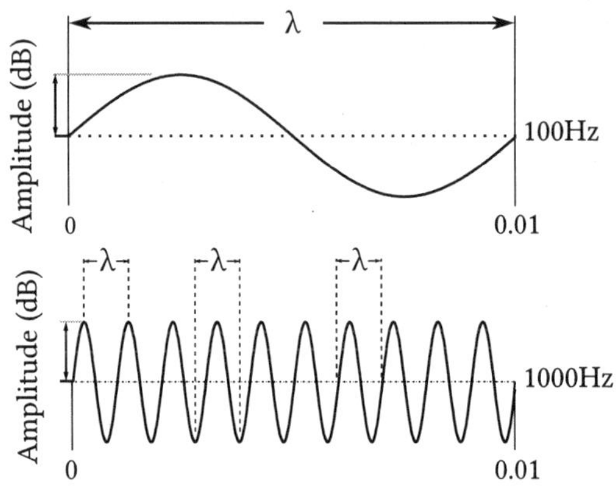

Figure 3.5 Wavelength of 100 and 1000Hz waves

Speed of Sound in Various Media

Medium	Speed (m/s)
Air	331
CO_2	259
Helium	965
Hydrogen	1290
Oxygen	316
Water	1433
Water vapor	405
Wood	3400

Talking in Helium

Normally, sound waves travel in air. However, if one inhales helium gas, the resulting sound is quite different. The difference with helium is its density. Vocal cords vibrate faster in gases like helium that are less dense than air, which is mostly nitrogen. When vocal cords vibrate faster, the pitch of the sound rises. Furthermore, the sound waves travel more quickly through helium, so the acoustic properties of the signal are changed so that the signal resonates with higher-frequency tones.

A cycle can begin at any point on a waveform, so it is possible to have two sound sources producing sine waves of the same frequency and peak amplitude that have different profiles at any one point in time. These waves are said to be *out of phase* with respect to each other. Phase is measured in degrees and one full cycle can be divided into 360°. The sine wave (as in Fig. 3.2) usually begins at 0 and increases to a maximum amplitude at 90°, then decreasing to 0 amplitude at 180° then continuing to a negative maximum at 270° degrees before returning to 0 amplitude at 360°.

Waveforms may be combined by merging their signals. If two identical waveforms are merged at 0, i.e. completely in phase with each other, the result is a waveform of the same frequency, but with twice the amplitude (twice as loud). If, however, the two identical waveforms are merged at 180° out of phase, then they cancel each other out, since each positive point has a corresponding negative point in the waveform. The result is a flat line and, thus, complete silence (Figs. 3.6 and 3.7).

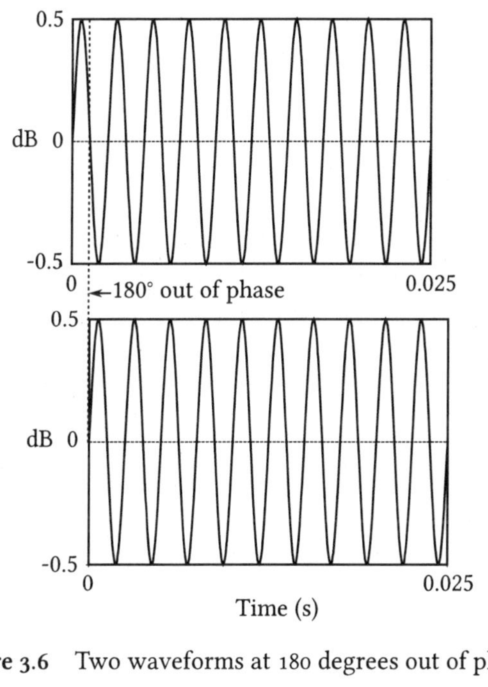

Figure 3.6 Two waveforms at 180 degrees out of phase

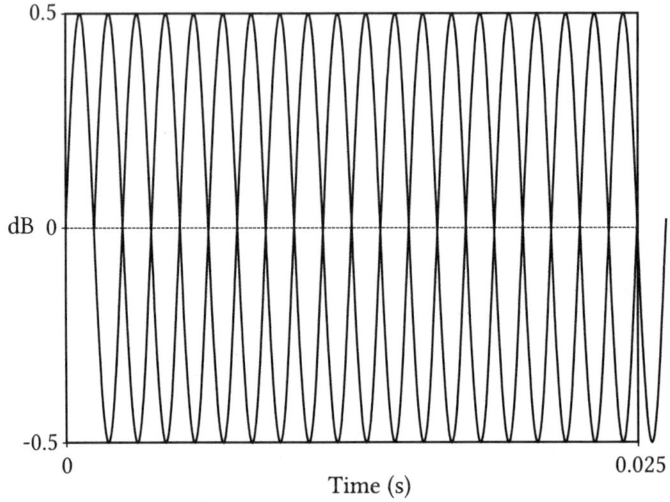

Figure 3.7 The two waveforms merged

When the waveforms are only partially out of phase, the result is a complex wave with some parts added and some parts subtracted from the original waveforms, as exemplified in Fig. 3.8.

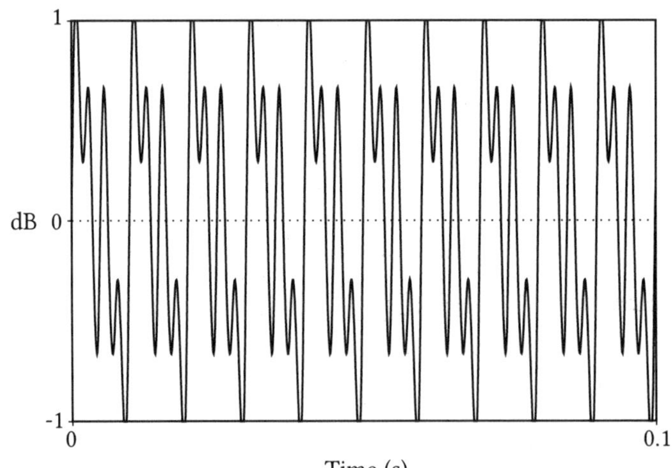

Figure 3.8 A complex waveform

Waveforms may be even more complex, involving even more elements combined to create typical speech sounds.

> One practical application of the concept of *phase* is the development of *noise-cancelling headphones*. These headphones use a technology referred to as *active noise control* (ANC) to reduce or eliminate extraneous noise. This technology involves the use of small microphones placed in the headphones and electronic circuitry that processes the output of the microphones, producing an out-of-phase copy of the signal in order to create an 'anti-noise' signal. This signal is then relayed to the headphone speakers, thereby canceling out the noise.
>
> This technology improves the quality of music by removing extraneous noise and can also help the headphone wearer to sleep or work comfortably in a noisy environment.

3.2 Equipment for Phonetic Analysis

In the early days of phonetic analysis, the equipment used to analyze acoustic data was bulky, difficult to use, and expensive. Recording devices used wax cylinders and large megaphones to record very short utterances (Fig. 3.9).

Figure 3.9 The Edison phonograph

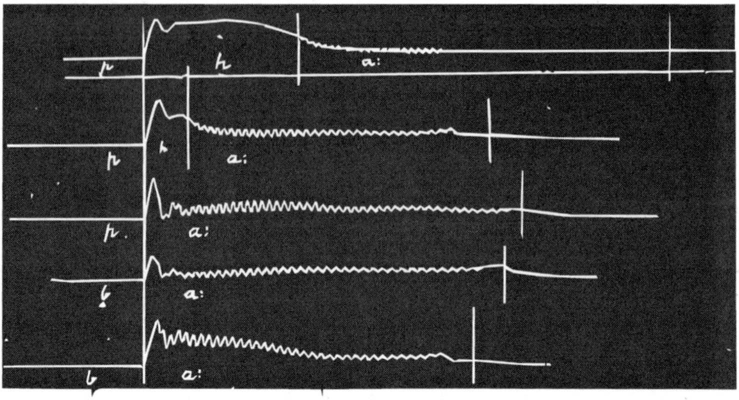

Figure 3.10 Tracings of pha:, pʰa:, pa:, b̥a:, ba: (Jones, 1918:172)

The *kymograph* was another piece of equipment that was used in the measurement of air pressure changes in the production of sound waves. The output of this machine was quite difficult to read, as shown by Fig. 3.10. Fig. 3.11 shows Professor Daniel Jones using the kymograph.

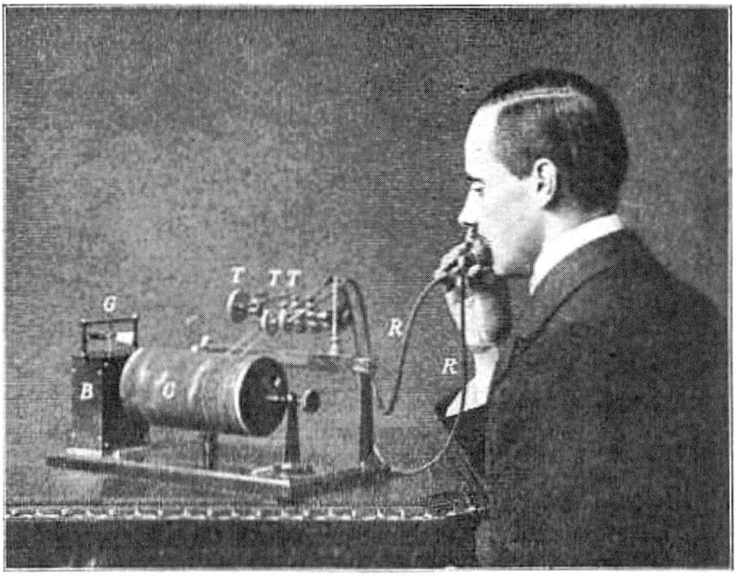

Figure 3.11 Daniel Jones and the kymograph (fr. Jones, 1918:169)

In the 1940s, the *sound spectrograph*, also referred to as the *sonagraph*, was developed, allowing phoneticians to record and analyze short utterances in a much clearer fashion than previously (Koenig et al., 1946). The spectrograph continued to be developed through the 1960s, culminating in the *Kay Sonograph.*

The development of the computer allowed ever-improving capabilities for the analysis of sound. The results are more accurate and more easily obtained than with the earlier equipment. By the late 1990s, readily accessible computers and software and easily available means to digitize sound made it possible for anyone to perform acoustic analysis of speech at a minimum of expense and difficulty.

3.2.1 Digitizing Sound

The first step in the use of computers to analyze speech is the recording and digitization of the sounds to be examined. The recording may be accomplished in several ways: (i) it may be recorded directly onto the computer in digital (rather than analog) format; (ii) some form of digital recorder such as a DAT recorder or other device may be used; (iii) alternatively, the sound may be recorded in analog format and then converted into digital format using software that converts incoming analog signals to a digital format. It is then transferred to the computer for analysis.

The most important piece of equipment in this process is the *microphone.* A good microphone will make good recordings even on a cheaper computer, but a poor microphone will only make poor recordings, even on the best computer. Hence, it is worth acquiring the best microphone that one can afford if you intend to make a lot of recordings.

In addition to the microphone, a good set of headphones will be useful for listening to the recordings, although this will not affect the quality of the recording or the analysis, so they need not be expensive. If you use them for long periods of time, comfort is perhaps the most important factor.

Finally, a computer with sufficient memory to run the phonetic software and for storing the digitized data is necessary. Computers with such capacity are readily available and most can perform the kinds of tasks necessary for what will be done here. It is not necessary to have an expensive or powerful computer, but it will be helpful if the computer has microphone and headphone connections. Most built-in microphones are not really suitable for phonetic research.

Microphones

There are two basic kinds of microphones that are most commonly used for recording speech: (i) dynamic and (ii) condenser. Dynamic microphones do not require any external power supply, which makes them good for work in the field. Condenser microphones, on the other hand, produce a high-quality audio signal but require a power source, which makes them a bit more inconvenient for use in the field.

Another consideration is how the microphone is connected to the recording device. The most common types are phone plugs, which connect directly to computers and most common stereo systems and XLR plugs, which tend to be found on the more professional equipment. In selecting a recorder/microphone combination, one must be careful to choose compatible units.

In the following section we will discuss the software that will be used to perform the acoustic analysis in this textbook.

3.2.2 Acoustic Analysis Software

In this section we will discuss several pieces of software that are freely available and accessible for anyone. We will use this software throughout the text as a way of analyzing phonetic data. In what follows we will learn the basics of using this software.

3.2.2.1 Audacity

Audacity is free, open source software for recording and editing sounds. It is a very useful tool for the phonetician and we will use it to record and edit data for phonetic analysis.

Since each version of Audacity is slightly different, it would not be practical to try to give exact instructions on using the program. Each version has basic instructions on how to use it so here we will discuss its use in only general terms. The basic steps for starting to use Audacity are:

1. Download the software for your operating system from the Internet at the Audacity home page at audacity.sourceforge.net.
2. Follow the instructions for installing it on your computer.
3. Open the software and follow the instructions for setting it up.

Once you have done this, you will be ready to do some basic things with the software. First of all, we will try a simple experiment.

1. Download a short sound file from the Internet or from some other source. It doesn't have to be short, but it is easier to work with short sound files and that is sufficient for present purposes.
2. Open the sound file, using the **Open** command from the **File** menu.

You should now see a window like Fig. 3.12.

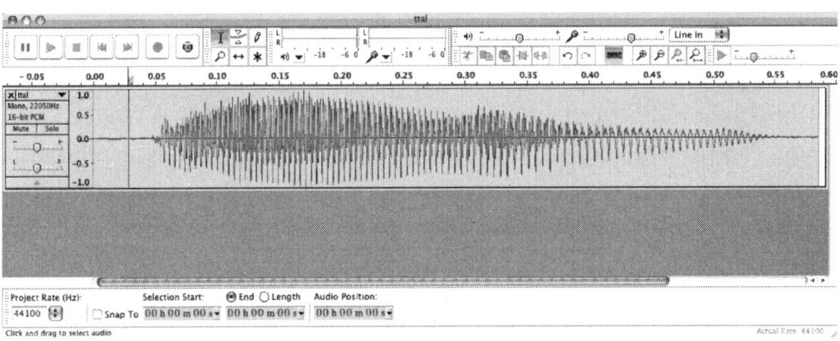

Figure 3.12 The Audacity window

The representation of the sound wave in Fig. 3.12, in this case the Korean word 딸 [t'al] 'daughter,' appears in the center of the window.

We will discuss the nature of the graphic later, but for now, notice that there is a row of buttons in the top lefthand corner. With these buttons, you can pause, play, stop, rewind or fast forward the sound, just like with any other recording device. There are also buttons for recording directly into Audacity, using a microphone connected to the computer.

For now you can just try playing with the software on an old file. You can use the **Export ... item** in the **File** menu to save the file at any time. If you want to just save the modified sound, you can select the portion you want and use **Export selection** .... After choosing **OK**, you will be presented with a save window that provides a number of different file formats to save in. For the time being, select WAV as the simplest, standard format (you can always change it later).

Now we can try some simple editing: first select a portion of the text from the middle of the sound wave. To do this, place your cursor at the start of the selection. There are two ways to select a piece, either (i) simply hold the mouse down and sweep across the piece you want to select or, (ii) click at the beginning, then hold down the SHIFT key, move your mouse to the end of the selection, and click again. Either way will give you a piece of the sound. Now, you can remove this piece by either using the 'scissors' icon (✄) in the Audacity toolbar or go to the **Edit** menu and choose **Cut**. Now that the piece is removed, you can place it in front of the existing material and paste it back in, using either the **Paste** button from the Audacity menu or the **Paste** command from the **Edit** menu. Now, try to listen to the result by playing it, using the **Play** button. It should be quite different from the original. If you want to save it, you can use the **Export selection** ... procedure, as discussed above.

3.2.2.2 Praat

The function of *Praat* (the Dutch word for "language") is somewhat different from that of Audacity. Audacity is most useful for recording and editing files, while Praat is best at doing acoustic analysis of the output of Audacity. As such, you will usually use Audacity first, to isolate the sounds you want to study, and then use Praat to study them.

Like Audacity, Praat is free, open source software. It is also a very useful tool for the phonetician, particularly for phonetic analysis. Since each version of Praat is slightly different, it would not be practical to try to give exact instructions on using the program. Each version comes with instructions on how to use it so here we will discuss its use in only general terms. Again, the basic steps for starting to use Praat are just like for Audacity:

1. Download the software that suits your operating system from the internet at www.fon.hum.uva.nl/praat/.
2. Follow the instructions for installing it on your computer.
3. Open the software and follow the basic setup instructions.

Once you have done this, you will be ready to do some basic acoustic analysis with the software. We will begin with the file created in the previous section using Audacity. When you first open Praat, it should look something like this:

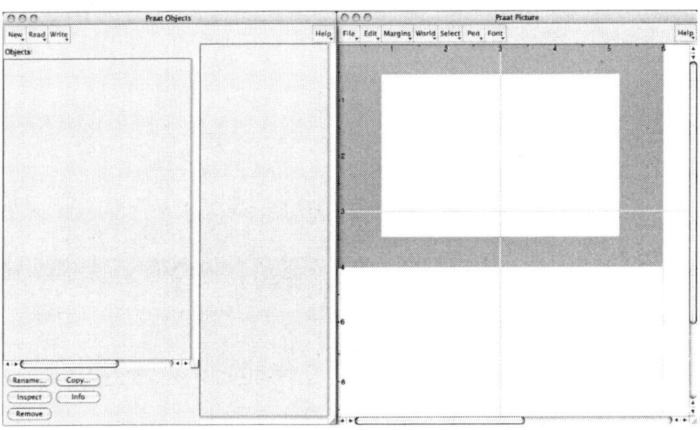

Figure 3.13 The Praat main windows

There are two windows: (i) the **Objects** window, on the left side, and (ii) the **Picture** window on the right side. The **Objects** window is where we select what is to be analyzed and decide how to do it. The **Picture** window is useful for producing a graphic representation of the analyzed data. For now, we will transfer the sound file to Praat:

1. In the **Read** menu, select **Read from file ...**

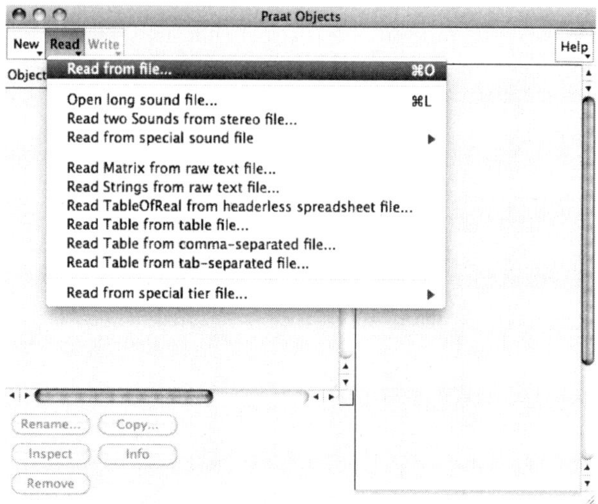

2. When the **Open File** window pops up, select the file to open.

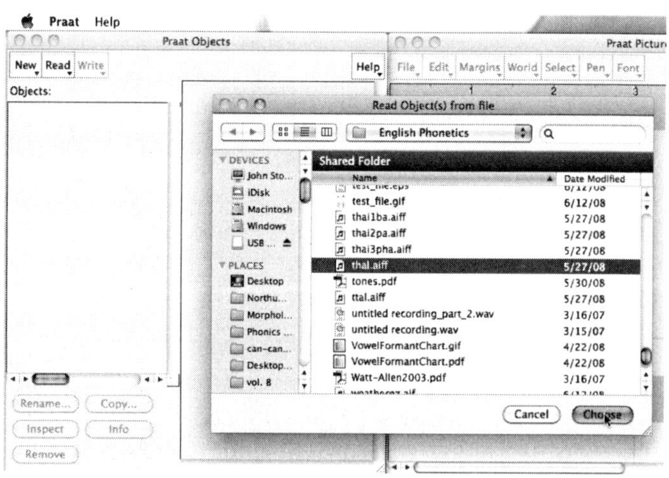

3. The file will appear in Praat's **Objects** list. Select it by clicking.

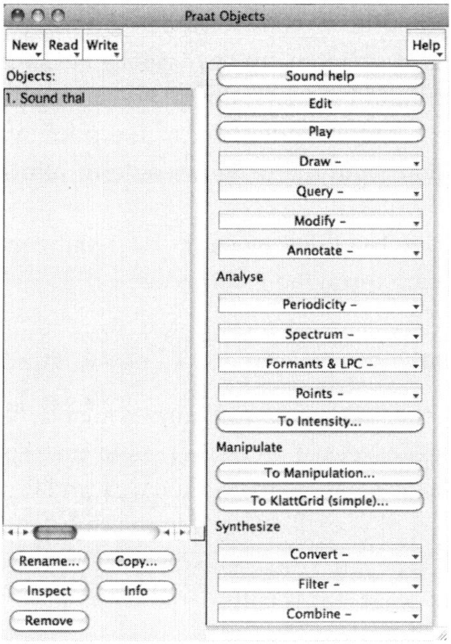

4. With the file selected, click on the Play button to confirm that it is the correct recording.
5. Now click on the **Edit** button.
6. This will bring up a new window with additional information.

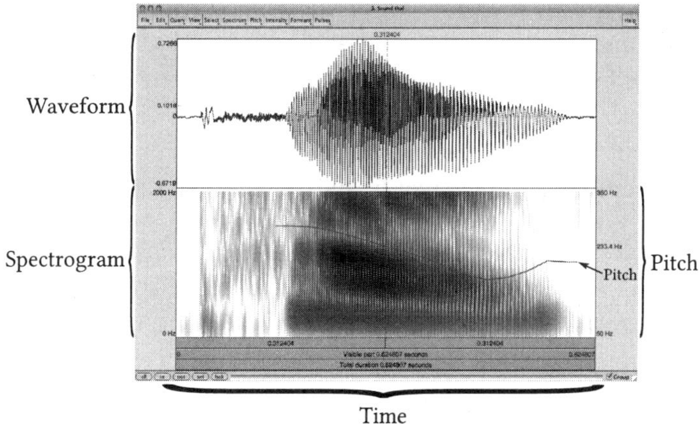

The top portion of the window contains the waveform of the sound with an indication of its intensity in decibels. Below that is a spectrographic representation of the sound with frequency marked on the left side of the window and an indication of the pitch with its frequency on the right. The bottom of the window contains information about the time.

We will return to the Praat program later and continue to use it to analyze phonetic data throughout this book.

3.2.2.3 Other Software

There are many other pieces of software available for doing acoustic analysis, of varying degrees of accessibility and cost. For the purposes of this book, we will focus on how to use Audacity and Praat, since they are two inexpensive, readily-available software programs that can be used for doing phonetic analysis. Other software may be introduced at the appropriate time and place if it is considered necessary or useful for some specific task.

3.3 Reading Spectrograms

One form of output of the acoustic software that was discussed above is the spectrogram. Spectrograms are graphic representations of the frequency of sound waves over time. They typically take a form something like in Fig. 3.14.

Throughout this book, you will be presented with various spectrograms representing different words and phrases. You should examine each spectrogram carefully, trying to understand the characteristics of the representation of each sound contained in the spectrogram so that you will become accustomed to reading and interpreting unfamiliar spectrograms.

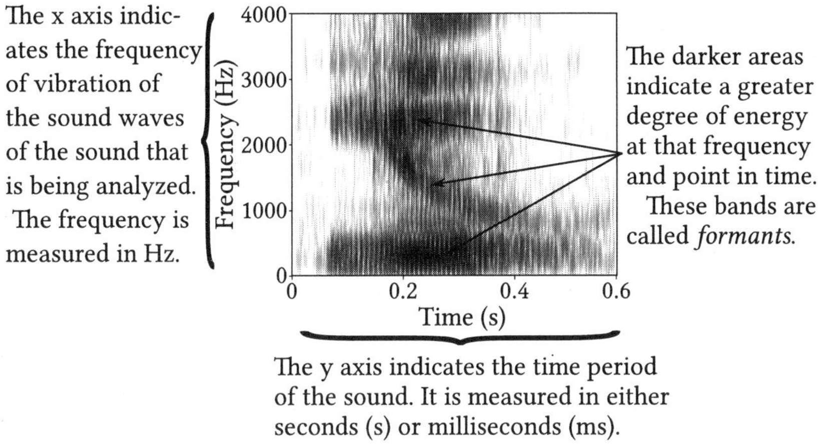

Figure 3.14 Reading spectrograms

Exercises

1. Record two Korean words using Audacity. Remove the first sound of each word and put it at the beginning of the other word. Save the file and edit it using Praat to produce a picture like that on page 45.
2. Download recordings of two English words from the Internet, using one of the online dictionaries that have sound files. Remove the last sound of each word and put it at the beginning of the other word. Save the file and edit it using Praat to produce a picture, as in Ex. 1.
3. How does active noise control work to remove noise?
4. Discuss the process of analyzing a sample of sound from beginning to end.

Further Readings

Ladefoged (1996) is a concise introduction to the field of acoustic phonetics, containing much valuable information on the subject. More recently,

Johnson (2003) provides detailed discussion of the subject. Ladefoged & Johnson (2010) is the most recent edition of the standard introductory text on phonetics.

Koenig et al. (1946) is a classic work on the development of the sound spectrograph. Zue (1976) is an earlier study on the use of the spectrograph for studying consonants by one of the leading specialists in reading spectrograms. Stevens (1998) provides a more advanced presentation of acoustic phonetics.

Keywords: Active noise control, amplitude, cycles per second, Hertz, peak, phase, waveform, wavelength.

Chapter 4

Applications of Phonetics

In the previous chapters we have discussed the various formal aspects of phonetics and some of the physics involved in measuring phonetic phenomena, as well as the anatomy and physiology employed in speech. In this chapter we will take a look at how phonetics may be applied in different fields.

Articulatory phonetics is concerned with the properties of sounds as they relate to articulation or sound production. The facts of physical manifestation are quite obvious: in exchanging information the speaker produces a sequence of sounds which they assume the hearer will be able to decode in order to obtain the information. This may then be followed by a signal from the hearer in response.

With respect to the infinite number of possible speech sounds, it is important to note that languages typically exhibit fewer than one hundred contrasting sounds, some much less. Rotokas, spoken in the South Pacific region, has only 11 distinct elements in its sound system, whereas !Xu, a Khoisan language spoken in Southern Africa, has one of the largest inventories with approximately 120 sounds.[1] Most languages have inventories somewhere between these two extremes.

[1] For further details about the range of possible segments in languages, see Ladefoged & Maddieson (1996); Maddieson (1984).

While there is a great range of possible languages and sounds, there are also certain limitations imposed on the speech system, including: (a) *physical impossibility*, the physical constraints on what are possible sounds, i.e., no language has a consonant that is made by touching the tongue tip to the vocal cords or the teeth to the back of throat; (b) *extra-linguistic emissions*, certain sounds not used as linguistic elements in any language, e.g., belches and grunts are not used as regular members of the system although they do convey meaning; and (c) *gaps in the system*, the possibility that a certain sound is not found in all possible environments in a language, e.g. there is no word-final [h] in English.

We should consider the possible sound systems of the world's languages to involve a wide range of choices constrained by universal and typological properties that linguists are still discovering.

4.1 Phonetic Transcription

In describing or discussing speech sounds it would be very inconvenient to have to constantly refer to instrumental representations such as wave-forms and spectrograms in order to represent the relationships between sounds. For this reason, it is standard practice for phoneticians, and linguists in general, to resort to a kind of shorthand notation instead. This shorthand representation is commonly referred to as a *transcription system*, and typically involves the use of a set of basic symbols representing the various consonants and vowels, combined with various additional symbols for supplementary modifications, often referred to as *diacritics*, in order to represent the sounds of natural language.

One of the benefits of using a transcription system is that it can be employed for any language being investigated. This means that, whatever language one encounters, the phonetic characteristics of the language will be clearly and easily represented, ensuring consistency and uniformity of presentation and interpretation. This also facilitates the comparison of languages and, thus, aids in the advancement of our understanding of universals and typology. We will now examine several different transcription systems used to represent speech sounds.

4.1.1 The International Phonetic Alphabet

The International Phonetic Alphabet or IPA, was first proposed in the later part of the 19th c. (Passy, 1888) as a system for representing sounds phonetically. It has been regularly revised and updated since then, the latest revision appearing in 2005.

The IPA (see Fig. 4.1) is a phonetic alphabet that assigns specific symbols to individual sounds that are generally agreed upon by phoneticians to be significant in one or more languages of the world. Each symbol is assigned to one and only one sound and any variation/modifications of these sounds are indicated by the use of additional diacritics included in the system.

In addition to symbols for segmental elements such as vowels and consonants, there are also special symbols to indicate such suprasegmental features as tone, stress, intonation, and length. These are indicated in the chart in Fig. 4.1.

Whenever linguists encounter new sounds in the languages they study, a revision to the IPA is debated and, if considered necessary, a representative symbol is suggested. Given the more than 5,000 languages estimated to exist currently and the limited amount of information on many of them, new sounds continue to be uncovered and the IPA will be revised as this occurs.

Since it is the most widely used system for transcribing words phonetically, the IPA will be used in this book for transcribing words phonetically except where practical orthographies are standard and the topic does not depend on narrow phonetic detail.

4.1.2 Alternatives to the IPA

There are several notable precursors to the IPA, including Alexander Melville Bell's *Visible Speech* (Bell, 1867, Fig. 4.2) and Henry Sweet's *Romic alphabet* (Sweet, 1880), based on Bell's system, as well as the *Shavian transcription system* commissioned by the famous playwright, George Bernard Shaw (Fig. 4.3).

THE INTERNATIONAL PHONETIC ALPHABET (revised to 2015)

CONSONANTS (PULMONIC)

	Bilabial	Labiodental	Dental	Alveolar	Postalveolar	Retroflex	Palatal	Velar	Uvular	Pharyngeal	Glottal
Plosive	p b			t d		ʈ ɖ	c ɟ	k ɡ	q ɢ		ʔ
Nasal	m	ɱ		n		ɳ	ɲ	ŋ	ɴ		
Trill	ʙ			r					ʀ		
Tap or Flap		ⱱ		ɾ		ɽ					
Fricative	ɸ β	f v	θ ð	s z	ʃ ʒ	ʂ ʐ	ç ʝ	x ɣ	χ ʁ	ħ ʕ	h ɦ
Lateral fricative				ɬ ɮ							
Approximant		ʋ		ɹ		ɻ	j	ɰ			
Lateral approximant				l		ɭ	ʎ	ʟ			

Symbols to the right in a cell are voiced, to the left are voiceless. Shaded areas denote articulations judged impossible.

CONSONANTS (NON-PULMONIC)

Clicks	Voiced implosives	Ejectives
ʘ Bilabial	ɓ Bilabial	ʼ Examples:
ǀ Dental	ɗ Dental/alveolar	pʼ Bilabial
ǃ (Post)alveolar	ʄ Palatal	tʼ Dental/alveolar
ǂ Palatoalveolar	ɠ Velar	kʼ Velar
ǁ Alveolar lateral	ʛ Uvular	sʼ Alveolar fricative

VOWELS

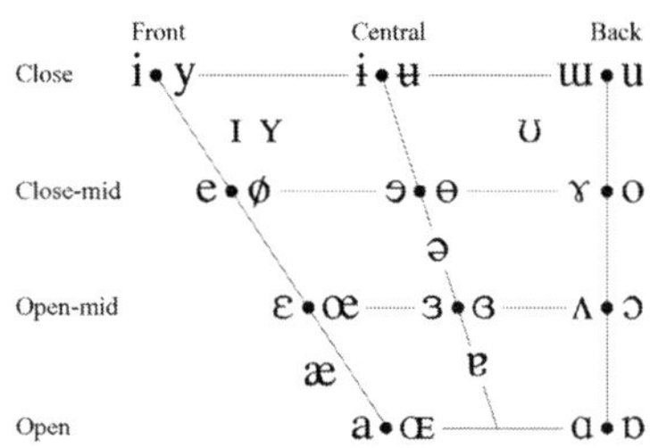

Where symbols appear in pairs, the one to the right represents a rounded vowel.

OTHER SYMBOLS

ʍ Voiceless labial-velar fricative
w Voiced labial-velar approximant
ɥ Voiced labial-palatal approximant
ʜ Voiceless epiglottal fricative
ʢ Voiced epiglottal fricative
ʡ Epiglottal plosive

ɕ ʑ Alveolo-palatal fricatives
ɺ Voiced alveolar lateral flap
ɧ Simultaneous ʃ and x

Affricates and double articulations can be represented by two symbols joined by a tie bar if necessary. t͡s k͡p

SUPRASEGMENTALS

ˈ Primary stress
ˌ Secondary stress ˌfoʊnəˈtɪʃən
ː Long eː
ˑ Half-long eˑ
̆ Extra-short ĕ
| Minor (foot) group
‖ Major (intonation) group
. Syllable break ɹi.ækt
‿ Linking (absence of a break)

DIACRITICS Some diacritics may be placed above a symbol with a descender, e.g. ŋ̊

̥ Voiceless	n̥ d̥	̤ Breathy voiced	b̤ a̤	̪ Dental	t̪ d̪
̬ Voiced	s̬ t̬	̰ Creaky voiced	b̰ a̰	̺ Apical	t̺ d̺
ʰ Aspirated	tʰ dʰ	̼ Linguolabial	t̼ d̼	̻ Laminal	t̻ d̻
̹ More rounded	ɔ̹	ʷ Labialized	tʷ dʷ	̃ Nasalized	ẽ
̜ Less rounded	ɔ̜	ʲ Palatalized	tʲ dʲ	ⁿ Nasal release	dⁿ
̟ Advanced	u̟	ˠ Velarized	tˠ dˠ	ˡ Lateral release	dˡ
̠ Retracted	e̠	ˤ Pharyngealized	tˤ dˤ	̚ No audible release	d̚
̈ Centralized	ë	̴ Velarized or pharyngealized	ɫ		
̽ Mid-centralized	e̽	̝ Raised	e̝ (ɹ̝ = voiced alveolar fricative)		
̩ Syllabic	n̩	̞ Lowered	e̞ (β̞ = voiced bilabial approximant)		
̯ Non-syllabic	e̯	̘ Advanced Tongue Root	e̘		
˞ Rhoticity	ɚ a˞	̙ Retracted Tongue Root	e̙		

TONES AND WORD ACCENTS

LEVEL		CONTOUR	
e̋ or ˥	Extra high	ě or ˩˥	Rising
é ˦	High	ê ˥˩	Falling
ē ˧	Mid	e᷄ ˦˥	High rising
è ˨	Low	e᷅ ˩˨	Low rising
ȅ ˩	Extra low	e᷈ ˧˦˧	Rising-falling
ꜜ	Downstep	↗	Global rise
ꜛ	Upstep	↘	Global fall

Figure 4.1 The International Phonetic Alphabet

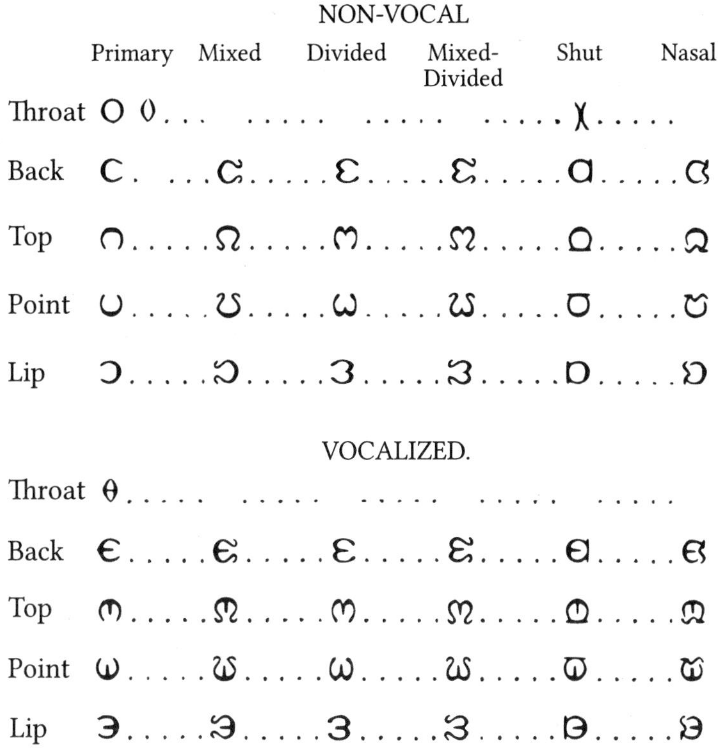

Figure 4.2 Bell's Visible Speech (Bell, 1882:59)

George Bernard Shaw (July 26, 1856–November 2, 1950) was an Irish writer and the author of *Pygmalion: A Romance in Five Acts* (Shaw, 1914), which introduced readers to the science of phonetics. This play was adapted for film, first as *Pygmalion* and later as *My Fair Lady*. Shaw was interested in orthographic reform and in his will he provided for Isaac Pitman to establish a *Shaw Alphabet*. A contest for the design of the new alphabet was won by Ronald Kingsley Read, who designed the new alphabet (Fig. 4.4).

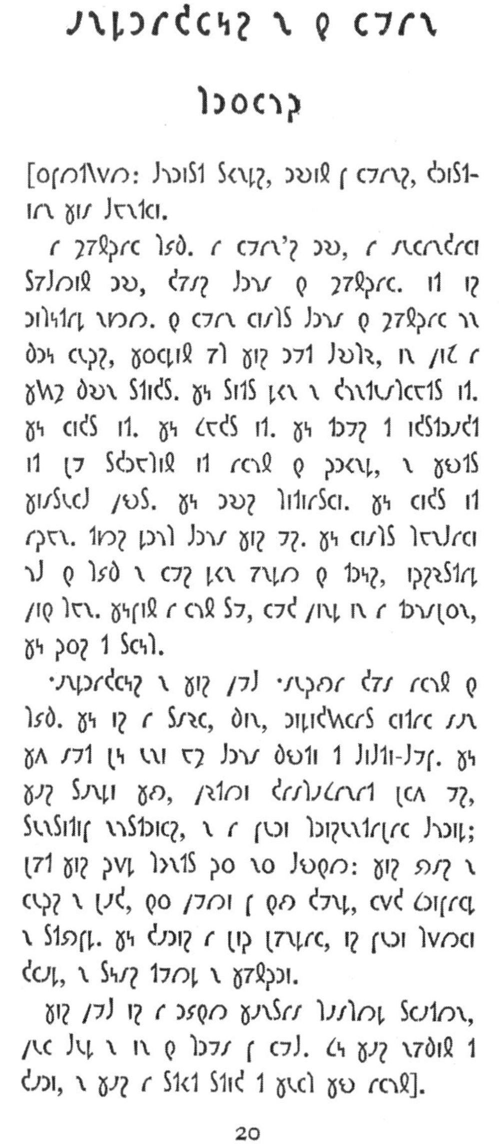

Figure 4.3 The first page of George Bernard Shaw's *Androcles and the Lion* in Shavian script (Shaw, 1962)

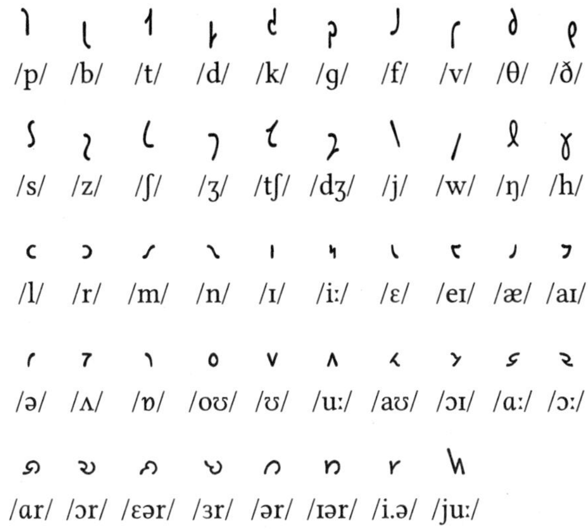

Figure 4.4 Shavian phonetic transcription

Contemporary alternatives to the IPA alphabet include the North Americanist transcription system which, for instance, provides distinct symbols for the affricates, assuming their independent status (Table 4.1). Thus, [č] represents the voiceless alveopalatal affricate represented by the digraph [tʃ] in the IPA, and [ǰ] represents the voiced variant, [dʒ]. For further details of the Americanist transcription system, the reader is referred to standard works such as Fromkin et al. (2006).

Americanist Symbol	IPA Symbol	Americanist Symbol	IPA Symbol
š	ʃ	y	j
ž	ʒ	ü	y
č	ʧ	ö	ø
ǰ	ʤ	r	ɹ
ñ	ɲ	ṭ	ʈ

Table 4.1 Americanist versus IPA symbols

There may also be transcription systems for special purposes, such as a working romanization for a specific language or group of languages. For instance, Korean is represented by one of several possible transcription systems, including the McCune-Reischauer (M-R) system, the Yale system, and a number of other variants. An example of this is provided in Table 4.2. Notice that there is considerable variation even in this small sample and this degree of arbitrariness is quite common in such *adhoc* kinds of transcription system.

Hangul	IPA	Yale	M-R
ㅍ	pʰ	ph	p’
ㅌ	tʰ	th	t’
ㅋ	kʰ	kh	k’
ㅈ	ʧ˙	c	ch

Table 4.2 Transcription systems for Korean

4.1.3 Using Hangul for Phonetic Transcription

While most modern phonetic transcription systems are based on the Latin alphabet (even Bell’s and Sweet’s), this is not a *requirement* of a suitable transcription system and is not necessary for the accurate representation of sounds. The main requirement of a good transcription system is that it maintains a clear and accurate relationship between sound and symbol, so that the exact pronunciation can be determined by anyone familiar with the system. As an example of this, let’s look at the use of Hangul as a phonetic alphabet. First of all, we can use the existing symbols with roughly their usual phonetic value (Table 4.3).

There are some symbols from Middle Korean that have not survived into Modern Korean may be reintroduced for this purpose, for instance, ㅿ could represent the first sound in English *zoo*, ㅹ could represent the first sound in English *fox*, etc. Furthermore, symbols may be re-assigned new values, just as Latin letter <B> is used in the IPA for a sound that

	Labial	Labiodental	Alveolar	Palatal	Velar	Glottal
Plain	ㅂ		ㄷ	ㅈ	ㄱ	ㆆ
Asp.	ㅍ		ㅌ	ㅊ	ㅋ	
Vd./Tense	ㅃ		ㄸ	ㅉ	ㄲ	ㆀ
Nasal	ㅁ	ㅱ	ㄴ		ㆁ	
Vl. Fric.	ㅸ	ㆄ	ㅅ	ㆅ	ㅎ	
Vd. Fric.	ㅹ	ㅹ	ㅿ			

Table 4.3 Using Hangul as a phonetic transcription system

is made by blowing air over the lips (sometimes referred to as 'giving the raspberry'). In addition, new symbols with specific values could be created, just as they are for the IPA, for example ʘ for the bilabial click sound found in some Khoisan languages.

Clusters of consonants can be constructed in a similar fashion to how they were in Middle Korean, e.g. ᄣᅢ 'time', Modern Korean 때. In this way, English words such as *school*, *spoon* and *spend* can be represented as ᄭᅮᆯ, ᄲᅮᆫ and ᄲᅦᇇ. In addition, the Hangul writing system already has a means to represent tonal distinctions, handed down from Middle Korean, and this could be adapted for more complex systems, thus Busan Korean [:눈] 'snow' can be shown to contrast with [·눈] 'eye' with respect to tone.

It should be remembered that using the Hangul system as a transcription system is different from using it as a writing system, so certain principles must be followed. For instance, sounds always have the same value, so both [ㄴ] and [ㄷ] must always be pronounced in the transcription of the English word ᄲᅦᇇ 'spend', which is only one syllable according to the representation.

The main aim of this discussion is to demonstrate that there is nothing inherently better about the Roman alphabet as a system for phonetic transcription, and other systems are equally, or even better, suited to the task.

4.2 Other Forms of Representation

In addition to phonetic transcription, there are other forms of representation that have their own specific purposes. These should be considered as different from phonetic transcription. Two examples of this type of system are: i) *Romanization* and ii) *Hangulization*. Such systems vary in the accuracy, consistency, and regularity with which they represent the sounds of a language and thus have varying degrees of utility for the representation of the target language. We will examine these systems briefly in the following two sections.

4.2.1 Romanization

Romanization refers to the use of the Roman alphabet to represent words from languages that normally use a non-Roman writing system. Romanization systems may be used for a variety of purposes. For instance, language specialists in an area where the languages use a non-Roman alphabet have traditionally opted for a romanized system that replicates quite closely the orthography of the languages under study. This type of system is useful for discussing language data where there is otherwise some difficulty in typesetting the native script, however it is not ideal for the novice, since it assumes prior knowledge of the language.

Another type of romanization is that intended for language learners in a pedagogical context. For example, the Chinese *Pinyin* system is a romanization system that reduces Standard Chinese pronunciation to a systematic representation employing Roman letters. The result is only partly phonetic in that certain symbols may represent more than one phonetic value: for instance <r> may represent either IPA [ɻ] or [ʐ] or [ɹ̟], depending on context and/or speaker. Furthermore, certain sounds employ two symbols combined (referred to as a *digraph*), such as <sh> for IPA [ʂ] or <ng> for IPA [ŋ]. With respect to vowel symbols, <u> may represent IPA [u] or IPA [y], based on the context: after most consonants it has the value of [u], but after <x,j,q,y> it signifies the vowel sound [y]. Pinyin, like most such romanization systems, works only for Standard Chinese and cannot be considered either international or phonetic.

A common example of the use of romanization is in the representation of names that common from languages that do not employ the Roman alphabet. For instance, Korean names such as 이 or 김 may be represented in a variety of ways, such as *Lee, Rhee, Yi,* for the former or *Kim, Khym,* or *Gim,* in the case of the latter. Such attempts at representing names are often inaccurate and may lead to mispronunciation in various ways. The issue of romanization is a very complex and difficult one, posing many challenges for those involved.

4.2.2 Hangulization

If romanization applies to the representation of non-Roman writing systems in a Roman alphabet, then we may employ the term *hangulization* to refer to the use of the Hangul writing system to represent words from other languages when they are represented in a Korean context. An example would be the titles of foreign movies or television programs, such as 프렌즈 [pʰɨɾɛndʒɨ] for the North American TV program 'Friends', in contrast to the title of the famous Korean movie 친구 [tʃiŋgu] 'Friends'. The former is a hangulization of the English word 'friends' and is not a loanword borrowed into Korean, but simply a way to represent the English name of this TV show, whereas the latter is the Korean word for 'friend'. Hangulization may also be used for advertising or for the names of shops, etc.

This highlights the difference between loanwords, which are borrowed into the language as part of the vocabulary, and hangulized forms, which are simply a representation in Hangul of an English (or other language) word or words.

4.3 Phonetic Fieldwork

In conducting fieldwork on an unknown or little-known language, one of the first steps is to reduce the spoken language to a so-called phonemic system, so that any data collected, such as wordlists or texts, can be represented simply and accurately.

One of the paradoxes inherent in this work is that one cannot determine the most suitable representation of the sounds of an unknown language until one records enough data to isolate the contrastive sounds of the language but, at the same time, one cannot record enough data until one has determined a means to accurately represent the contrasts of the language. Since this level of representation cannot be determined immediately, one must begin by recording all the phonetic detail possible, assuming that anything may be contrastive in the language. Then, after careful examination and analysis, one can arrive at a simpler system that focusses on just the relevant contrasts of the language.

It is for this reason that fieldworkers begin by transcribing all data in what is known as a *narrow phonetic* format, recording as much detail as possible. Sometimes this will involve instrumental analysis for certain difficult aspects of the research, but for the most part it is taken as a task of hearing what the speaker says and writing it down in a reasonably accurate approximation.

At this stage, it is also usual to record the data for subsequent analysis using some form of recording device, e.g. computer, tape recorder, minidisk, etc., but accumulated recordings can quickly becoming overwhelming, so unless the ultimate goal is a detailed phonetic analysis of the language, most linguists soon move on to a more phonemic level, where only the contrastive sounds of the language are recorded, without all of the fine phonetic detail. This level of detail can be recorded in written transcription using the IPA or some other system.

4.4 Speech Recognition and Synthesis

Speech recognition and synthesis both involve the use of computer hardware and software to recognize and synthesize human speech. This research has applications in a number of areas, including information technology, telephone systems, assistive technology for the disabled, and for military and security uses.

Speech recognition (sometimes referred to as *voice recognition*) is used to refer to systems that can recognize spoken language and convert it to a digital format that can be manipulated by a computer. Once the data has been converted it may be used in a variety of ways. For instance, it may convert the spoken language into written language, known as speech-to-text processing. Alternatively, it may be employed in an automated system to provide or record information provided by the speaker. It may be used to convert speech to computer commands to perform various functions or to act as access control to some system. Speech recognition is particularly challenging when it must recognize a broad range of possible speakers whose voices vary substantially. In order to accomplish this, a detailed knowledge of phonetics is crucial.

Speech synthesis is the artificial production of human speech using a computer system. It may take the form of a text-to-speech (TTS) system, which converts written text into speech. This may be useful in applications for the disabled, such as for those who are blind or who have difficulties seeing. This type of application can 'read' to the individual, making it possible to ease the burden on reading. It can also be used to 'speak' for those with difficulties communicating verbally, as in the case of Stephen Hawking, the famous Cambridge University physicist, who has a form of motor neuron disease that has made it difficult for him to communicate verbally. Speech synthesis has made it possible for him to lecture and give talks using a computer. The quality of a speech synthesizer may be judged by its similarity to the human voice and by its ability to be understood. An intelligible text-to-speech program allows people with visual impairments or reading disabilities to listen to written works on a home computer. Detailed knowledge of phonetics is necessary to design and construct high-quality speech synthesizers.

Developers in both of these areas must have a good understanding of the field of phonetics so that the systems they develop can model human speech in the most natural way. Just imagine the possible variation in the voice quality of different people and individual variation in pitch and loudness and you can easily see that the task is a very complex one requiring extensive knowledge of phonetics.

Substantial progress has already been made in many areas of this field, but there is still much to be done before we have 100% accuracy in recognizing voices and creating synthesized versions of them.

4.5 Speech-Language Pathology and Audiology

Two very important areas involving phonetics are i) *speech-language pathology*, sometimes referred to as *speech therapy* or *speech and language therapy* and ii) *audiology*, the study of hearing-related functions.

Speech-language pathology deals with a wide range of language communication disorders, ranging from accent reduction to cleft palate disorders and aphasias. Therapists assess speech difficulties and develop programs for addressing the problems they diagnose. These may be simple treatments for problems such as changing or improving one's pronunciation or may involve long-term treatment of serious medical conditions, such as the different types of aphasia.

Audiology focuses on the study of hearing and related disorders by means of examination, diagnosis and treatment through hearing aids or referral to medical specialists. Audiologists determine whether someone can hear within the normal range or whether there is hearing loss in specific ranges of hearing (high, middle, or low frequencies). If an audiologist determines that a hearing loss or abnormality is present, they will provide recommendations to a patient as to available solutions (e.g. hearing aid, cochlear implants, surgery, medical referrals). Specialists in these fields must have an extensive knowledge of phonetics, in addition to more specialized training in their specific areas.

4.6 Forensic Phonetics

Forensic phonetics is a relatively new field of study which employs phonetic analysis to assist in the investigation and prosecution of criminal activities that are related to speech. Specialists in this area analyze speech patterns to attempt to identify specific characteristics of the speaker, including social and dialectal background.

Voice identification may be important during investigation or criminal proceedings when there exists a recording in connection to a crime where the identity of the speakers are in question. These can include situations such as the recording of conversations, telephone threats that have been recorded by the recipient, or other crimes where there is recorded evidence involving unidentified voices.

There has been much discussion in the literature regarding the notion of a 'voiceprint', analogous to a fingerprint, that may be used to confirm the identity of a speaker with a high degree of certainty, but this is still quite controversial. However, there is much debate among phoneticians as to the legitimacy of this comparison. While fingerprints are seen as unique to an individual, it is still not clear what aspects of an individual's voice are unique. In any case, this is an important area of study and one that may prove to be invaluable in the area of the law.

The above are just a few of the possible applications of phonetics to real world problems. We will not explore these aspects of phonetics any further here but references for this kind of research are included in the **Further Readings**.

Exercises

1. Use the Hangul writing system to transcribe the following English words phonetically. You may modify the system by creating new symbols or changing existing symbols to suit the purpose.

   a. spot
   b. tops
   c. cry
   d. strength

2. Discuss three practical applications of phonetics with examples of how it can be used in these areas.

3. Discuss the differences between a writing system, a romanization, and a transcription system. You may have to refer to other sources of information in your answer.

4. Convert the Shavian transcription of George Bernard Shaw's *Androcles and the Lion* in Fig. 4.3 into regular English orthography.

Further Readings

For a good presentation of the IPA symbols and other phonetic symbols, Pullum & Ladusaw (1996) and International Phonetic Association (1999) are particularly useful. Ladefoged (2003) is an excellent discussion of phonetic fieldwork by an acknowledged leader in the field. Gordon (2003) and Maddieson (2001) are shorter discussions concerning similar issues. Ladefoged (1997) explores the use of phonetic instruments in the field, while Gick (2002b) examines the use of ultrasound techniques. Ladd & Himmelmann (2008) and Himmelmann (2006) discuss the study of prosody in phonetic fieldwork.

Jurafsky & Martin (2008) is a good introduction to the field of language processing, including speech-related technology. Dutoit (2001) and Taylor (2009) discuss the topic of text-to-speech technology. Damico et al. (2010), Minifie (1994), Van Riper & Erickson (1996), and Zemlin (1997) introduce the various areas of speech-language pathology, including those directly related to phonetics.

Baldwin & French (1990), Hollien (1990, 2001), Nolan (1991), and Rose (2002) are fairly recent works on the subject of forensic phonetics and speaker identification.

Keywords: digraph, hangulization, International Phonetic Alphabet, language typology, phonetic fieldwork, romanization, speech pathology, speech therapy, universals.

Part II

The Study of Sounds

Chapter 5

Vowels and other Syllabic Segments

In this chapter, we consider the nature of vowels and other elements that behave as if they were vowels. In addition, we will examine the additional modifications that may alter vowels in certain ways, including length, tenseness and nasalization. We will examine both the acoustic and articulatory properties of these vowel or vowel-like elements in a general, cross-linguistic fashion.

5.1 The Nature of Vowels

Vowels are important in all languages and are the central element in most syllables. They are often described as the *head*, i.e., the crucial core of the syllable and the thing that may bear stress in the word. Native speakers' feelings about the number of syllables in a word are based on the number of vowel-like sounds in the word.

Phonetically, we can say that vowels are speech sounds made by shaping the oral cavity in a particular way, while allowing the free passage of air from the lungs, without any turbulence or restriction. Catford (1988:123) describes vowels as a "class of pulmonic pressure sounds normally voiced, with a maintainable central oral approximant or resonant dorso-domal, or pharyngeal articulatory channel." We can interpret this as meaning that vowels are voiced sounds made by egressive airstream with an articulation along the center of the tongue or back of the throat.

We typically describe vowels based on their position within the oral cavity, supplemented by any secondary articulations such as tone, stress, nasality, etc. The IPA chart of the vowels is based on the position of the vowels vis-à-vis the shape of the oral cavity, as shown in Fig. 5.1.

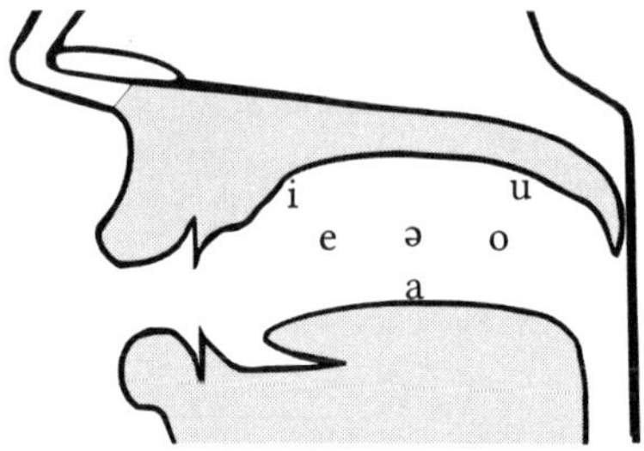

Figure 5.1 Vowel Space

This configuration gives us a graphic representation like that in (5.1), where the vowels of Fig. 5.1 are presented. The chart has basically the same shape as that in the IPA chart (Fig. 4.1) and follows the placement of the vowels in the vowel space.

(5.1) **Vowel inventory**

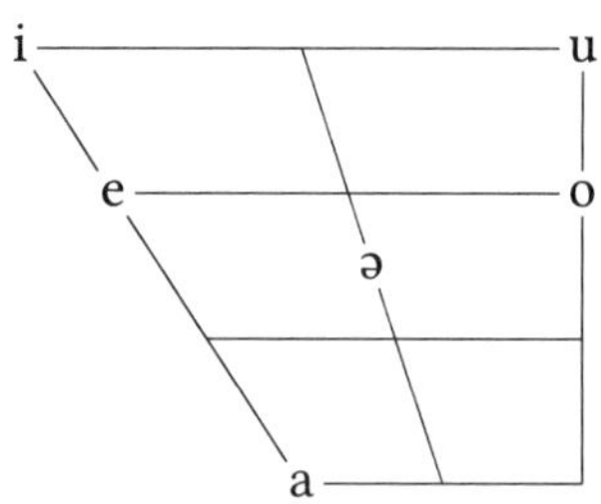

We will examine the English vowels in more detail in Ch. 9, but here we will take a look at the criteria for distinguishing and describing vowels crosslinguistically.

5.2 Vowel Criteria

The first question to ask before discussing the quality of vowels is what distinguishes vowels from other segments? If we examine obstruent consonants, for instance, we note that they are unable to bear stress or tone and, in almost all cases, cannot be the head of a syllable.[1]

If obstruent consonants cannot behave like vowels, then what about sonorant consonants? Typically, sonorant consonants aren't central in the syllable and so do not act as the head of the syllable, but certain syllabic sonorants may do so, for instance, the final sound in the English words *bottom, button, bottle, butter*, etc. In such cases, while the syllabic sonorant may act as the head of the syllable, there may be certain restrictions placed on it. For instance, such syllables can never bear the stress in English. On the other hand, syllabic sonorants may bear tone in Cantonese, so it is best to consider their behavior *vis-à-vis* the language in which they appear. We should assume that they are not exactly the same as vowels, but behave in a similar way in some contexts.

To return to our examination of the primary criteria for describing vowels, we can isolate several key properties which help us to distinguish among the vowels. They are presented in (5.2).

(5.2) **Vowel criteria**

a. Distance between the top of the tongue and roof of the mouth
b. Retraction or extension of the tongue
c. Shape of the lips

These three criteria may be reduced to the phonetic properties in (5.3).

(5.3) **Vowel properties**

a. Height:	high	mid	low
b. Backness:	front	central	back
c. Shape of lips:	plain	rounded	spread

[1] Two languages that are purported to have syllabic obstruents are Bella Coola, spoken in British Columbia, Canada (Bagemihl, 1988) and Berber, spoken in Northwest Africa (Dell & Elmedlaoui, 1985, 1988).

In the IPA, vowel height is measured in four levels, with the mid range separated into *close-mid*, the higher range of mid, and *open-mid*, the lower part of the range. Furthermore, high is referred to as *close* and low as *open*. These descriptors refer to the degree of opening of the mouth and the distance of the tongue from the roof of the mouth. In addition to the primary criteria for vowels, there are additional criteria, such as those in (5.4).

(5.4) **Further vowel properties**

a. Tenseness, involving tension in the muscles of the vocal tract
b. Oral versus nasal, i.e., whether the velum is raised or lowered to affect the flow of air through the nose
c. Length or duration of the vowel sound

Bearing these criteria in mind, we now move on to an examination of what are referred to as the *Cardinal Vowels*.

5.3 Cardinal Vowels

The Cardinal Vowels are an idealized interpretation of the vowels which places them at absolute points within the vowel space. This idea was first proposed by the British phonetician, Daniel Jones, in the early 20th century (Jones, 1917).

The basic idea of the Cardinal Vowels is that three of them, [i], [u], and [ɑ] have articulatory definitions that place them at relative points within the oral cavity. [i] is produced with the tongue as far forward and as high in the mouth as is physically possible, with the lips spread. [u] is produced with the back of the tongue as far back and as high in the mouth as is possible, with the lips rounded. The third vowel, [ɑ], is produced at the other extreme, with the tongue as low and as far back in the mouth as possible. This gives three reference points from which the other vowels can be placed.[2]

[2] This notion has been taken up in recent theories of phonology such as Dependency Phonology (e.g., Ewen, 1995) and Government Phonology (e.g., Kaye, 1989).

The other vowels are 'auditorily equidistant' between these three vowels and are arranged in four degrees of height: close, close-mid, open-mid, and open. These distinctions provide eight reference points, numbered from 1 to 8, known as the *Primary Cardinal Vowels*, shown in Fig. 5.2.

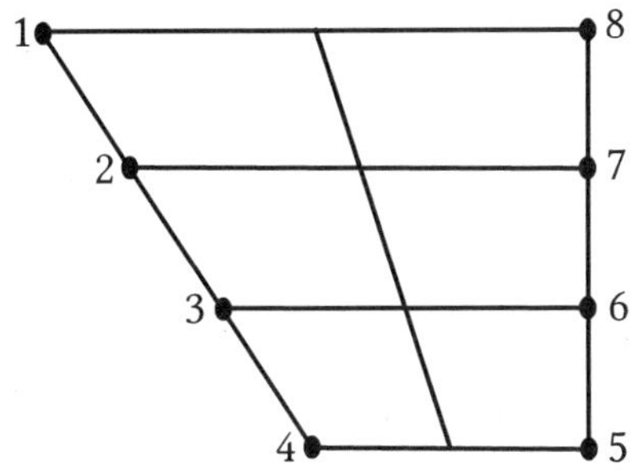

Figure 5.2 The primary cardinal vowel positions

There is also a second set of cardinal vowels having the opposite values for lip rounding of the Primary Cardinal vowels. These are referred to as the *Secondary Cardinal Vowels*, and they are numbered from 9–16 in the chart (Fig. 5.3).

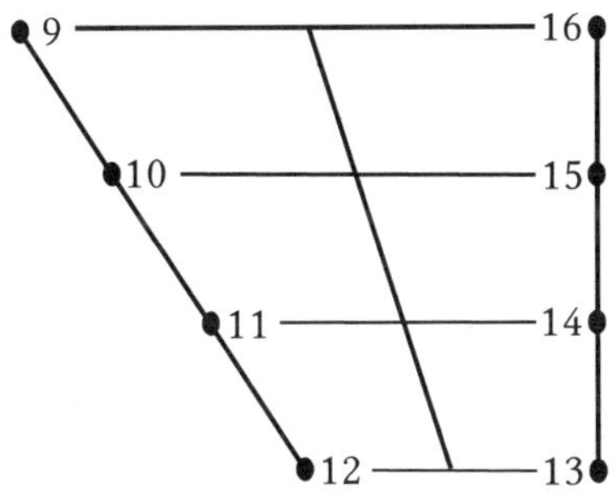

Figure 5.3 The secondary cardinal vowel positions

If we fill in the primary and secondary cardinal points with the appropriate IPA vowel symbols, the chart will be as in Fig. 5.4, indicating all the primary and secondary cardinal vowels.

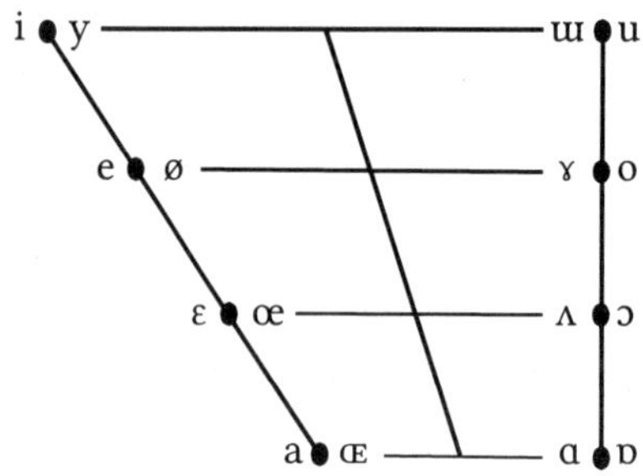

Figure 5.4 The cardinal vowels

There are still some obvious gaps in the cardinal vowel system, in particular in the center area of the chart. Abercrombie (1967: 161) states that "there are six more secondary cardinal vowels. They consist of three pairs of vowels, the vowels in each pair having the same tongue posture but one being unrounded and the other rounded. All are central vowels ...." These additional vowels are shown in Fig. 5.5, filling in the central area of the vowel chart.

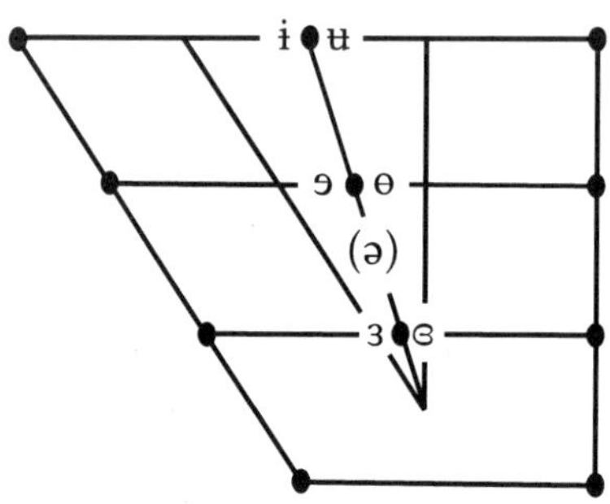

Figure 5.5 The additional secondary cardinal vowels

There are still vowels missing from the IPA chart, but these may be filled in with reference to the cardinal vowels, for instance [æ] is between cardinal vowels 3 and 4. Note that [ə] is included in the chart in Fig. 5.5 in parentheses, since it is a very common vowel in the languages of the world, even though it is not one of the cardinal vowels.

5.4 Acoustic Properties of Vowels

The primary indicator of vowel quality is *formant frequency*. Formants are the frequency *foci* (singular: *focus*) that appear as dark bands of concentrated energy on spectrograms. They are, in fact, harmonics of the fundamental frequency (F_0), and are thus labelled F_1, F_2, F_3, etc.[3]

5.4.1 Vowel Place and Formants

The formant with the lowest frequency concentration is F_1, the second F_2, and so on. The two first formants are usually sufficient to distinguish a vowel, indicating the quality in terms of vertical and horizontal position (sometimes referred to as *height* and *backness*, respectively). The first formant has a higher frequency for a low vowel (such as [a]) and a lower frequency for a high vowel; and the second formant has a higher frequency for a front vowel and a lower frequency for a back vowel.

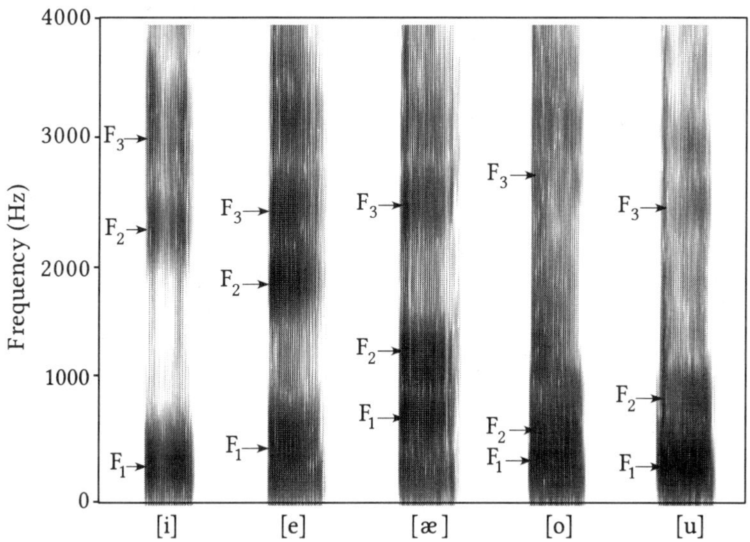

Figure 5.6 First three vowel formants for [i, e, æ, o, u]

3 A harmonic is a multiple of the fundamental frequency (F_0), so if the fundamental frequency is f, the harmonics have frequencies 2 x f (F_1), 3 x f (F_2), etc. Thus, if the fundamental frequency is 100 Hz, F_1 is 200 Hz, F_2 is 300 Hz, etc.

In Fig. 5.6, the F_1 of [i] and [u] are the lowest and as the F_1 rises, the vowel lowers or becomes more open. With F_2, the front vowels have the highest frequency and the back vowels the lowest. In fact, there is a clear correlation between the two main vowel criteria and the first two formants: a lower F_1 correlates with a higher vowel and a lower F_2 correlates with a more back vowel.

We can plot the first two formants for the various vowels in a chart format to make their relationship clearer. When doing so, the usual practice is to plot the F_1 on the x-axis and the F_2 on the y-axis, as shown in Fig. 5.7.

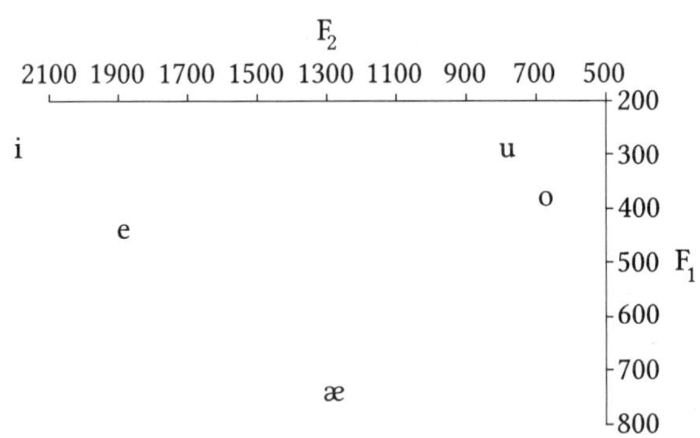

Figure 5.7 Vowel formant plot for the vowels in Fig. 5.6

There are software programs to assist with doing the vowel plot[4] or one can use a spreadsheet program like *Microsoft Excel* or simply make a graph and plot the points to indicate the vowel space by hand.

5.4.2 Vowel Rounding and F_3

F_3 is useful in describing some aspects of vowel quality, such as lip rounding. We can see that the round vowels have a much greater distance between F_3 and F_2 than the corresponding non-round vowels due to the lowering effect of lip rounding on F_2.

[4] A good example of such a program is the *JPlotFormant* program.

If we examine the French high front vowels, which involve a contrast between [i], e.g. *si* [si] 'if', *lit* [li] 'bed', and [y], e.g. *su* [sy] 'knew (p.p.)', *lu* [ly] 'read (p.p.)', we can see the differences in the formants of the unrounded and rounded vowels. Compare, for instance, the formant frequencies of the French vowels in Fig. 5.8.

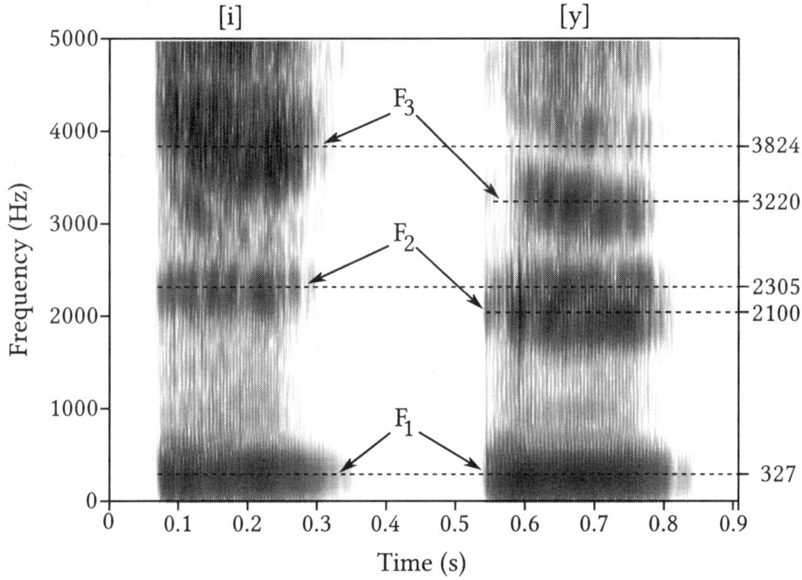

Figure 5.8 Formant frequencies of high front vowels

Fig. 5.8 demonstrates that F_1 is more or less the same for both [i] and [y] (327 Hz), showing that they are both high vowels. F_2 is also quite similar (2305 Hz vs. 2100 Hz), indicating that they are front vowels, although there is a slightly lower value for [y]. However, the most obvious indicator of the roundness of [y] is F_3, which is much lower in [y] (3220 Hz) compared to [i] (3824 Hz), due to the lip rounding.

Thus, F_3 is a useful indicator of lip rounding, especially in those cases where this is the only difference between segments, as in the case of French or German front high vowels. F_3 may also correlate with various other vowel properties, such as nasalization, but this will be discussed later.

5.5 Secondary Articulations

In this section we discuss the secondary vowel articulations. Vowels may have additional modifications that can affect their pronunciation in various ways. These changes may be phonetic, phonemic, or morphophonemic in nature. In what follows, we will discuss four secondary effects commonly applied to vowels, beginning with vowel length.

5.5.1 Vowel Length

One process that affects the nature of vowels is *vowel length*. In some languages vowel length contrasts in a meaningful way, the only difference between the meaning of words being whether the vowel is held for a greater or lesser duration, as exemplified by the data from the North American language, Nuuchahnulth, in (5.5).

(5.5) **Nuuchahnulth vowel length**

yatʃ	'dogfish'	ya:tʃ	'warped, bent out'
wa	'to coil'	wa:	'to say'
mas	'healed up'	ma:s	'baking on open fire'
k̓ʷa	'break'	kʷa:	'move backwards'

The waveform display in Fig. 5.9 shows the difference between long and short vowels in the Nuuchahnulth words *k̓ʷa* 'break' and *kʷa:* 'move backwards'. Measuring the vowel portion of the waveform, *k̓ʷa* extends from 0.16s to 0.3s giving 0.14s in duration, whereas the vowel of *kʷa:* extends from 0.115 to 0.32s, a length of 0.205s. This means that the vowel of *kʷa:* is approximately 68% longer than the vowel of *k̓ʷa*, indicative of a significant vowel length difference.[5] Thus, *kʷa:* 'move backwards' is said to have a long vowel, whereas *k̓ʷa* 'break' has a short vowel.

This example from Nuuchahnulth shows that vowel length is contrastive in the language: if one does not observe the difference between

[5] It is important to note that long vowels are not usually *twice* as long as short vowels. The difference is typically in the range of 50% greater duration for long vowels, that is, they are 1½ times the length of a short vowel.

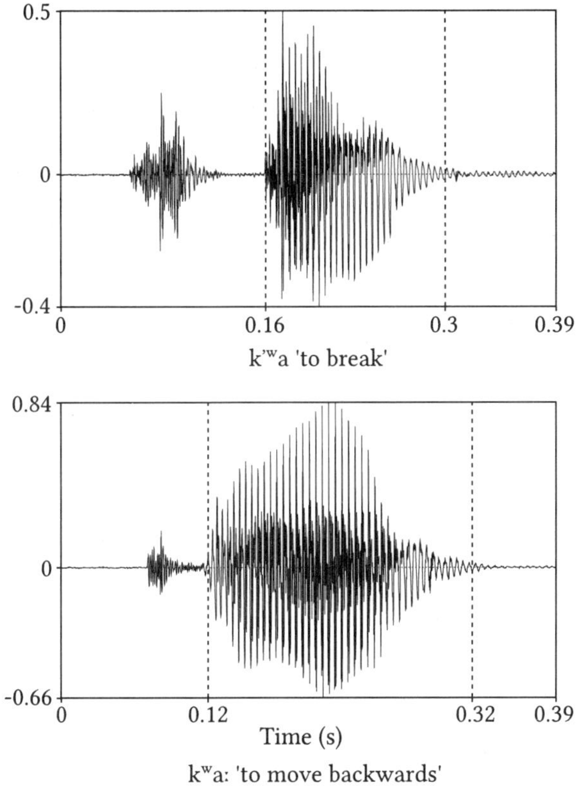

Figure 5.9 Nuuchahnulth vowel length

long and short vowels, one will make errors in the pronunciation of words, leading to potential misunderstanding.

It has been claimed that Korean has a limited degree of vowel length distinction, occurring only in the first syllable of the word. Thus, the examples in (5.6) are claimed to make minimal differences in vowel length. In each case the first member of the pair has a short vowel and the second member has a long vowel.

(5.6) **Korean vowel length**

[mal] 말 'horse'	[maːl] 말 'language'
[pam] 밤 'night'	[paːm] 밤 'chestnut'
[nun] 눈 'eye'	[nuːn] 눈 'snow'

Nevertheless, for many speakers of Korean, there is no length difference in such words, so it would appear to depend on factors such as age and dialect as to whether vowel length is significant or not. We will discuss the nature of English vowel length in detail in Ch. 9.

5.5.2 Tense/Lax Distinctions

Another modification of the vowel system, found in English and other languages, is the distinction between *tense* and *lax* vowels. Jones (1918: 19-20) puts it in the following way:

> Another element which is considered by many to be of importance in determining vowel quality is the state of the tongue and lips (more especially the former) as regards muscular tension. Vowels produced while the tongue is in a state of considerable muscular tension are called *tense vowels.* Those produced while the tongue is not in a state of muscular tension but is held loosely, are called *lax vowels.*

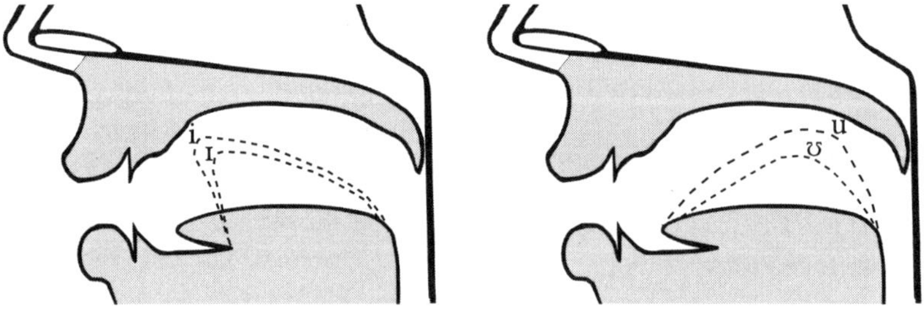

Figure 5.10 Tense/lax vowel distinctions

As can be seen in the outlines of tongue shapes for the tense and lax high vowels in Fig. 5.10, the tongue is obviously in a greater degree of tension when making [i] or [u], since it must stretch further in either case. Jones further states that he does not completely agree with this characterization, but many phoneticians have adopted it to describe the difference between the pairs of English vowels in (5.7).

(5.7)	**Lax**		**Tense**	
	bit	[bɪt]	beat	[biːt]
	soot	[sʊt]	suit	[suːt]

It is clear that there is a meaningful difference between such pairs of vowels in English, but that not all languages make such a distinction.

> Korean does not have a lax/tense distinction for vowels. Consequently, this difference presents certain challenges for Korean learners of English, since pairs like *fit/feet*, *soot/suit*, etc. are contrastive in English and therefore problems of miscomprehension may result from mispronunciation of such vowels.

5.5.3 Advanced Tongue Root (ATR)

A similar effect to the tense/lax distinction is that of Advanced Tongue Root (ATR). As the name suggests, this articulation involves extending the tongue outward, so that in pairs such as [ɪ]/[i], [i] is considered to involve a greater forward movement of the tongue root (Fig. 5.11). This feature occurs in the vowel harmony systems of a number of languages.

In Somali, a Cushitic language of eastern Africa, there is a harmony system that requires that all the vowels in a word agree in terms of their value for ATR, i.e. they are either all [+ATR] or all [-ATR]. The vowel pairs differing in ATR are presented in Fig. 5.12 from Saeed (1993).

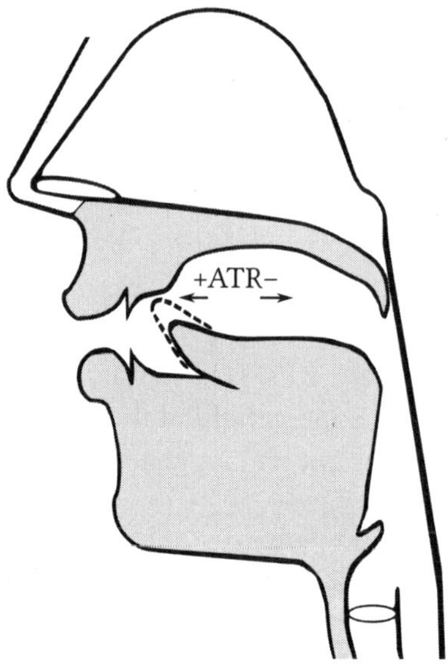

Figure 5.11 Advanced Tongue Root (ATR)

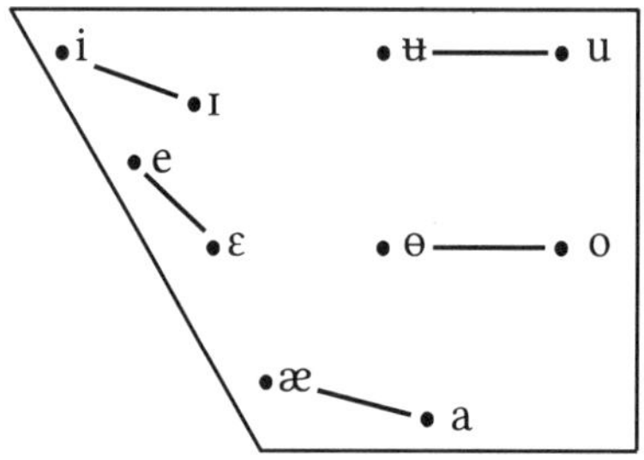

Figure 5.12 Somali ATR vowel pairs

Examples of the application of ATR harmony in Somali are provided in (5.8), where you can see that, in the words in the first column, all the vowels are non-ATR, while in the words in the second column, the vowels are all ATR. This demonstrates the relevance of ATR in this vowel system.

(5.8) **Somali vowel harmony**

a. [dɪːday] '(I) fainted'		[diːdæy] '(I) refused'
b. [qɵdɛːn] '(they) dug'		[rogeːn] '(they) turned over'

We will not go any further into the Somali data, but the relevant issue is that the secondary articulation of ATR may be important for deciding which vowel quality to employ in a particular word.

5.5.4 Nasalization

The majority of vowels in the world's languages are what are referred to as *oral vowels*, i.e., vowels made with the air passing only through the mouth or oral cavity. All languages have this kind of vowel. However, there are also languages that make use of a further modification of vowels by lowering the velum to permit the passage of air through the nasal cavity in addition to the oral cavity. Vowels of this sort are referred to as *nasal vowels* or *nasalized* vowels.

Languages such as French and Navajo have contrastive nasal vowels, as can be seen from the examples in (5.9), from French.

(5.9)

Nasal Vowel	**Oral Vowel**
[bõ] bon 'good'	[bo] beau 'handsome'
[tõ] ton 'tone'	[to] tot 'soon'

Spectrographically, nasalization of the vowel appears as increased darkening of the vowel formants overlain with additional resonances due to the passage of air through the nasal cavity, in effect, an additional resonating chamber, as shown in Fig. 5.13.

English does not have contrastive nasal vowels like French, but vowels may become nasalized in English when they are adjacent to nasal consonants. For instance, a word like *none*, with a vowel between two nasal consonants, will be pronounced with some degree of phonetic nasalization, i.e., [nʌ̃n]. This type of nasalization is completely predictable from the environment and is non-contrastive.

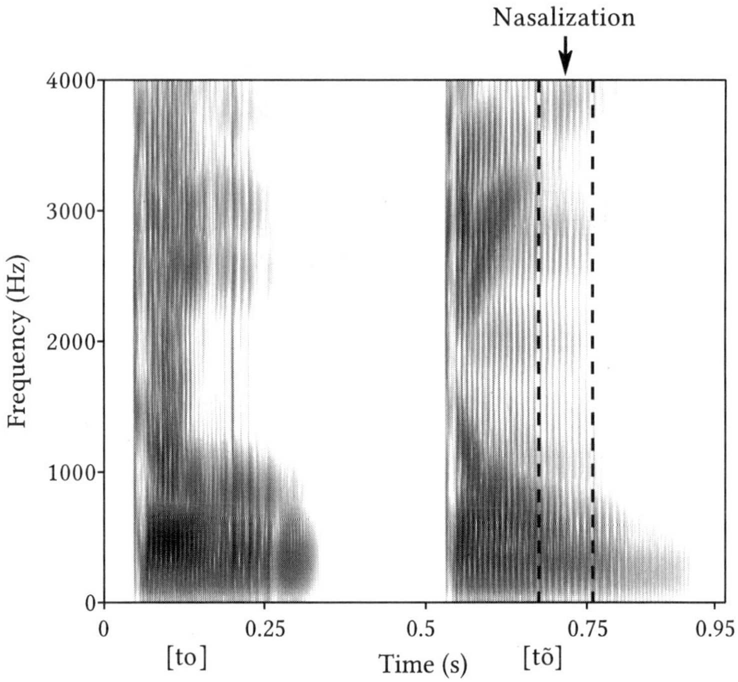

Figure 5.13 The French words *tot* [to] 'early' and *ton* [tõ] 'tone'

Interestingly, some varieties of Korean appear to have a process of *denasalization*. This involves removing or reducing the nasal feature of consonants in certain contexts, resulting in an oral stop, for instance, using [dɛ] (or perhaps: [ⁿdɛ]) instead of [nɛ] for 네 'yes' (cf. Yoshida, 2008).

5.6 Diphthongs

Diphthongs (이중모음) are a kind of vocalic segment that involves a complex articulation. The word *diphthong* comes from Greek and means 'two sounds,' and that is what diphthongs are: vowels that combine two vowel qualities into a single unit.[6] They are usually represented by combining the monophthongs that begin and end them, i.e., the two parts of the sound. So *high* contains a diphthong consisting of [a] + [ɪ] giving [haɪ] and *how* contains a diphthong consisting of [a] + [ʊ] giving [haʊ], as shown in Fig. 5.14.

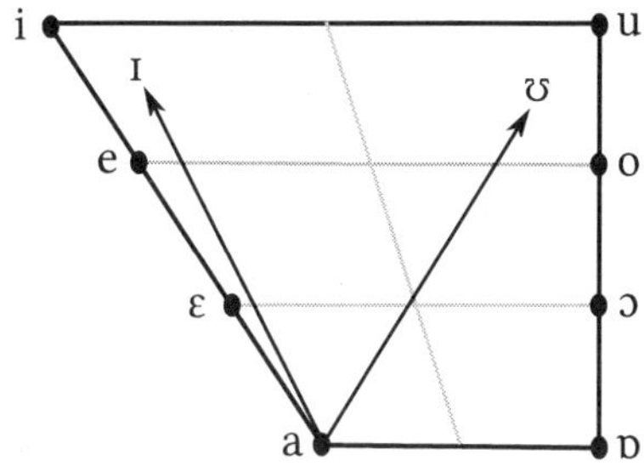

Figure 5.14 Representing diphthongs [aɪ] and [aʊ]

When two vowels come together in this way, one vowel is always less prominent than the other. If the first is less prominent, we describe this as a *rising diphthong*, since its prominence increases towards the second member of the diphthong, for example, *you* [ɪ͗u] or [i̯u]. The [̯] below the vowel indicates the less prominent vowel, which is sometimes represented by the corresponding semivowel, [j] or [w]. If, on the other hand, it is the second member that is less prominent, then we refer to this as a *falling diphthong*, e.g., [a͗ɪ] or [aɪ̯] in the word *high*.

Note the formant transitions of the diphthongs [aɪ], [ɔɪ] and [aʊ] in the words *buy*, *boy*, and *bow*, respectively, in Fig. 5.15. This spectrogram clearly demonstrates the special characteristics of diphthongs. What can be readily observed is a clear movement from one formant position to the other across the formant bands. Thus, it is relatively easy to recognize diphthongs on spectrograms, since they show a transition from one vowel position to another. To determine the specific diphthong, one simply measures the formants at or near the two edges of the diphthong,

6 *di*- 'two' + *phthongos* 'voice, sound'. Plain vowels are known as *monophthongs* (단모음) < *mono* 'one' + *phthongos*.

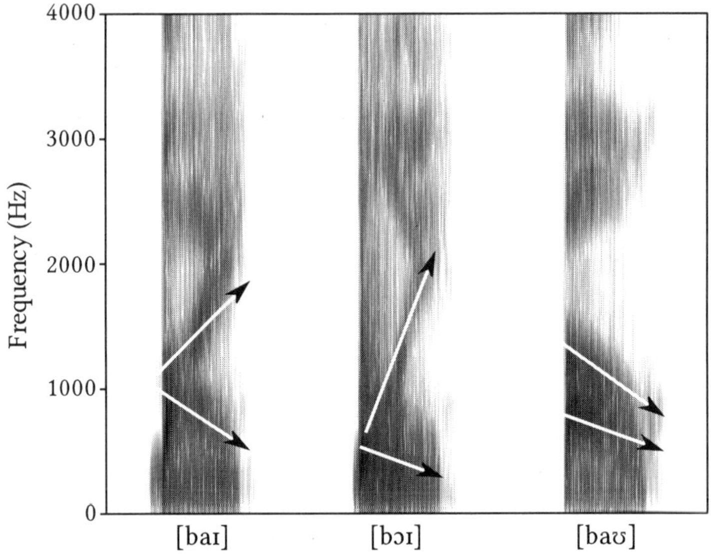

Figure 5.15 Examples of diphthongs 'buy', 'boy', and 'bow', showing the formant transitions of [aɪ], [ɔɪ] and [aʊ]

giving the vowel components of the diphthong and then combines them to form the diphthong.

Diphthongs are relatively common in the languages of the world, but there is some variation in the types of diphthongs that may be encountered in a language. For instance, Korean does not have falling diphthongs like English [ai̯] in *high.*[7] So, when Korean learners of English pronounce English words containing diphthongs, such as *cake*, in order to replicate the English diphthong, they break it into two monophthongs, [e] and [i], giving a bisyllabic form [ke.ik]. This is most likely a consequence of the absence of such diphthongs in Korean.

[7] The one possible exception is ㅢ [ɨi̯]. However, most Korean speakers reduce this to [e] in the majority of contexts and to [ɨ] or [i] in a few others.

5.7 Syllabic Sonorants

When we refer to syllabic sonorants (성절 자음), we actually mean syllabic sonorant *consonants*, although vowels are also syllabic sonorants. Syllabic sonorant consonants are found in a number of languages of the world, although they are much less common than vowels or diphthongs. They are basically sonorant consonants, such as nasals or liquids, that function as the head of a syllable, i.e., as if they were a vowel. Often there are special constraints on such segments, restricting their occurrence in certain ways.

5.7.1 Relationship to Vowels

Syllabic sonorant consonants are similar to vowels in that they may: i) act as a syllable nucleus; ii) play a role in syllable counting; and iii) may bear tone and/or stress, depending on the language.

They are different from vowels because they: i) don't exhibit length distinctions: no short versus long; ii) don't participate in harmony processes, such as ATR harmony (cf. §5.5.3); iii) don't exhibit tense/lax differences; and iv) don't combine to form diphthongs.

5.7.2 Tone on Syllabic Consonants

An example of tone on syllabic consonants can be seen in Cantonese, where syllabic nasals bear tone, just like vowels, and are contrastive phonologically. Examine the data in (5.10). The tone in these examples is indicated by the IPA system of employing a vertical bar [|] with a horizontal line marking the point and direction of the tone, e.g., [˨˧] indicating a tone that rises from quite low to the mid point of the scale, [˧˩] a mid tone that falls to the bottom of the range, and [˧˥] a mid tone that rises to high.

(5.10) **Cantonese syllabic consonants**

a. [m˧˩] 唔 'not'		[m˧˥] 嘸 'huh?'	
b. [ŋ˨˧] 五 'five'		[ŋ˧˩] 吳 'Woo (surname)'	

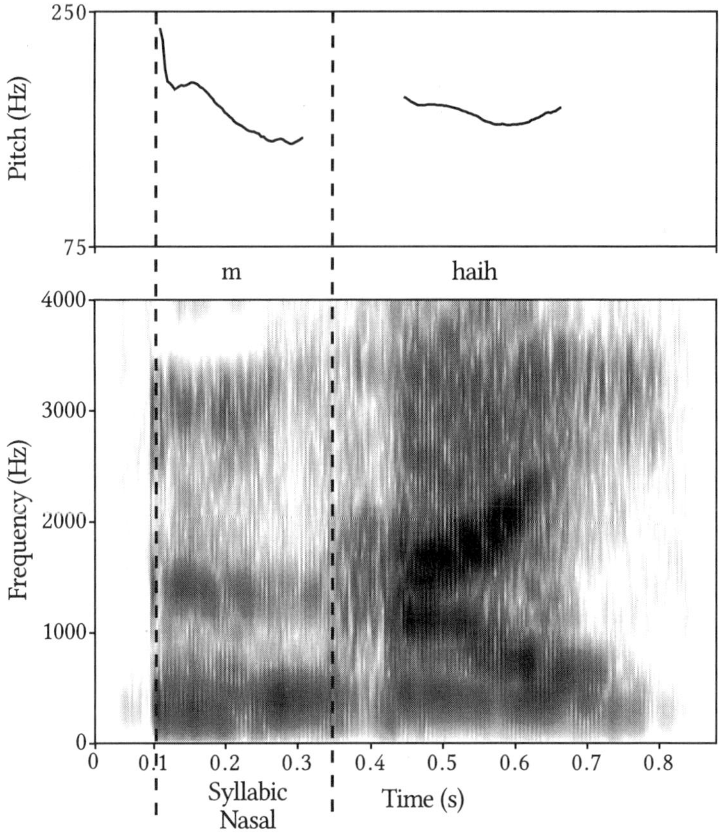

Figure 5.16 The Cantonese phrase *m̀ haih* [m̩˩ haɪ˨] 'is not'

Notice that a change of tone signals a change in meaning in the pairs of forms in (5.10a and b). We can see that syllabic nasals act very much like vowels and are contrastive in Cantonese. Fig. 5.16 provides a spectrogram of the syllabic nasal [m̩] in the Cantonese form *m̀ háih* 'is not', showing the tone contours on the nasal.

In English, syllabic consonants appear frequently. The nasals, [m] and [n], and the liquids, [l] and [ɹ], can all be syllabic in the appropriate context. Syllabic sonorants are a property of a number of languages, including Cantonese and English, but do not appear to exist in Korean.

5.7.3 Acoustic Properties of Syllabic Sonorants

As can be seen from Fig. 5.16, syllabic sonorants have formants that are very similar to vowel formants, although usually somewhat lighter in intensity. They are also typically longer than their non-syllabic consonantal counterparts. Furthermore, since they may bear tone, as in Cantonese, they will show pitch on a pitch track, just as with vowels.

In general, syllabic sonorants behave like vowels and should be analyzed as if they were vowels, although they may be more limited in their distribution and less prominent on a spectrogram. We will revisit English syllabic sonorants in Ch. 9.

Exercises

1. Make a recording of yourself saying the vowels [i e a o u] and analyze them. Provide a table giving the F_1 and F_2 of each vowel and discuss any difficulties you experience with the analysis.

2. Analyze the diphthongs in the words *tie*, *tow*, and *toy*. Provide a table indicating the F_1 and F_2 of each part of each diphthong.

3. Provide the IPA symbols for the vowels in the following Korean words.

   a. 보다   c. 캐나다

   b. 고양이   d. 한글

4. Provide the IPA symbols for the vowels in the following English words.

   a. elephant   c. usual

   b. scenery   d. sofa

Further Reading

Recommended additional readings for this chapter include Ladefoged & Johnson (2010) and Lieberman & Blumstein (1988), for general phonetic description. Chiba & Kajiyama (1941) and Peterson (1951) are early studies of vowel phonetics and are certainly worth reading.

For detailed discussion of vowels, Ladefoged & Maddieson (1990) contains a wealth of information. Lindblom (1986) and Schwartz et al. (1997) discuss the phonetic universals of vowels, while Lindau (1978) and Nearey (1977) discuss vowel features.

Whalen & Levitt (1995) discusses the specifics of the fundamental frequency of vowels, while Johnson et al. (1993) studies individual differences in the production of vowels. Wood (1979) uses radiographic evidence for studying vowel articulations.

Keywords: Cardinal vowel, formant, fundamental frequency, harmonic, monophthong, rising/falling diphthong, syllabicity, vowel space.

Chapter 6

Consonants I

In this chapter we will examine some of the fundamental properties of consonants, including how they are articulated and how to recognize and analyze them. We will begin with an examination of the various types of airstream mechanisms, responsible for the control of the flow of air into and out of the vocal tract. Then we will examine the different states of the glottis and the effects that may be achieved by manipulation of the vocal cords. Finally, we will examine the various manners of articulation that result from the two previous factors and how to analyze them using phonetic software.

6.1 Airstream Mechanism

Airstream mechanism refers to the means of moving the air in and out of the respiratory/speech system and its interactions with the various types of articulations available, and may be divided into three separate possibilities: (i) *pulmonic* (폐의), the most common type of airstream mechanism, which involves the use of the lungs to move the air; (ii) *glottalic* (성문의), which involves the movement of the larynx either up or down to create air pressure, and finally (iii) *velaric* (연구개의), the least common, which involves a closure created by the back of the tongue at the velum, resulting in suction when released.

Table 6.1 illustrates the various possible combinations for both outward (egressive) and inward (ingressive) air movement, providing IPA symbols for the different sound types. The blank spaces are unattested.

	Egressive	Ingressive
Pulmonic	p, t, k	–
Glottalic	pʼ, tʼ, kʼ	ɓ, ɗ, ɠ
Velaric	–	ʘ, ǁ, ǂ

Table 6.1 Airstream Mechanisms

The following sections will describe the various realizations of these different airstream mechanisms in more detail.

6.1.1 Egressive versus Ingressive Air

Egressive air (Fig. 6.1) involves the movement of air outwards from whatever source, typically from the lungs, but also possibly from creating pressure by closing the glottis and forcing the air outwards from there. It is the most common airstream direction in language.

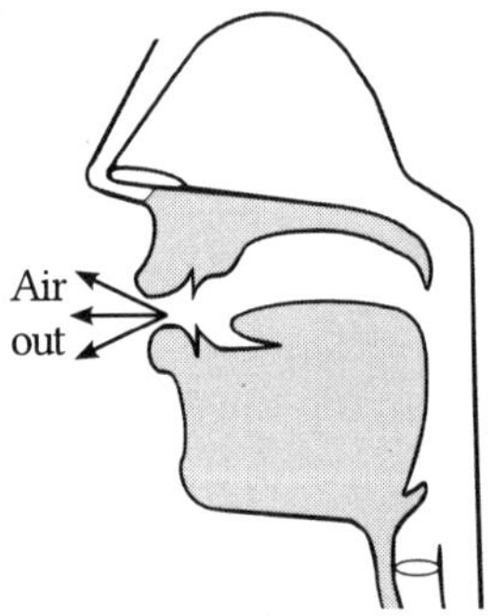

Figure 6.1 Egressive Airstream

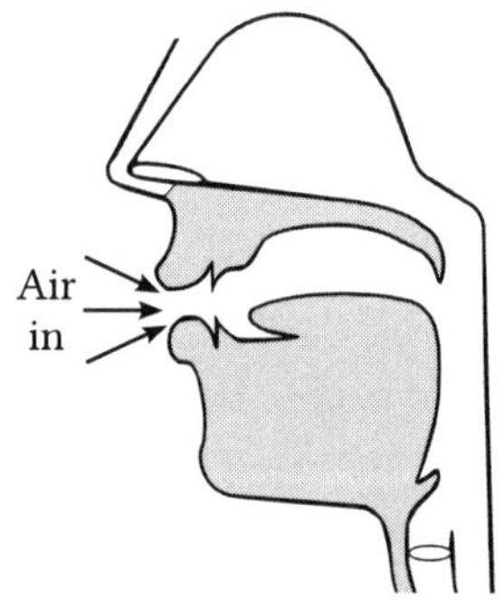

Figure 6.2 Ingressive Airstream

Ingressive airstream (Fig. 6.2) is produced by closing the glottis and lowering the larynx, creating inward suction. It may also be caused by closing off the mouth at the velum and then releasing the closure.

6.1.2 Pulmonic Action

Pulmonic airstream is the most common type of airstream mechanism encountered in the languages of the world. Unlike some of the other types of airstream mechanisms which are restricted to a limited number of languages, pulmonic airstream is found in *every* spoken language: it is the only mechanism employed in English and many other languages. It involves the use of the lungs in combination with the diaphragm to move air through the vocal tract.

As indicated in Table 6.1, only pulmonic egressive airstream, that is, the outward movement of air, is found as a natural linguistic expression of pulmonic air, although it is possible to also produce ingressive pulmonic airstream, by trying to talk while inhaling. We will meet many instances of pulmonic egressive airstream in the remainder of this book.

6.1.3 Glottalic Action

Air may also be drawn into or forced out of the vocal tract by means of the raising or lowering of the larynx. In the case of glottalic egressive sounds, the glottis is closed tightly and then the larynx is moved upward (Fig. 6.3), creating air pressure (Fig. 6.4). Upon releasing the closure, the air explodes outward (Fig. 6.5), creating the phonetic effects associated with *ejective* sounds.

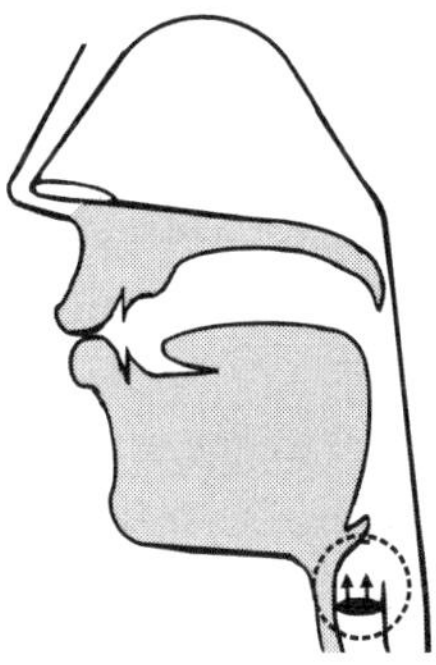

Figure 6.3 Larynx raised

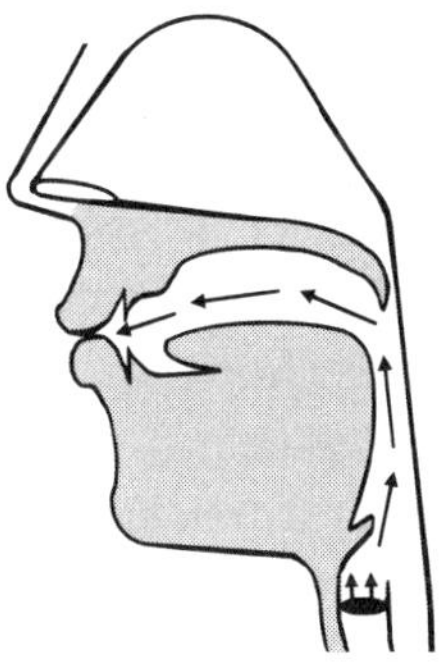

Figure 6.4 Pressure increases

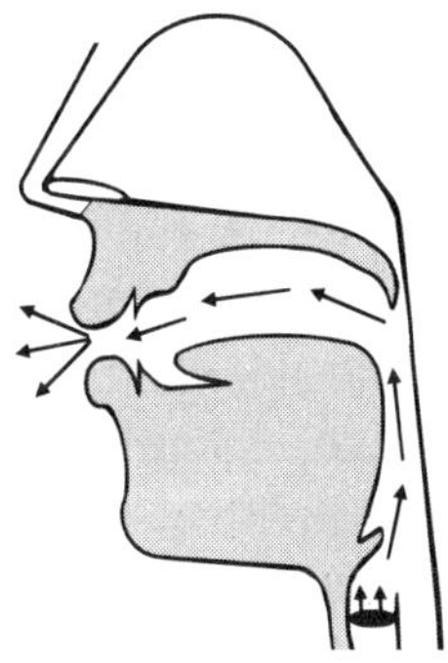

Figure 6.5 Air explodes

The opposite situation may also exist, with the air being sucked into the oral cavity due to the lowering of the larynx (Fig. 6.6), thereby creating suction (Fig. 6.7). In such cases, the air first rushes in, producing an *implosive* sound (Fig. 6.8), and then almost immediately is reversed into egressive air due to the following sound typically being an air egressive segment such as a vowel.

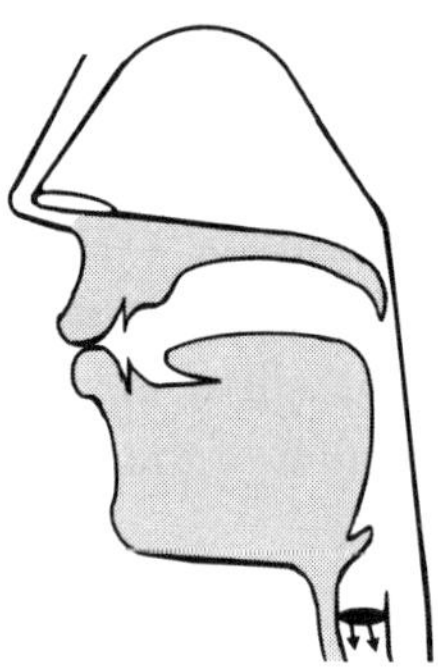

Figure 6.6 Lowering

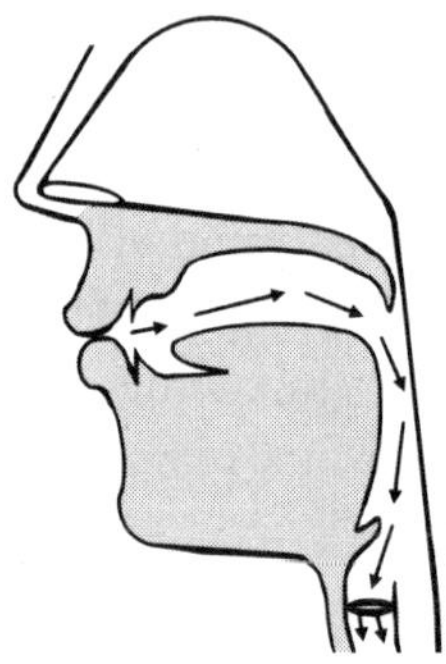

Figure 6.7 Pressure builds

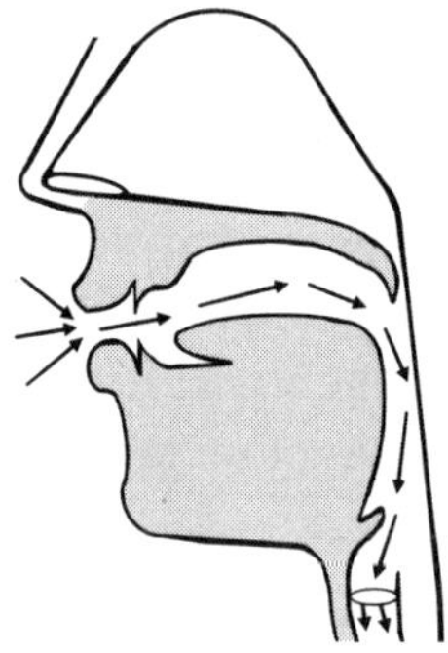

Figure 6.8 Air implodes

6.1.4 Velaric Action

Velaric action is an airstream mechanism that involves the oral cavity alone. This is perhaps the rarest of all airstream mechanisms linguistically, and is encountered as a linguistic feature in only a small number of languages spoken in the southern part of Africa.[1]

In this case, the back of the tongue is used to close off the oral cavity at the velum and an additional closure is made further forward within the oral cavity. Retraction of the velar closure creates suction, producing a sound referred to as a *click*, as shown in Figs 6.9–6.11.

Zulu, a Southern Bantu language spoken in South Africa, employs dental [ǀ], alveolar [ǃ], and lateral [ǁ] clicks regularly in its vocabulary. The sounds were borrowed originally from the neighboring Khoisan languages in order to augment the Zulu sound system. Examples of clicks

[1] It appears as an extralinguistic feature in many languages, including English, where exclamations expressing disapproval such as *tut tut* or *tsk tsk* involve velaric suction.

from Zulu, illustrating the different basic clicks, are provided in (6.1). Each of these basic click types is subject to further modification in manner of articulation, including voicing, aspiration, and nasalization, giving 15 contrastive clicks in total in Zulu.

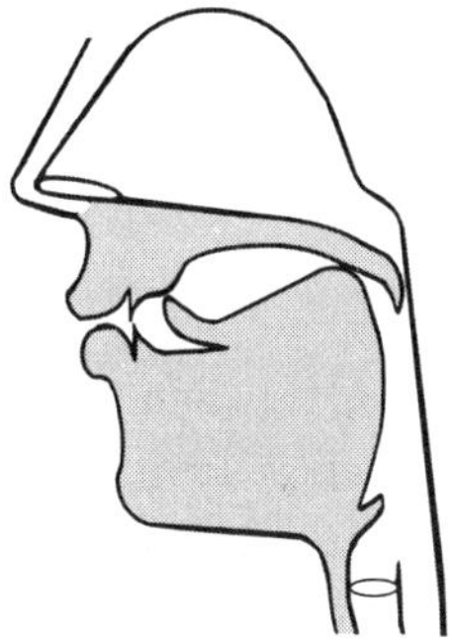

Figure 6.9 Velum closed

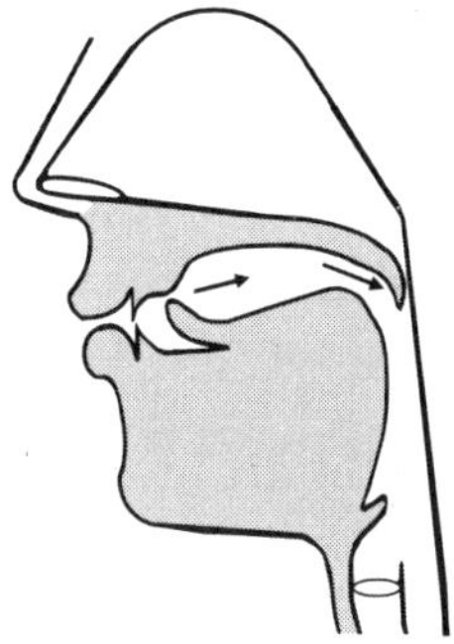

Figure 6.10 Vacuum created

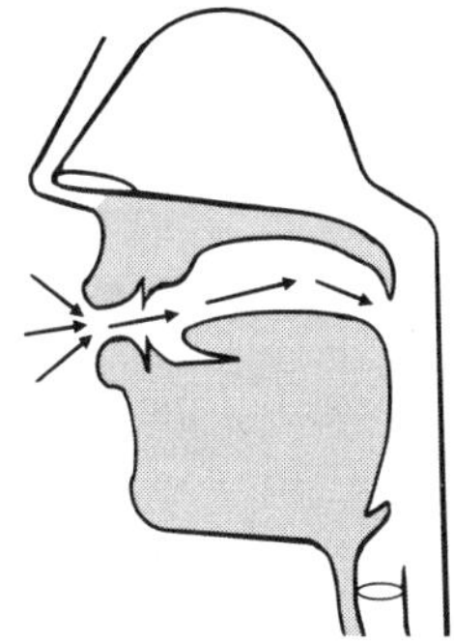

Figure 6.11 Release

(6.1) **Zulu clicks**

Click	Zulu	IPA	Meaning
[ǀ]	icici	[iǀiːǀi]	‘earring’
[ǃ]	iqaqa	[iǃaːǃa]	‘polecat’
[ǁ]	ixoxo	[iǁɔːǁo]	‘frog’

The introduction of clicks into Zulu and other Southern Bantu languages is an interesting sociolinguistic phenomenon. It arises from a custom referred to as *hlonipha* which refers to a kind of taboo avoidance by women of the names of their father-in-law or other senior males related to their husband. When Zulu men married Khoisan women, the women substituted sounds from their own language, i.e. clicks, to modify Zulu names, making them acceptable. Over time, the clicks became part of the regular phonological system.

6.2 States of the Glottis

As discussed in §2.2.2, the vocal cords are flexible ligaments that may be manipulated in a number of ways in order to produce different effects that may affect the production of a sound. The two most important factors are: (i) the degree of closure of the vocal cords, and (ii) their degree of vibration, as discussed below.

6.2.1 Open versus Closed Glottis

One possible manipulation of the vocal cords is to spread them apart, creating an easier passage for the air, producing a voiceless sound, such as [p] or [s]. This is common to all languages. Alternatively, the vocal cords may be brought together, shutting off the flow of air and producing what is called a glottal stop, [ʔ]. If the vocal cords are completely closed and the larynx is raised, then the effect will be one of glottalization, as discussed on page 91 for ejectives, which exhibit a popping sound that is quite distinctive.

The glottal stop is a pulmonic egressive plosive articulated at the glottis by tightly closing the vocal cords. It is, by definition, a stop, since it stops the flow of air and, necessarily voiceless, since it is impossible to vibrate the vocal cords while simultaneously holding them shut. Because it is pronounced in the larynx, it has no place of articulation in the vocal tract and no tongue-front features, such as *coronal* or *distributed.*

For many linguists the glottal stop is considered to be the maximally underspecified (= neutral) consonant and it often acts as a default consonant for breaking up sequences of vowels. It may be found at the beginning of German words that otherwise begin with a vowel, such as *Apfel* 'apple' [ʔap͡fl̩] or *Insel* 'island' [ʔinsl̩]. It may also occur in some speakers pronunciation of English words containing a sequence of vowels, such as *cooperate* [kʰoʊˈʔapəˌreɪt] or *reintroduce* [ˌriʔɪntrəˈd(j)us] to break up the sequence of vowels.

A further possibility is partially closing the vocal cords to produce a narrow passage of air without vibration. This happens when we whisper or speak softly.

6.2.2 Vibration

One of the most important aspects of the manipulation of the larynx is the presence or absence of concomitant vibration of the vocal cords. When this occurs, a number of effects may be observed, the most important of which is *voicing*.

Voicing (유성성) involves the vibration of the vocal cords (성대) during the articulation of a sound (Fig. 6.12), similar to the vibration created when you pluck the string of a guitar or kayageum. It is a characteristic of both obstruents and sonorants, including vowels.

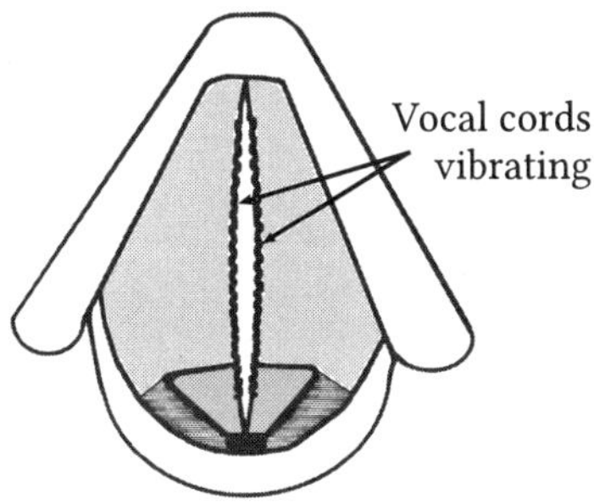

Figure 6.12 Voicing

You can feel the vibration of the vocal cords if you place your fingers on your larynx and say *zzzzz*, which is a voiced sound; now compare this with *sssss*. There should be less vibration with [s]than with [z], since [s] is voiceless. Examples of voiced segments include [b], [m], [j], and [a].

Voicing is a significant contrastive factor in the sound systems of the majority of languages. It is present in all languages and is the normal state for sonorants. It appears in the obstruent systems of many languages, including English, e.g., the first sound in *pin* versus *bin*. As such, it is an important phonetic modification of sounds.

Some languages make use of a somewhat more complex process referred to as *breathy voice* (유성 기식음). This involves the vibration of the vocal cords while they are partially open (Fig. 6.13). Hindi is an example of a language that makes such a distinction among its plosives, as shown in (6.2), where the raised [ʱ] indicates breathy voice.

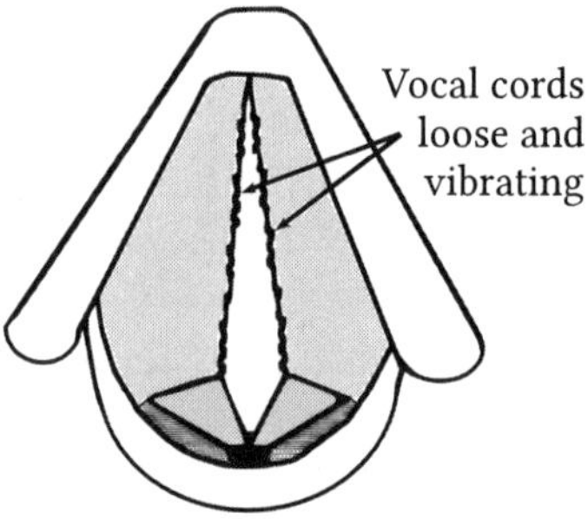

Figure 6.13 Breathy voice

(6.2) **Hindi consonants** (fr. Ladefoged, 2005:141)

	Vl. Plain	**Vl. Asp.**	**Voiced**	**Breathy Voice**
a.	pal 'care for'	pʰal 'blade'	bal 'hair'	bʱal 'forehead'
b.	tal 'beat'	tʰal 'plate'	dal 'lentil'	dʱar 'knife'
c.	kal 'era'	kʰal 'skin'	gal 'cheek'	gʱal 'confusion'

The final category of voicing types is *creaky voice* (협착음) or *laryngealization* (후두음화), an effect achieved by bringing the vocal cords close together and making them vibrate loosely, as in Fig. 6.14. Creaky voice may be used in English as a marker of hesitation and is found as a regular, contrastive marker of sonorant consonants in certain languages of the Pacific Northwest.

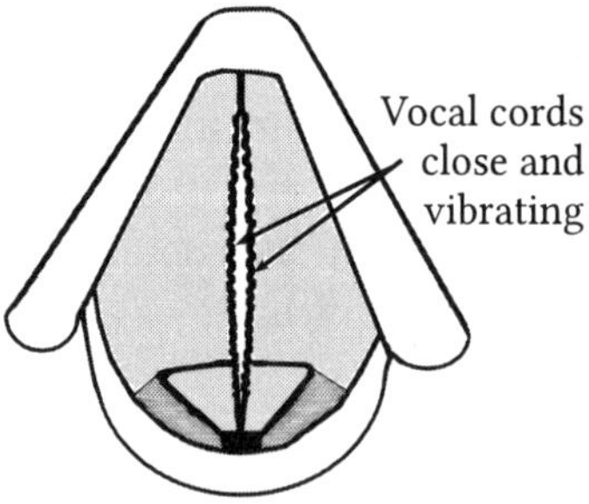

Figure 6.14 Creaky voice

6.3 Manners of Articulation

Manner of articulation (조음 방식) involves the manipulation of the vocal tract in order to produce certain vocal qualities. In what follows, we discuss a number of such manipulations, including the following: plosives, fricatives, affricates, nasals and approximants.

6.3.1 Plosives

One aspect of manner of articulation is that concerned with the production of plosives (파열음)/stops (폐쇄음). This involves an interruption in the flow of air through the oral cavity (구강), followed by a release with an accompanying burst of air, referred to as the *stop burst.* Note that air may pass through the nasal cavity while there is a stoppage in the oral cavity, in which case the segment is referred to as a *nasal stop.*

Plosives are found in all languages. In English, they include the first sound in the words *pot, bought, tot, dot, cot* and *got* and in Korean, the first sound of the words 검 'sword', 껌 'chewing gum', 컵 'cup', 달 'moon', 딸 'daughter', 탈 'mask', 밤 'night', 뺨 'cheek', and 팔 'arm'.

The term *stop* refers to the interruption of airflow, whereas *plosive* refers to the release phase of the segment, when the air *explodes* from the oral cavity. *Stop* is used generally for nasal stops, which have no explosive component.

6.3.2 Fricatives

Fricatives (마찰음) constitute another class of manner of articulation. They involve the continual flow of air along a narrow passage within the oral cavity, resulting in turbulence and noise, similar to the spray of water that occurs when you restrict the flow from a water hose by putting your finger over the end. With fricatives, the articulators are adducted until only a narrow passage remains for the air to flow.

Fricatives may be articulated at many different places within the oral cavity. They constitute a particularly large class of sounds in English, including the last sound in each of the following words: *tough, have, bath, bathe, toss, nose, dish*, and *rouge*. [h], as in the first sound in *high* or *help*, is also considered a fricative by many linguists.[2]

Korean has far fewer fricatives than English, typically only [s], [s'] and [h],[3] which presents a challenge for Korean learners of English, who must learn to make numerous new fricative sounds when acquiring English pronunciation.

6.3.3 Affricates

Affricates (폐찰음) are complex segments consisting of two main parts: i) a full closure like that of a stop and ii) a subsequent partial opening like that of a fricative, resulting in a complex, two-part sound. The IPA describes such sounds by means of the two symbols that represent the two different parts of the complex sound, using what is sometimes referred to as a *digraph*. Thus, a combination of [t] and [s], as in the first sound in the German word *Zeit* 'time,' is represented as [ʦ] or sometimes as [t͜s], using a ligature (합자) to show the close relationship of the two sounds. Similarly, a combination of [t] and [ʃ], which appears in the first sound of the English word *chip*, is realized as [ʧ].

English has two affricates, [ʧ], as in *church, choose*, and [ʤ], as in *judge, gym*. Korean has three distinct affricates, as in the first sound in the words 잘 'good' [ʧal], 친구 'friend' [ʧʰɪŋgu], and 쪽 'page' [ʧ'ok].

Other affricates encountered in languages include German [p͜f] in *Pferd* 'horse', French [p͡s] in *psychologie* 'psychology', Nuuchahnulth [t͜ɬ] in *tɬuɬ* 'good', and Zulu [k͜x] in *krakra* 'bitterness'.

6.3.4 Nasals

Nasal stops constitute a special class of consonants that involves stoppage of the airflow at some place in the oral cavity, while allowing the air to

---

[2] See Kean (1972) for the view that [h] should be considered a sonorant.

[3] Some Korean dialects have merged [s] and [s'], resulting in a single coronal fricative.

continue to pass through the nasal cavity (비강), creating a stop with a nasal timbre or quality.

Almost all languages have at least one nasal consonant. English has the three nasals found at the end of the words *comb* [m], *fan* [n], and *tongue* [ŋ]. Korean has the same three nasals in the same positions as the English nasals, e.g., *kɔm* 검 'sword', *pʰan* 판 'board', *toŋ* 동 'East'. In both English and Korean, the velar nasal [ŋ] does not occur at the beginning of words.

6.3.5 Approximants

Approximants (접근음) are sounds that involve a partial closure in the oral cavity that is not as constricted as with the fricatives and thus does not create turbulence or noise. There are both *central*, meaning that the main flow of air is over the center of the tongue, and *lateral* approximants, in which the airflow is around the sides of the tongue.

In English, [ɹ], [l], [j], and [w] are all approximants. The first two are distinguished by central versus lateral, and the last two are semivowels, effectively consonantal counterparts of the vowels [i] and [u], respectively. We will examine the various kinds of approximants in the following sections, beginning with the r-sounds.

6.3.5.1 Rhotics

Rhotics are r-like sounds and come in a number of varieties. They may be *flapped* (탄설음), as in Korean 사람 [saɾam] 'person', which involves a single tap of the tip of the tongue against the alveolar ridge, *trilled* (전동음), as in Spanish *perro* [pɛro] 'dog', which involves multiple taps of the tip of the tongue or repeated taps of the uvula, as in the French *r-grasseyé* in the word *Paris* [paʀi], or *bunched*, as in English *hair* [hɛɹ]. Rhotics may also occur at various places in the oral cavity, including dental, alveolar, retroflex and uvular places of articulation.

We will examine the typical English rhotic, described as 'bunched' or 'retroflex', in more detail in Ch. 11.

Spanish actually has two rhotics, [ɾ] and [r]. The Spanish words *pero* [ˈpeɾo] 'but' and *perro* [ˈpero] 'dog' contrast in just that respect: the choice of rhotic is crucial to being understood in Spanish.

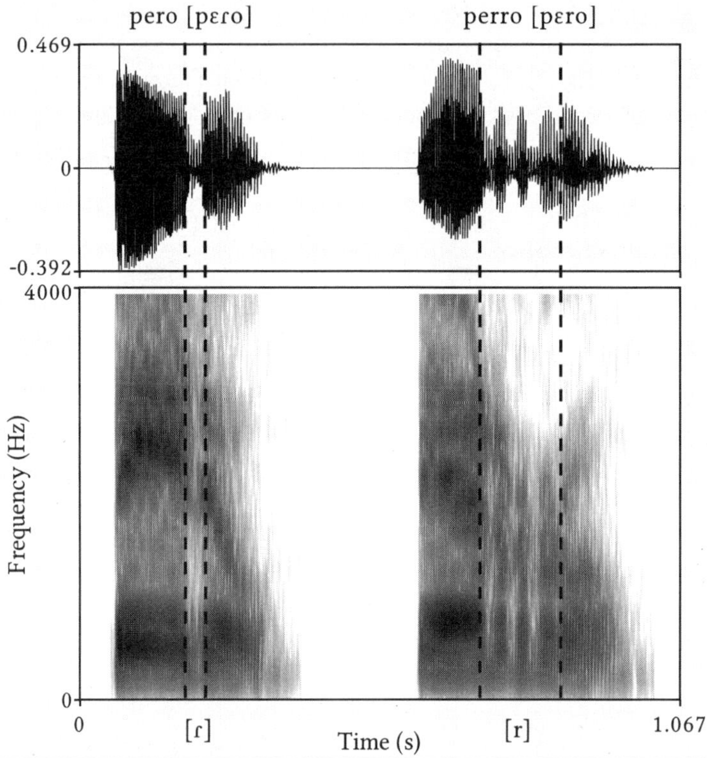

6.3.5.2 Laterals

Laterals (설측음) are the l-sounds that occur in many languages. Perhaps the most common lateral is the alveolar lateral approximant, [l], which is found in English words such as *luck*, *lemon*, *leaf*, etc.

English also has another lateral, referred to as *dark l* or *velarized l*, which is only found at the end of the syllable. This lateral also occurs in languages like Russian, where it may also appear at the beginning of the syllable. This is shown by the spectrogram of the two Russian laterals, [ɫa] and [lʲa], in Fig. 6.15. Velarized laterals are represented by the symbol [ɫ] and palatalized laterals by [lʲ].

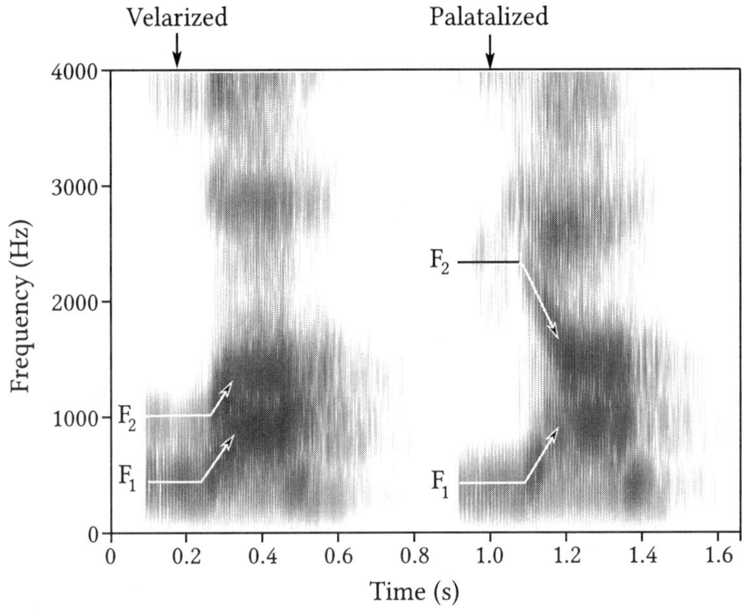

Figure 6.15 Russian laterals: [ɫa] and [lʲa]

The Korean lateral in words like 쌀 [s'aɭ] 'rice' or 발 [paɭ] 'foot' is more like a retroflex [ɭ], made with the tongue curled up toward the hard palate. This type of lateral also occurs in many languages of India, such as Hindi. In addition to these, Spanish has a palatal lateral [ʎ] in words like *lluvia* 'rain' or *pollo* 'chicken', much like the l-sound in the Korean word 한류 'Korean Wave'.

6.3.5.3 Semivowels

Semivowels (반모음), often referred to as *glides* (전이음), are approximants that share properties of both consonants and vowels. They share most of their place features with vowels, but they appear in the position of consonants, that is, either at the beginning or the end of the syllable.

Semivowels are found in every language and a sound may alternate sometimes between being a consonant and a vowel, depending on its position. For example, the Korean root 기다리 [kidaɾi] 'wait' becomes 기다려 [kidaɾjɔ] with the attachment of the suffix /-ɔ/ IMPERATIVE. Both Korean and English have semivowels, but the way they behave is slightly different in the two languages. We will see further examples of this later on in the book.

This concludes the discussion of the basic manners of articulation and we will now move on to examine the various types of sounds that result from these different modifications.

6.4 Analyzing Consonants

In this section we will look at various techniques used for the acoustic analysis of the consonants we have discussed above. We will focus on some of the basic aspects of this analysis using Audacity and Praat, as discussed in Ch. 3.

6.4.1 Voicing

We have already discussed the general properties of voicing in §6.2.2, so here we will focus on how to recognize voicing in the output of the acoustic software. We know that voicing is the result of the vibration of the vocal cords, but how is this manifested in terms of acoustic analysis?

Let's take a look at our example of *ssss* versus *zzzz* from §6.2.2. We know that *ssss* is voiceless, while *zzzz* is voiced, but how does this difference appear in a phonetic analysis? To find out, we follow the same procedure discussed in §3.2.2, but this time we will *create* the sound files using Audacity to record them, and then analyze them with Praat.

1. Open Audacity and select **New** from the **File Menu**.

2. Make sure a microphone is connected to the computer and that the software is set for line in: 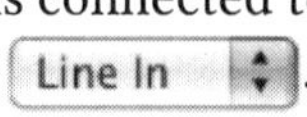
.

3. Set the microphone volume to high: 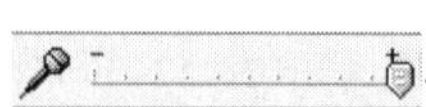.

4. Press the record button to record. After recording, press stop.

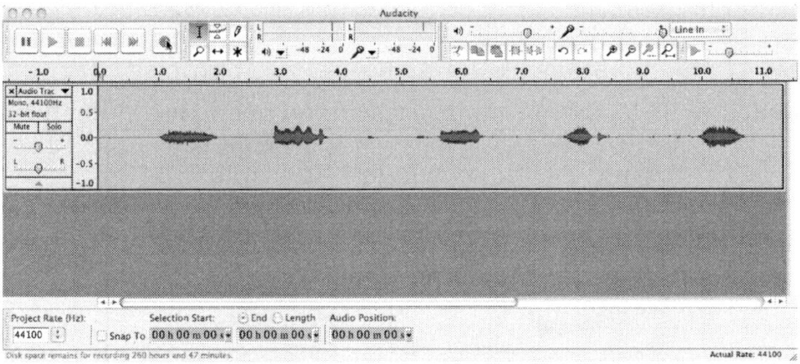

5. Select the recorded sounds.

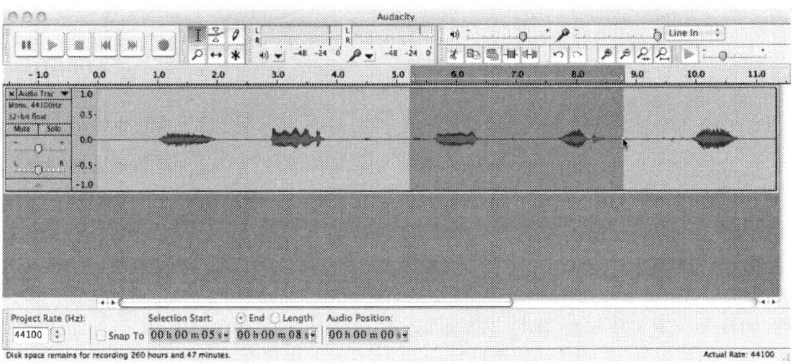

6. From the **File Menu**, select **Export Selection**....

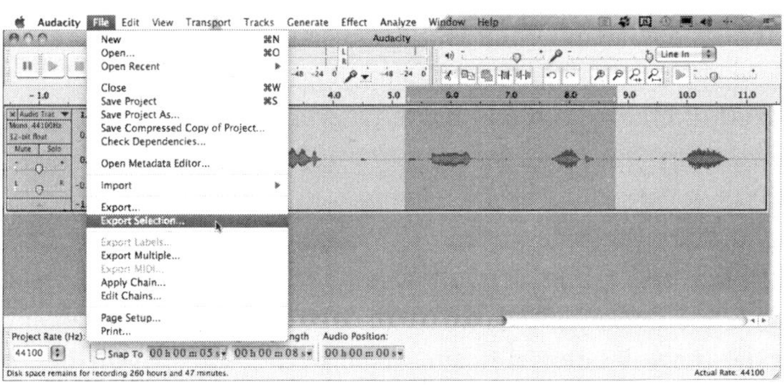

7. Choose a name for the sounds and save as WAV files.

Once the sounds have been recorded digitally, they can now be input into Praat, just as in §3.2.2.2 and then analyzed to see what differences exist between *ssss* and *zzzz*.

1. Read the file(s) into Praat from the **Read** menu, using **Read from**....
2. Select them in the **Objects** window and choose **Edit**.
3. The analysis window provides us with the waveform on top and the spectrogram on the bottom.

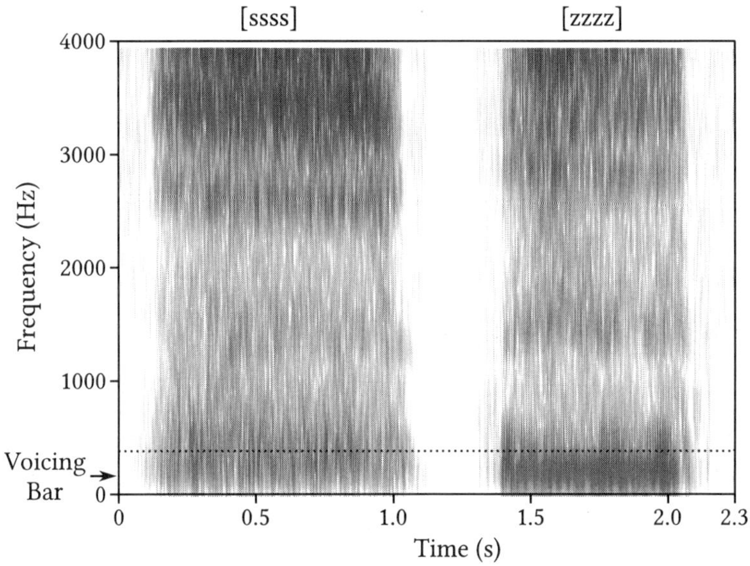

Figure 6.16 *ssss* versus *zzzz*

The resulting spectrogram is shown in Fig. 6.16. The most important indicator of voicing that is shown in Fig. 6.16 is in the low frequency area at the bottom of the spectrogram in the range from 0 to approximately 200Hz. Notice that, while [ssss] shows no significant variation at the bottom, [zzzz] is substantially darker at the bottom of the spectrogram. This greater darkness is referred to as a *voicing bar*, and is a primary indicator of voicing in the spectrogram. All kinds of voiced sounds, including vowels, show this voicing bar.

6.4.2 Properties of Plosives versus Fricatives

Fig. 6.16 demonstrates the general acoustic properties of fricatives, i.e., substantial turbulence by the vertical striations indicating noise. Compare this with the acoustic properties of the plosive [t] in the utterance *ata* in Fig. 6.17.

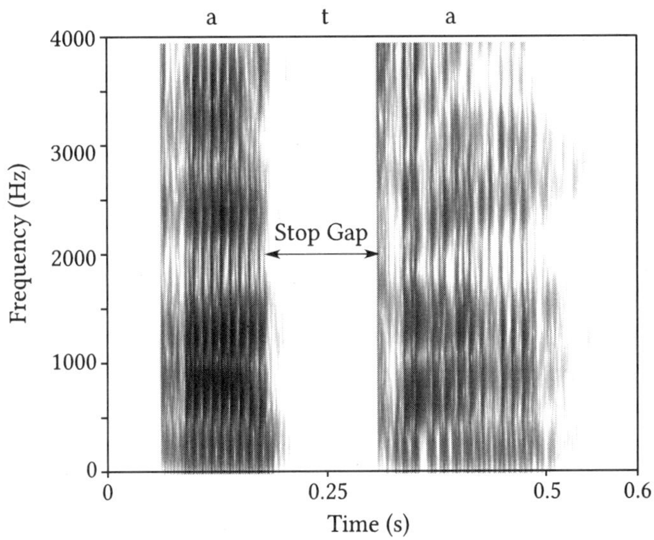

Figure 6.17 Stop gaps

In this spectrogram, the plosive is represented by the white space between the vowels. This space is often referred to as a *stop gap*, which is basically a period of silence. This is the nature of plosives, which involve the closure or interruption of airflow. We will see later how to distinguish different plosives by the affects they have on adjacent sounds, but for now the stop gap will be the most useful indicator of a plosive.

6.4.3 The Nature of Nasals

Nasals, as discussed in §6.3.4, are a special kind of stop that blocks the airflow in the oral cavity while allowing it to continue through the nasal cavity. They are sonorant consonants, which means that they have a certain degree of resonance in the vocal tract and so will appear as darker bands of energy than plosives, although not usually as strong as vowels. This is exemplified in the English word *man* in Fig. 6.18.

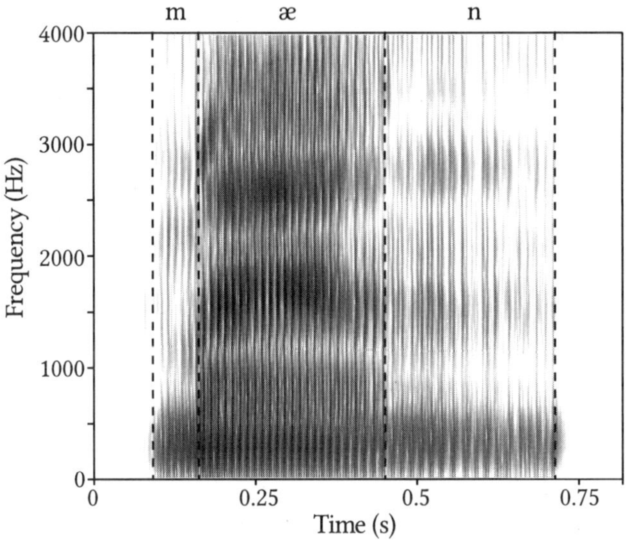

Figure 6.18 Acoustic properties of nasal consonants

As can be readily observed in this spectrogram, the nasal consonants, [m] and [n], show dark bands of energy before and after the vowel, respectively. The final nasal [n] is rather longer simply by virtue of being at the end of the utterance. This greater length is not a property of the sound but rather of its position. Note that the bands of energy associated with the nasals are not as strong as those of the vowel itself. This reflects the consonantal nature of the nasals.

6.4.4 Approximants

Approximants are consonants formed without sufficient closure to stop the flow of air like plosives, or to cause the turbulence found with fricatives. They include the rhotics, laterals and semivowels. Their acoustic analysis is similar to that of the nasal and we can see that, as sonorants, they have greater intensity than the obstruents, but less than the vowels, generally. Fig. 6.19 provides examples of three different approximants, [ɹ], [j], and [l] in the English word *royal.*

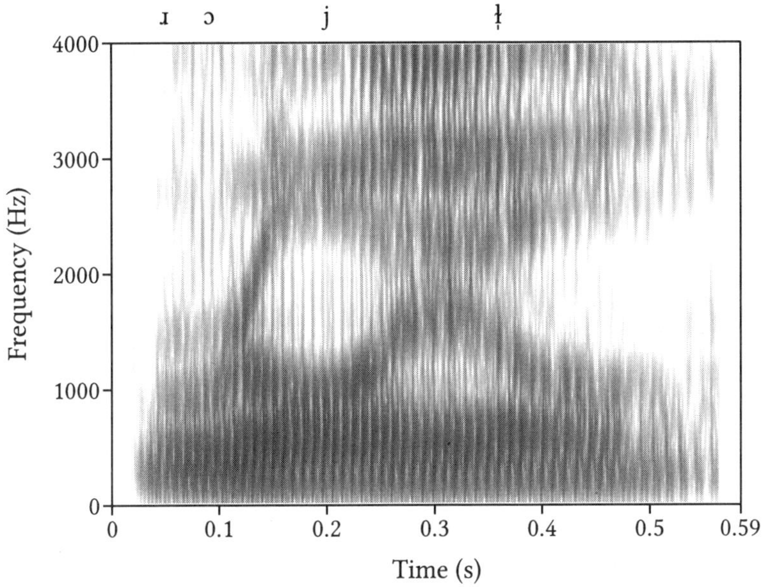

Figure 6.19 Spectrogram of *royal*

Approximants tend to have specific formants, related to their acoustic properties. This will be discussed in greater detail in Ch. 11.

Exercises

1. Analyze recordings of English speakers pronouncing the following words.

pɪt	'pit'	bɪt	'bit'
tæn	'tan'	dæn	'Dan'
kɪl	'kill'	gɪl	'gill'

2. Compare the results of the previous exercise with your own recordings of the following Korean words. They should occur inside a single morpheme if possible.

tal	달	'moon'	t^hal	탈	'mask'
pul	불	'fire'	p^hul	풀	'grass'
pal	발	'foot'	p^hal	팔	'arm'

3. What is the function of the larynx in the modification of speech sounds? What kind of modifications are possible?

Further Readings

Recommended additional readings for this chapter come from several sources. For general phonetic description, Ladefoged & Johnson (2010) and Lieberman & Blumstein (1988) are excellent. For a detailed study of the consonants of the world's languages, Ladefoged & Maddieson (1996) contains a wealth of information.

Lindblom & Maddieson (1988) examines the typology of consonant systems and Cho & Ladefoged (1999) investigates voice onset timing in a variety of languages. Henton et al. (1992) studies the nature of plosives, Catford (1990) investigates glottal consonants and Clements & Osu (2002) examines air pressure factors in the production of stops. Butcher (2004) deals with the fortis/lenis distinction in consonants.

For Korean, Cho et al. (2002), Kim et al. (2002), and Kim (2004) all look at various aspects of the phonetics of Korean plosive consonants.

Keywords: affricate, airstream mechanism, approximant, manner of articulation, obstruent, pulmonic airstream, rhotic, semivowel, sonorant, stop gap, voicing bar.

Chapter 7

Consonants II

In this chapter we continue our examination of the properties of consonants, focusing on the place within the vocal tract where consonants are formed and the kinds of secondary modifications that may be made to change their pronunciation in various ways. We then look at how to analyze these various characteristics acoustically using the software discussed in Ch. 3.

7.1 Places of Articulation

The configuration or shape of the oral cavity will decide the nature of the sound made, since it will determine the structure of the resonating chamber in which the sound resonates, just as altering the volume of liquid in a bottle will affect the sound produced by blowing into the bottle. To modify the quality of a speech sound, one may manipulate the larynx, vary the flow of air, move the velum up or down, or change the shape of the vocal tract. We have already explored the first three in the preceding chapter, so here we will focus on the last of these factors.

We will proceed through the various configurations of the vocal tract individually to make clear the nature of the structures that produce a given sound, starting with a presentation of the *places of articulation* (조음 위치), as shown in Fig. 7.1.

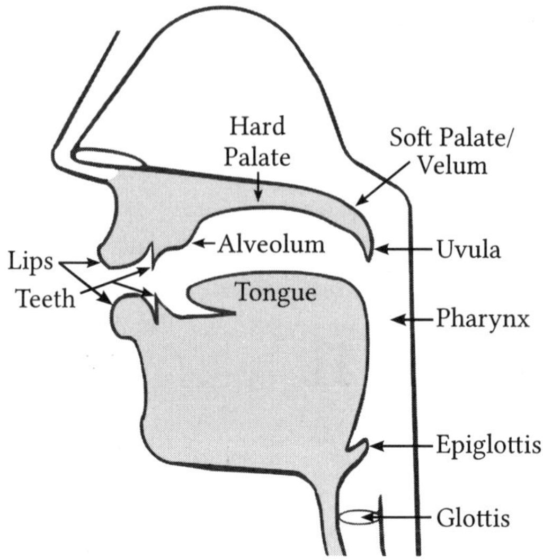

Figure 7.1 The places of articulation

7.1.1 Labial Sounds

Labial sounds (순음) are made by contact or approximation of the lips, possibly along with various secondary manipulations. The lips may also act as a secondary characteristic of a sound, as when the lips are rounded in labialized consonants like [k^w] or [t^w].

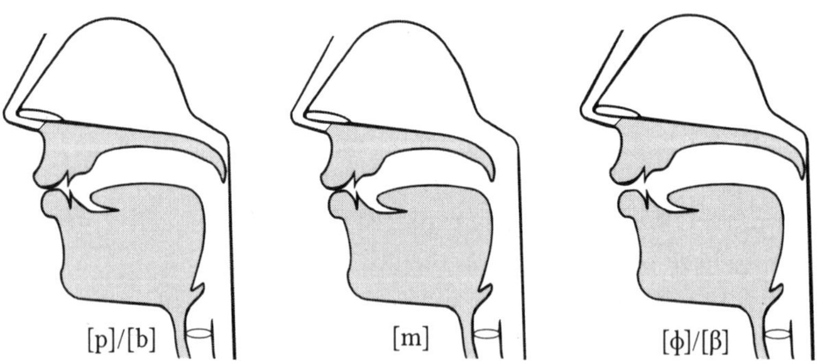

Figure 7.2 Bilabials

Bilabial sounds (양순음) involve the use of both lips and produce sounds such as those described in Fig. 7.2. The sounds may be stops, affricates, fricatives, nasals or any other type which employs the lips. Examples from English include *mom, pop, baby*, etc. Bilabial fricatives are found as the first sound in the Japanese word *ɸɯton* 'futon' and the third sound in the Spanish word *kuβa* 'Cuba'.

Labiodentals (순치음) involve only the lower lip in conjunction with the upper teeth and produce sounds as shown in Fig. 7.3. Labiodentals in English include the first consonants in *fat* and *vat*, and the nasal in the word *emphasis* [ɛɱfəsɪs] (in relaxed speech, due to assimilation to the following [f]). These sounds do not occur in Korean and are difficult for Korean learners of English, who often substitute [pʰ] for [f] and [b] for [v].

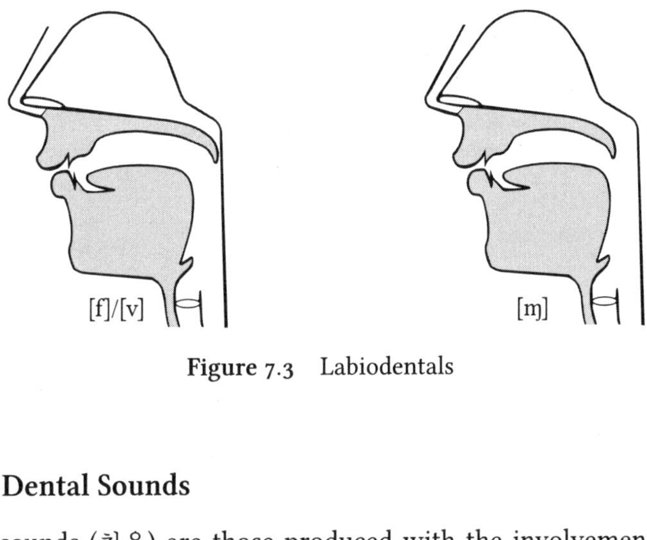

Figure 7.3 Labiodentals

7.1.2 Dental Sounds

Dental sounds (치음) are those produced with the involvement of the teeth, typically with either the lips or the tip or blade of the tongue. Dental sounds may also be of several types, depending on the active articulator.

Interdental sounds (치간음) are those made by placing the tongue between the teeth, as in the first sounds in the English words *think* and *though* (Fig. 7.4). These sounds are relatively rare crosslinguistically, and are not found in Korean. Nevertheless, they contrast with both [f] and [v] on the one hand, and [s] and [z] on the other in the English fricative system and must be distinguished carefully.

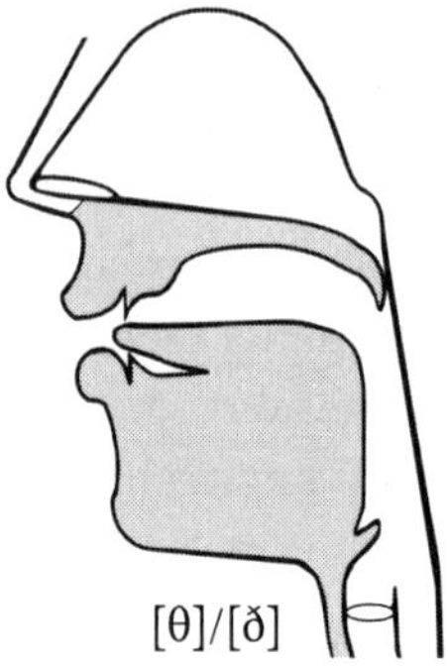

Figure 7.4 Interdentals

When the tongue is raised to the back of the upper teeth, then a dental sound is produced. Such sounds may be fricatives, affricates, plosives or other varieties involving this type of articulation, as in Fig. 7.5.

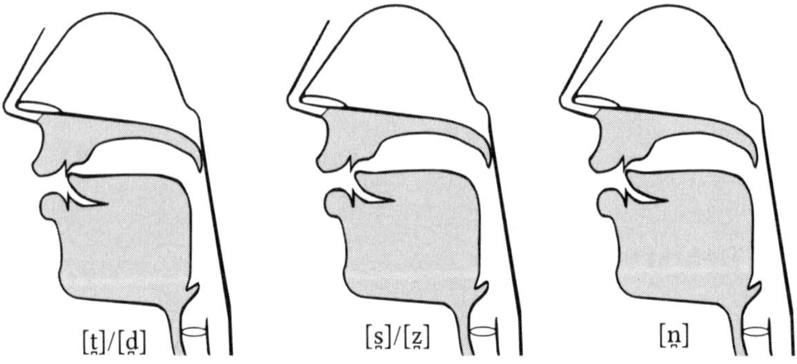

Figure 7.5 Dentals

In English, dental sounds may arise from assimilation to adjacent interdental sounds, such as the nasal consonant in the word *tenth* [tʰɛn̪θ]. Korean has dental plosives, fricatives, and the dental nasal [n̪].

7.1.3 Alveolar Sounds

Alveolar sounds are those articulated behind the teeth at the alveolar ridge. They are often very similar to dentals and the co-occurrence of both types of plosive in a single language is rare, although certain Dravidian languages such as Malayalam are claimed to have such distinctions. Fig. 7.6 gives examples of alveolar sounds.

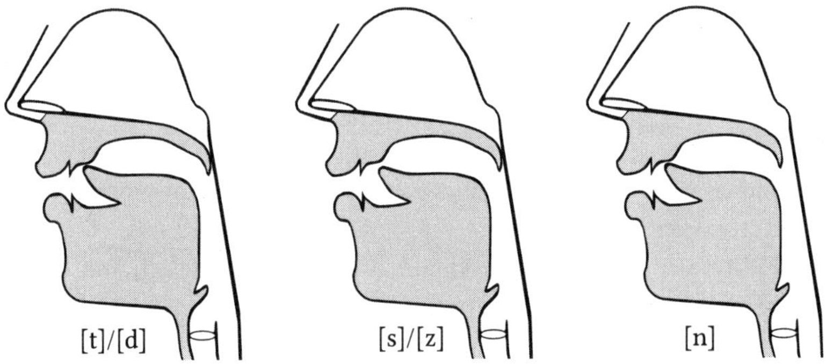

Figure 7.6 Alveolars

In English, alveolar sounds include the initial consonants in *tie*, *do*, *no*, *sew*, *zoo*, *lie*. They constitute the largest class of sounds in English according to place of articulation.

7.1.4 Palatal Sounds

Sounds made in the region of the hard palate are referred to as *palatal* sounds (경구개음). They typically involve the contact or approximation of the *blade* of the tongue towards the hard palate, producing a distinctive effect which may be described as *alveopalatal* (치경구개음), as shown in Fig. 7.7. Such sounds are relatively common in the languages of the world.

Examples of alveopalatal sounds in English include the consonants in the words *shoe*, *chew*, and *Jew*. The nasal in the word *new* may also be palatalized in some dialects, in which case it is represented by the symbol [ɲ] in the IPA. Also, the last sound in the word *garage*, although

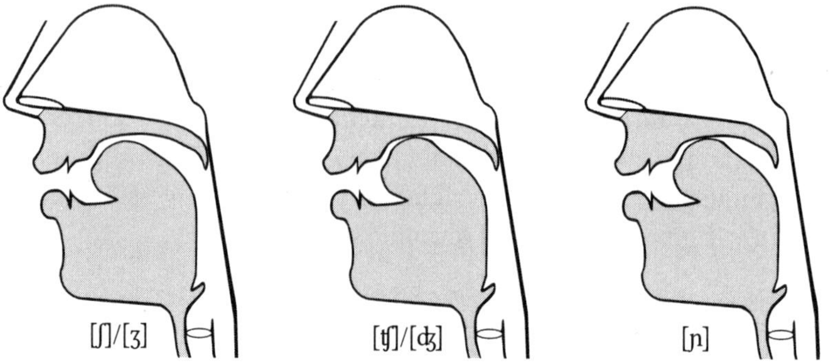

Figure 7.7 Alveopalatals

this sound is quite rare in English, found mainly inside of words such as *treasure*, *pleasure*, *measure*, etc.

In addition to the alveopalatal consonants, both English and Korean have a palatal approximant, [j], in words such as *yes*, *yeast*, *you*, 약, 여자, as shown in Fig. 7.8.

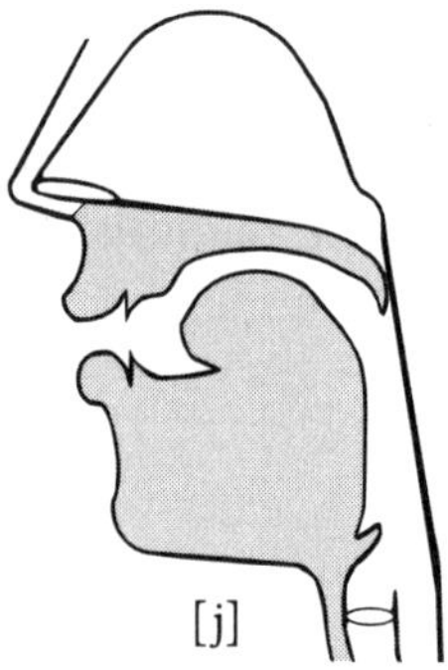

Figure 7.8 The palatal semivowel

7.1.5 Retroflex Sounds

Retroflex sounds (반전음) are made by bending the tip of the tongue back (from Latin *retro* 'back' *-flex* 'bend'), causing the tip or underside to make contact with the hard palate. In terms of position, they are *palatal* in nature, the difference being in the shape of the tongue (Fig. 7.9).

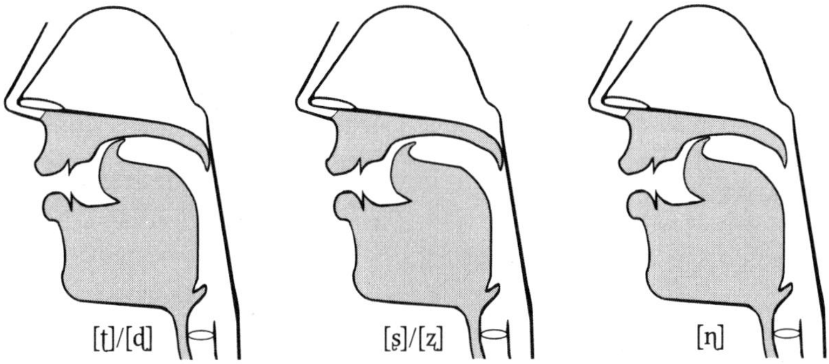

Figure 7.9 Retroflexes

English is not usually considered to have retroflex sounds, although some linguists regard the English [ɹ] as retroflex when pronounced by some native speakers (see §11.2 for further discussion of this issue). The English spoken on the Indian subcontinent uses retroflex sounds for the corresponding alveolar sounds of Standard English, reserving the dental plosives to represent the English interdentals. The Korean pronunciation of ㄹ at the end of the syllable is similar to the retroflex [ɭ], e.g., 물 [muɭ] 'water', 살 [saɭ] 'flesh', 골 [koɭ] 'village'.

7.1.6 Velar Sounds

Velar sounds (연구개음) are those which are produced by moving the back of the tongue in the direction of the velum or soft palate. They include plosives, fricatives and nasals, as shown in Fig. 7.10.

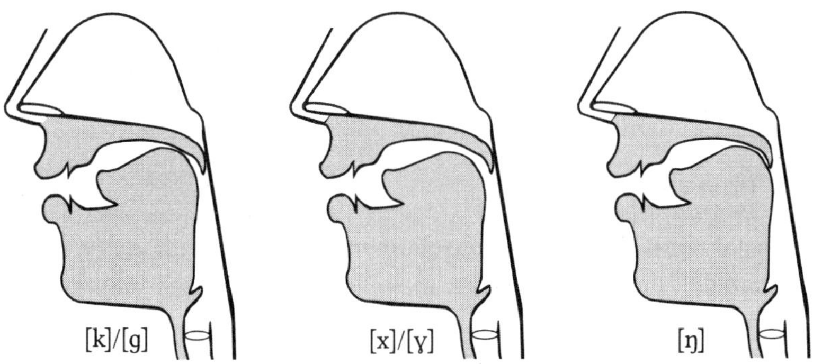

Figure 7.10 Velars

In English, words such as *book*, *bag*, *bang* all end in velar sounds. Korean words such as 길 'street', 칼 'knife', 끝 'end' all begin with velar plosives of different types. Korean also has a velar nasal but, as in English, it only appears at the end of the syllable, e.g., 공 'ball'.

Velar contact is also important in velaric ingressive airstream articulations, such as are found in the *clicks* (흡기음) of some Southern African languages, discussed earlier in §6.1.4.

7.1.7 Uvular Sounds

Uvulars (구개수음), as in Fig. 7.11, are articulated in a similar fashion to velars, although with the back of the tongue retracted to make contact with the uvula, rather than with the velum. Such sounds are less common than velars among the languages of the world, although they do occur in some well-known languages such as French and Arabic.

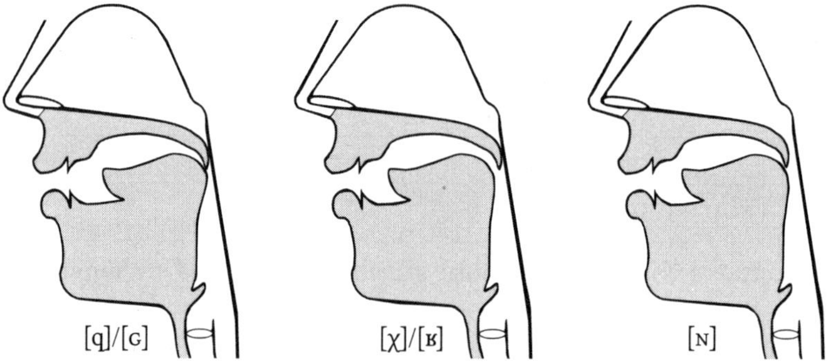

Figure 7.11 Uvulars

Neither English nor Korean makes use of uvulars,[1] but the Parisian dialect of French uses a uvular [ʁ] in words such as *Paris*, *France*, etc.

7.1.8 Pharyngeal Sounds

Pharyngeal sounds (인두음) are relatively rare in the languages of the world but do occur in Arabic, a major world language, as well as in

[1] However, see §11.2.4 on the Northumbrian burr.

numerous less commonly studied languages, such as the North American language, Nuuchahnulth (Kim, 2003). The production of pharyngeals, as in Fig. 7.12, involves the constriction of the pharynx, accomplished by retracting the tongue root towards the back wall of the pharynx. Neither English nor Korean make use of pharyngeal sounds.

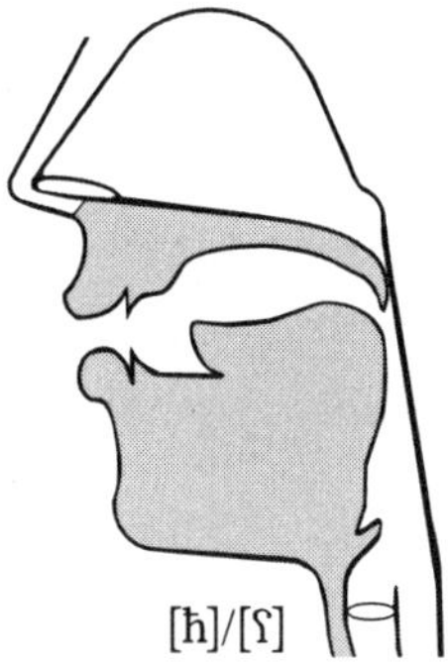

Figure 7.12 Pharyngeals

7.1.9 Glottal Sounds

Glottal sounds (성문음) involve no point of contact within the oral cavity but are, instead, the result of the degree of opening or closure of the glottis, in combination with the passage of air. Sounds such as glottal stops [ʔ] (성문폐쇄음) and glottal fricatives [h]/[ɦ] (성문마찰음) arise in such situations, as shown in Fig. 7.13.

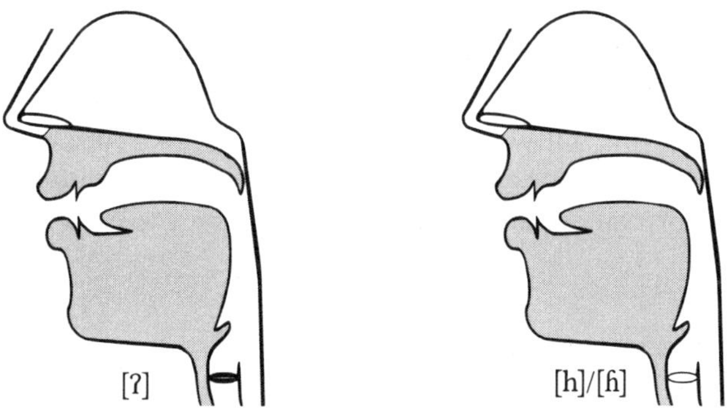

Figure 7.13 Glottals

Glottal stop [ʔ] is a common consonant in many varieties of English, where it replaces other sounds, but it is never contrastive. For example, the word *water* may be pronounced [wɔʔɑː] in London English. In English, the glottal stop always substitutes for some other sound of the standard variety, but in other languages it may serve a contrastive function, for instance, Nuuchahnulth *ʔuyi* 'when' versus *ʕuyi* 'medicine'.

This concludes the discussion of the basic points of articulation and we will now move on to examine the variation found in sounds due to different kinds of secondary modifications.

7.2 Secondary Articulations

Secondary articulation refers to the modifications made to segments that produce some additional phonetic or phonological effect. These may be contrastive effects or simply automatic concomitant phonetic effects on the segment.

7.2.1 Gemination

Gemination (쌍자음) involves the doubling of consonants, causing an increase in the length of time that a consonant is held before its release. Because this requires an increase in duration, it is not easily perceived at the edges of words and is most commonly found inside words. This may occur in languages under certain conditions and may produce contrasts or simply phonetic modification. It may be used to distinguish between similar words or may be an effect of combining forms, or may be simply a phonetic correlate of some structure. Examine the data in (7.1), from Japanese.

(7.1) **Gemination in Japanese**

kata 'shoulder'	ka**tt**a 'bought'
kita 'came; arrived'	ki**tt**a 'cut; sliced'

In Japanese, the doubling of consonants creates contrasts in meaning and so, the gemination is phonologically significant and failure to geminate a consonant will result in an incorrect form.

In Korean, there are also examples of consonant gemination, such as those in (7.2).

(7.2) **Korean Gemination**

manajo	많아요	'be many'	ma**nn**ajo	만나요	'let's meet'
noɾæ	노래	'song'	no**ll**a	놀라	'be surprised'
pɔɾida	버리다	'throw away'	pɔ**ll**e	벌레	'worm'

From these examples it is clear that Korean has contrastive gemination like Japanese. However, there are not many single morphemes that are distinguished by the existence of gemination in Korean.

The English data in (7.3) provide examples of gemination resulting from compounding but not, as in Japanese or Korean, *phonemic* gemination. In English, geminate consonants are never found inside a single morpheme: they only arise across morpheme boundaries when one morpheme ends with the same consonant that begins the next morpheme. This form of gemination is often referred to as *false gemination.*

(7.3) **English compounds and gemination**

[d:]	buil**dd**own	[t:]	ca**t-t**ail
	mi**dd**ay		whi**tet**ail
	hea**dd**ress	[m:]	broo**mm**an
	ai**de-de**-camp		co**mbm**aker
[n:]	pe**nkn**ife	[s:]	hou**ses**tead

In the waveform in Fig. 7.14 it is clear from the time scale that the geminated [d:] of *midday* is much longer than the single [d] of *middle.*[2]

[2] Doubled consonant letters in English spelling do not necessarily equate with duration. They often demonstrate laxing of a preceding vowel, e.g. *later* versus *latter.*

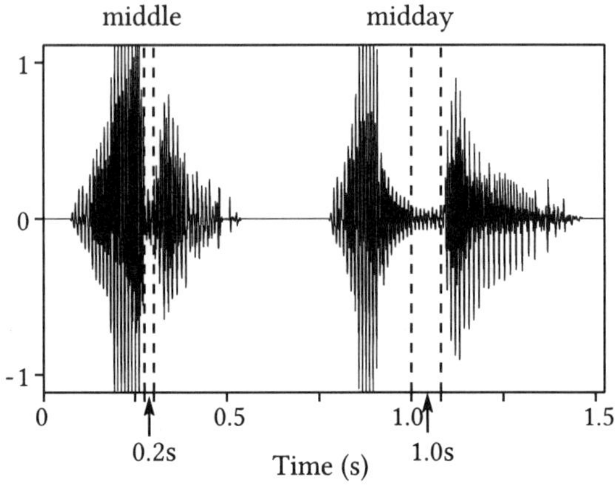

Figure 7.14 Length and gemination: *middle* versus *midday*

This variation in gemination suggests that there is something lexical about gemination in English, but that it only occurs when different morphemes are joined. This is quite different from the Japanese case, which may be morpheme-internal.

In Nuuchahnulth, there is an active phonetic process of consonant gemination which occurs whenever a single consonant occurs between two vowels, especially when the first vowel is short (Stonham, 1999). This happens in order to close the preceding syllable, while at the same time providing an onset for the following one (7.4).

(7.4) **Gemination in Nuuchahnulth**

a. hi**tt**a**kk**ʷists — 'it came across'
   ʔu**ss**u:tɬ — 'he died'

b. mu:tʃi:ɬnakħatɬ — 'it took four days now'
   qʷij̓i:ħawu:si — 'why he died'

Notice that the consonants in (7.4a) are geminated when found in this context, but the consonants in (7.4b) are not, when either: (i) the preceding vowel is long, (ii) the consonant is a sonorant or (iii) when there is an adjacent consonant. This type of gemination is purely phonetic and is conditioned by the environment, reflecting a pressure to avoid light syllables.

In this section, we have seen examples of gemination at several different levels of the grammar. This process may be purely phonetic, as in Nuuchahnulth, purely lexical, as in Japanese and a few cases in Korean, or it may be morphophonological, that is, operate across morpheme boundaries, as in English and in many cases in Korean.

7.2.2 Aspiration

Aspiration (기식) involves the opening of the glottis immediately following the articulation of a sound, producing an audible burst of air accompanying the main segment. As such, aspiration is a secondary characteristic of certain consonants, principally voiceless plosives and affricates.

In English, aspiration is a feature of these sounds in syllable-initial, stressed position. In other positions, aspiration is weak or non-existent. In clusters with preceding [s], such as *spot*, *stop*, *skip*, there is no aspiration of the plosive. Examine the data in (7.5).

(7.5) **Aspiration in English**

Initial	**After [s]**	**Final**
[pʰɪt] 'pit'	[spɪt] 'spit'	[lɪp˺] 'lip'
[tʰɔp] 'top'	[stɔp] 'stop'	[nɔt˺] 'not'
[kʰɔt] 'cot'	[skɔt] 'Scot'	[nɔk˺] 'knock'

As can be seen from this data, voiceless plosives are sometimes aspirated, but it is not contrastive. On the contrary, it is entirely predictable from the position of the plosive in the word. We can see the difference in *pit* and *spit* by examining spectrograms of the two words, as shown in Fig. 7.15. Compare this with Korean voiceless stops, which may be aspirated or unaspirated, as in (7.6).

It is clear from this data that aspiration is contrastive in Korean: if you remove the aspiration you produce a different word. Thus, aspiration in Korean differs from English in terms of its contrastive force.

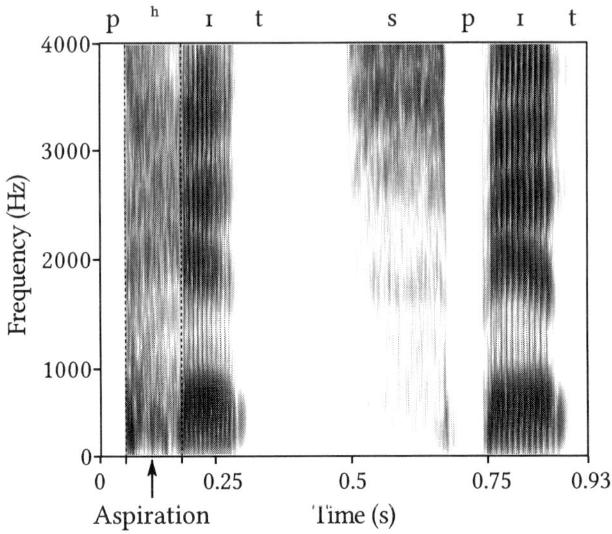

Figure 7.15 Spectrograms of *pit* and *spit*

(7.6) **Aspiration in Korean**

Unaspirated	**Aspirated**
[pal] 발 'foot'	[pʰal] 팔 'eight'
[tal] 달 'month'	[tʰal] 탈 'mask'
[kɨn] 근 'muscle'	[kʰɨn] 큰 'big'

7.2.3 Palatalization

Palatalization (구개음화) involves the addition of a palatal sound, [j], to a segment, thereby creating a new segment with this additional feature. This process is common in many languages, but we will restrict our investigation here to English and Korean.

Our first case comes from English. In English, there is a difference between palatalized and non-palatalized plosives before the vowel [uː], as shown by the examples in (7.7). In (7.7a) we see a contrast between labials—one group is obligatorily non-palatalized while the other group is obligatorily palatalized. In (7.7b) the same generalization holds of the velar consonants. However, with the alveolar consonants (7.7c), there is a potential contrast, but it varies from dialect to dialect. Clearly there are obligatorily non-palatalized forms, but the potentially palatalized forms are variable for this feature. This is described here as *optional*, but is related to dialect more than personal choice. As a broad generalization, British speakers tend to palatalize while North American speakers tend not to.

(7.7) **Palatalization in English**

	Non-palatalized	**Obligatory Palatalization**	**Optional Palatalization**	**Yod Coalesced**
a.	poor	pure		
	booty	beauty		
	food	feud		
	moon	immune		
b.	coop	cube		
	ghoul	(vir)gule		
	who	hue		
c.	tomb		tune	[ʧun]
	doom		dune	[ʤun]
	noon		nude	[ɲud]
	loon		lewd	[ʎud]
	soon		suit	[ʃut]

There is also an extreme version of the palatalized forms in (7.7c), presented in the final column. This so-called *Yod-coalescence* shows that the palatalization can be extended so that the consonants actually *change* their place of articulation, becoming actual alveopalatal consonants.

Our second example of palatalization comes from Korean where, in certain contexts or certain dialects, sounds may become palatalized when followed by either [i] or [j]. The examples in (7.8) illustrate the different contexts where palatalization may occur.

(7.8)	Word	Gloss	Palatalized Form
a.	곳+이	'place-SUBJ'	[koʃi]
	인터넷+이	'internet-SUBJ'	[intɔneʃi]
b.	기 + 어	'crawl-IMP'	[kʲəː]
	띠 + 어	'wear a belt-IMP'	[t'ʲəː]
c.	김치	'kimchi'	[ʧimʧi]
	길	'street'	[ʧil̚]

The examples in (7.8a) are instances of obligatory palatalization: a general rule of Korean that palatalizes [s] before [i]. All speakers apply this rule. (7.8b) contains examples of optional palatalization where [i] re-syllabifies as palatalization on the preceding consonant, reducing the syllable count by one. The examples in (7.8c) come from the Cheju dialect and, along with numerous other examples, demonstrate a greater degree of palatalization before [i] in this variety of Korean.

What should be clear from the preceding examples is that palatalization is a very common process in language and may take various forms, phonetic, phonological or lexical.

7.2.4 Labialization

The process of labialization (순음화) involves the addition of the labial consonant [w] to a segment, resulting in a rounded segment. This may be an underlying contrast in the language or may be derived via some process. We will examine cases from both English and Korean.

In English, labialization is contrastive for alveolar and velar points of articulation (7.9a & b), but only rarely for labial consonants (7.9c). The restriction on labials, which is found in many languages, may be related to the labiality of [w] itself.

(7.9) **Labialization in English**

a.	tin	[tʰɪn]	twin	[tʷɪn]
	deign	[deɪn]	Duane	[dʷeɪn]
	seep	[siːp]	sweep	[sʷiːp]

b.	keen	[ki:n]	queen	[k^{w}i:n]	
	gone	[gɔn]	guano	[g^{w}ɔnoʊ]	(< Spanish)
c.	bond	[bɔnd]	bwana	[b^{w}ɑnə]	(< Swahili)
	paw	[pɑ]	(petits) pois	[p^{w}ɑ]	(< French)

Korean also exhibits cases of labialization for alveolars and velars, as shown in (7.10). As in English, labials are much less likely to exhibit labialization.

(7.10)	[t^{w}eʤi]	돼지	'pig'
	[and^{w}e]	안돼	'don't'
	[k^{w}a.il]	과일	'fruit'

In the case of Korean, there is also an active, optional process of *delabialization*, which removes the rounding effect, resulting in forms such as [t^{w}eʤi] 돼지 'pig' becoming [teʤi]. One consequence of this process of delabialization is that Korean learners of English often fail to maintain the distinction between English pairs of words like *keen* and *queen* or *kick* and *quick*.

7.2.5 Glottalization

Glottalization (성문음화) involves the closing of the glottis with concomitant raising of the larynx to create air pressure in the oral cavity. This is subsequently released, creating a distinctive popping sound, that is easily perceived.

While this process is fairly common in the languages of the world, we do not usually encounter it in English, although there is a process known as *preglottalization* that is found in some varieties. In these dialects, the preglottalized consonants have a glottal stop, [ʔ], before the consonant in the coda, e.g. *what* [ˈwɒʔt], *thank you* [ˈθæʔŋk ˈju:], etc.

Some phonologists treat the Korean tense consonants, ㅃ ㄸ ㄲ ㅆ ㅉ, as glottalized ([p' t' k' s' tʃ']), although the acoustic effect is somewhat different. We will not explore this process any further here.

7.2.6 Velarization

Our final secondary modification of segments is *velarization* (연구개음화), a process that involves the raising of the back of the tongue toward the velum during the production of a sound. In English, this is most commonly encountered in the so-called dark *l*, that results from English *l* appearing in the rhyme of a syllable. The resulting velarized *l* is represented by the symbol [ɫ] and is found in words such as *tall*, *hill*, *bottle*, etc. In some varieties of English, velarization may lead to a change to [w], the labiovelar approximant.

Other languages, such as Russian and Polish, make a clear distinction between plain l [l] and velarized l [ɫ] in their vocabulary, as discussed in §6.3.5.2.

7.3 Acoustic Properties of Consonant Place

As mentioned earlier, the place of articulation of a consonant may be determined in a spectrogram by its effects on the surrounding segments. In the following we will examine the different effects associated with each place of articulation, focussing on the three main places, labial, alveolar, and velar.

7.3.1 Labials

Labial consonants, such as [p], [b], or [m], tend to have a lowering effect on the F_1 and F_2 of neighboring vowels so that one sees a downward trend in the formants as the vowel approaches the labial consonant. This is a prototypical property of labiality.

If we examine Fig. 7.16 closely, we can see that the area of the first formant that is closest to the labial consonant, [p], is lower than the average for F_1 for the vowel. This demonstrates the lowering effect of the labial consonant on the adjacent vowel and provides us with a useful heuristic for determining the place of articulation. In reading spectrograms, this downward trend of the formant is an important feature to note.

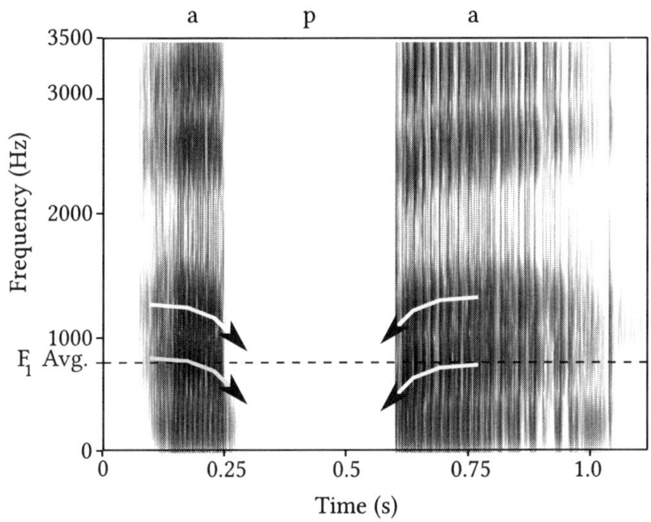

Figure 7.16 Effects of [p] on F_1 and F_2 of vowels in [apa]

7.3.2 Alveolars

Alveolar consonants tend to have less obvious effects on the adjacent vowel formants, so the formants remain more or less level, as shown by the F_1 and F_2 of the vowels in the nonsense word [ata] in Fig. 7.17. The same effects would be true for any of the other alveolar consonants.

As can readily be seen, alveolars tend to have little or no effect on the shape of the adjacent vowel formants. This absence of a clear effect on the vowel may be taken as an indicator of an alveolar sound. Thus, the marker of alveolar consonants is the levelness of the vowel formants and the absence of effects on their edges.

7.3.3 Velars

Velar consonants tend to have a raising effect on F_2 and a lowering effect on F_3, as shown in Fig. 7.18. This moving together of the two formants is often referred to as a *velar pinch*, since it appears as a pinching effect of a velar consonant on adjacent vowel formants.

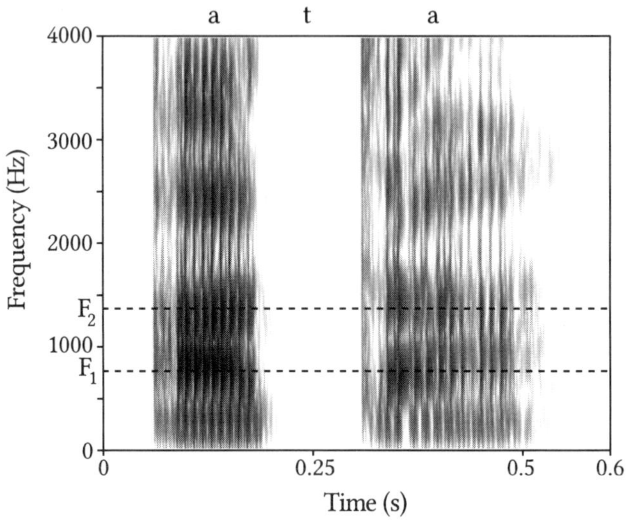

Figure 7.17 Effects of [t] on F_1 and F_2 of vowels in [ata]

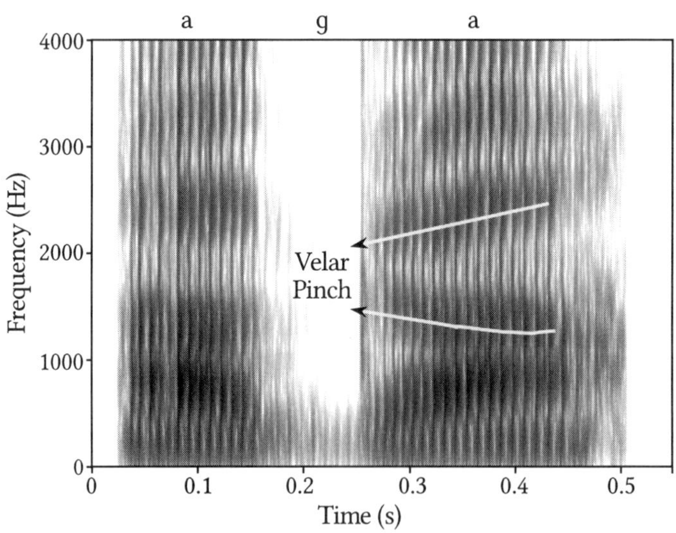

Figure 7.18 Effects of [g] on F_1 and F_2 of vowels in [aga]

There are other effects on adjacent vowels that may be caused by consonants, but we will restrict ourselves here to the most common cases, which we have discussed above. We will introduce any additional effects on vowel formants as we encounter them.

Exercises

1. Aspiration in English and Korean

   Examine the following data and decide in each case how aspiration is used. Provide a description of the phenomenon for each case.

   a. *English*

spɪt	'spit'	p^{h}ɪt	'pit'
stæn	'Stan'	t^{h}æn	'tan'
skɪn	'skin'	k^{h}ɪn	'kin'

   b. *Korean*

tal 달	'moon'	t^{h}al 탈	'mask'
pul 불	'fire'	p^{h}ul 풀	'grass'
pal 발	'foot'	p^{h}al 팔	'arm'

2. Give five examples of gemination in Korean. They should occur inside a single morpheme if possible.
3. Give five examples of consonant palatalization in English.
4. Discuss the acoustic correlates of place of articulation for consonants and how they are manifested in the spectrogram.

Further Readings

Recommended additional readings for this chapter come from several sources. For general phonetic description, Ladefoged & Johnson (2010) and Lieberman & Blumstein (1988) are excellent. For a detailed study of the consonants of the world's languages, Ladefoged & Maddieson (1996) contains a wealth of information. The earlier Maddieson (1984) contains extensive inventories of the consonant systems of many languages.

Stevens & Blumstein (1978), Kurowski & Blumstein (1987) and Delattre et al. (1962) discuss acoustic correlates of place of articulation among plosives, nasals and fricatives, respectively.

Keywords: aspiration, delabialization, gemination, glottalization, labiality, palatalization, point of articulation, velar pinch.

Chapter 8

Prosodic Analysis

In this chapter, we examine the prosodic properties of language from a phonetic perspective, including tone, stress, pitch accent, and intonation. Prosodic analysis involves those aspects of the phonetic system that are traditionally referred to as *prosody* (운율학) (see, for example, Firth, 1948). The study of prosody includes the examination of tone, stress, and pitch accent systems, as well as higher level phrasal and sentential intonation. We begin with a brief examination of tone.

8.1 Tone

Tone systems (음조) are relatively common in the languages of the world, especially in East and Southeast Asia, Central America, and Sub-Saharan Africa. There are a number of types of tone systems, but they all share one common property: a change in *pitch* may result in a change in meaning, although all combinations are not necessarily attested.

8.1.1 Pitch

Before discussing the relationship of pitch to tone, we must first understand the nature of pitch. Pitch is a term used to refer to variations in fundamental frequency (F_0). Fig. 8.1 is a typical sentence in Cantonese: *yìhgā néihdeih tèngjyu ngóh góng* ‘now you (pl.) listen (to what) I say’.

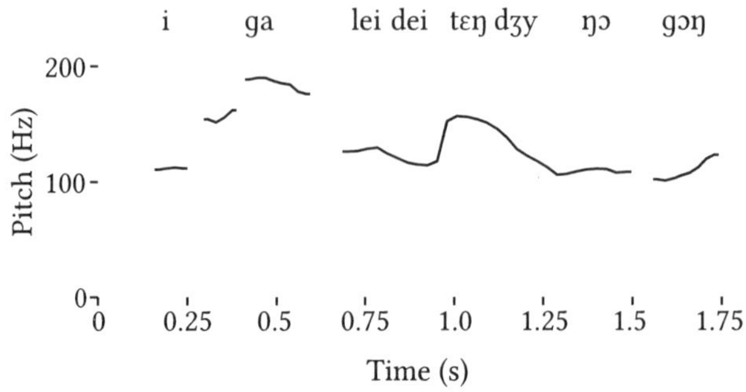

Figure 8.1 A Cantonese sentence

As can be seen in Fig. 8.1, the fundamental frequency of the speaker's voice, indicated on the left side of the pitch track as 'Pitch (Hz)', ranges from approximately 100–195Hz over the course of this sentence. This will vary according to the speaker: typically, males' pitch ranges from around 50–180Hz and females from about 100–300Hz, although these are only rough estimates. Each individual has their own specific range within these limits.

The variation in pitch in this example is not related to phrase or larger intonational units, but varies from syllable to syllable in unpredictable ways. This is very typical of tone languages, where each syllable or morpheme (sometimes they are the same) may exhibit its own pitch. In the most basic situation, each syllable is assigned a specific lexical tone, giving rise to lexical differences between otherwise identical words, as shown by the example in (8.1) from Standard Chinese.

(8.1) **Standard Chinese tones**

a. [ma˥] 媽 'mother'
b. [ma˧˥] 蔴 'hemp'
c. [ma˨˩˦] 馬 'horse'
d. [ma˥˩] 罵 'scold'

Note: ˥ marks high, ˧˥ rising, ˨˩˦ falling-rising, and ˥˩ falling tone.

These differences are clearly contrastive and there are a number of examples like this one which confirm that tone is a contrastive lexical property of Standard Chinese and, in fact, of all Chinese varieties. In Standard Chinese, the tones are maximally distinct, involving not only pitch level, but also changes in pitch level. This distinction is an important one: tones may occur at different levels of pitch, e.g. high, mid, low, but they may also involve a transition from one level to another. Such cases are referred to as *contour tones*. To facilitate perceptual saliency, maximal differences of tone configuration are preferred in tone systems.

8.1.2 Analyzing Tone

Now that we have some idea of the nature of tone, we can examine how to analyze tone using software. First of all we must find a sample of tone to analyze. As an example, we can use a recording of the four Standard Chinese words discussed in (8.1). The recording is first digitized using Audacity as discussed earlier and then a WAV file is created with just the four words *mā* 'mother', *má* 'hemp', *mǎ* 'horse', and *mà* 'scold'. This is then loaded into Praat as done previously in §3.2.2.2. We then select **Edit**, providing a window as in Fig. 8.2.

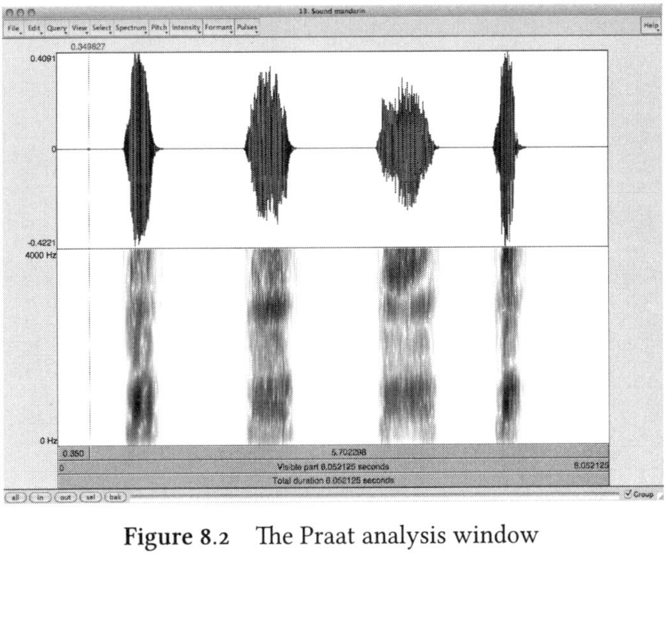

Figure 8.2 The Praat analysis window

Since tone is the focus here, and this is best shown by a pitch track, we first remove the spectrograph window from the display, by deselecting SHOW SPECTROGRAM in the **Spectrum** menu item, as in Fig. 8.3.

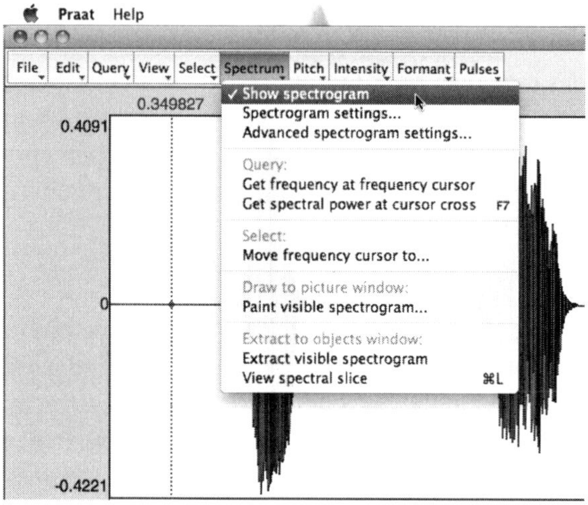

Figure 8.3 Turning spectrographic analysis off

This leaves only the waveform window. Now we turn *on* the pitch analysis window by selecting it under PITCH in the menus, as shown in Fig. 8.4.

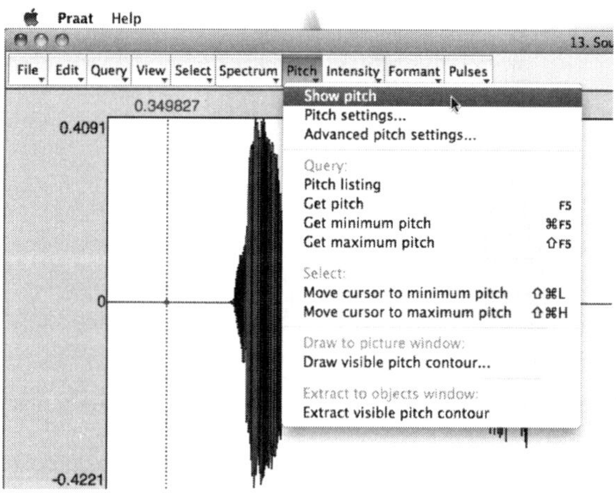

Figure 8.4 Turning pitch analysis on

This provides us with a graphic presentation of the variation in fundamental frequency, measured in Hz, of the tones of the four words, *mā* 'mother', *má* 'hemp', *mǎ* 'horse', and *mà* 'scold', as shown in Fig. 8.5.

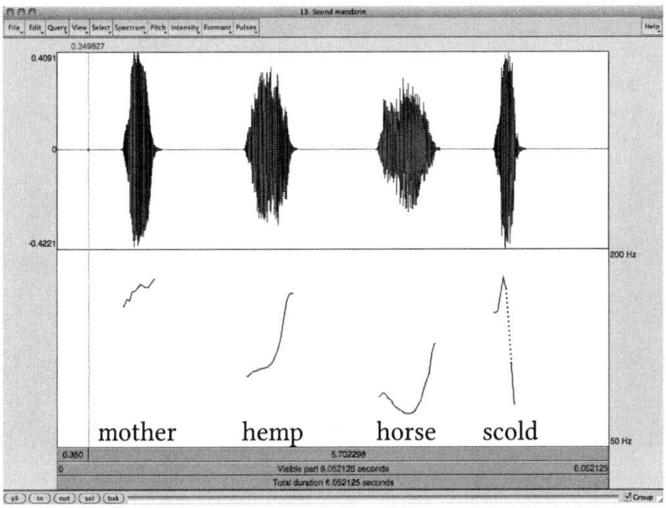

Figure 8.5 The tones of the four Mandarin words *mā* 'mother', *má* 'hemp', *mǎ* 'horse', and *mà* 'scold'.

There are several adjustments that can be made to the pitch display to make the analysis clearer. First, one can adjust the *range* of analysis. Since different speakers have different pitch ranges, this can be very useful. To adjust this setting, we must open the Pitch menu and select Pitch settings…, as in Fig. 8.6.

In the pitch settings window, we can adjust the pitch range by entering appropriate numbers in the two boxes, left for bottom of the range, right for top of the range. Choose **Hertz** for the unit of measurement and **curve** for the **Drawing method**. As for the **Analysis method**, *autocorrelation* is preferred for intonation studies and *cross-correlation* for tone studies. Note that it is possible to measure the pitch at any point by placing the cursor at the desired position and clicking. As shown in Fig. 8.7, the pitch at that point appears on the right side of the window, in this case 179Hz.

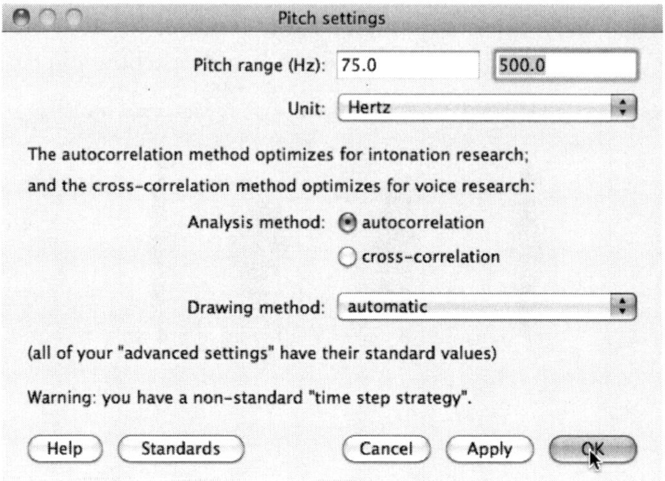

Figure 8.6 The pitch setting window

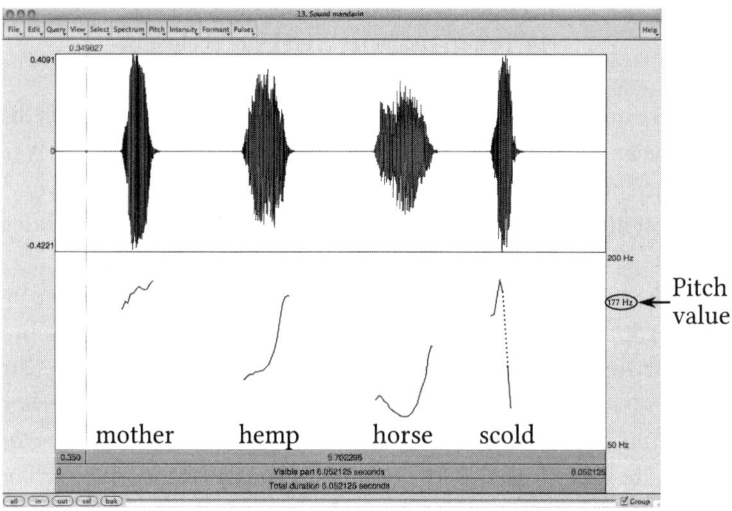

Figure 8.7 Pitch indication on right of window

The pitch track of the data can be saved as a graphic in various formats for presentation purposes. This is done by selecting **Extract visible pitch contour** from the PITCH menu. The result will be an entry in the PRAAT OBJECTS window entitled *Pitch untitled.* If you close the **Edit** window and return to the PRAAT OBJECTS window you can select *Pitch untitled* and then rename it by pressing the **Rename** button at the bottom of the window. This is useful for selecting the proper file when you have many objects in the PRAAT OBJECTS window.

Now, select the pitch track again and choose **Draw** from the menu on the right side (Fig. 8.8).

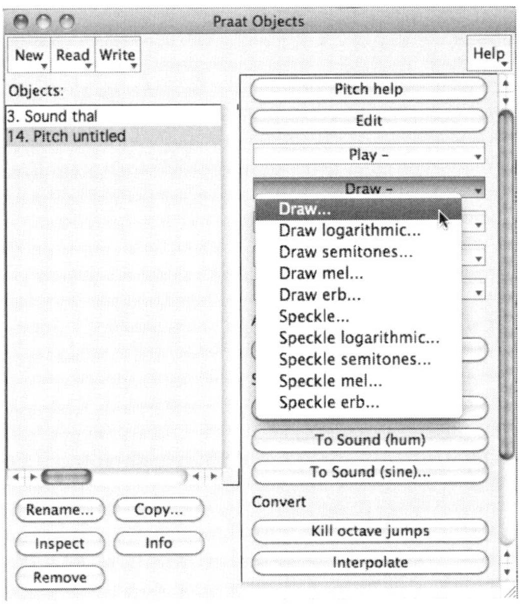

Figure 8.8 Creating a graphic of the pitch track

This will give you a new window entitled **Pitch: Draw**, as in Fig. 8.9. This window allows you to specify the time range and frequency range of the resulting graphic. It also allows you to tick a box labeled *Garnish* which will provide a basic format for the graphic. Later on you can learn alternative ways to do this but this is sufficient for now. The result of this is shown in Fig. 8.10.

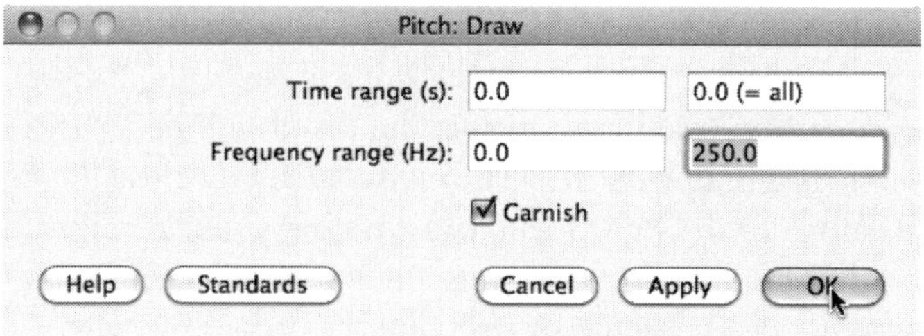

Figure 8.9 The Pitch: Draw window

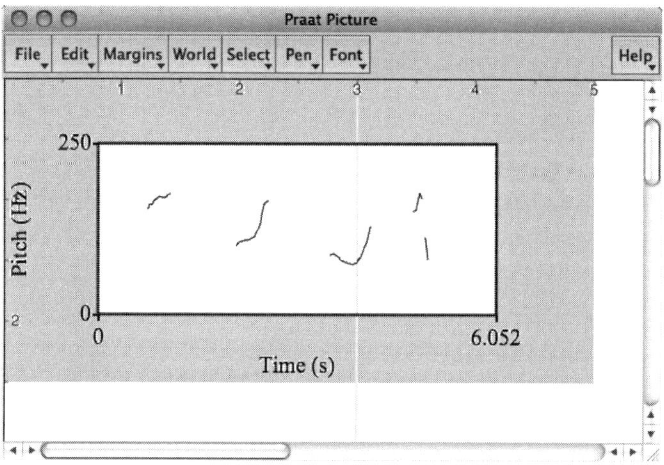

Figure 8.10 The graphic of the pitch track

This graphic may now be saved as a file that can be inserted into other documents. This is done by choosing one of the items in the **File** menu, for example *Write to EPS file...*, as shown in Fig. 8.11. The final output is shown in Fig. 8.12. This may be used like any other graphic file.

Praat can be very useful for analyzing the pitch levels and contours found in a language. There are a number of additional settings that we have not yet explored in this short discussion and you are encouraged to experiment with them.

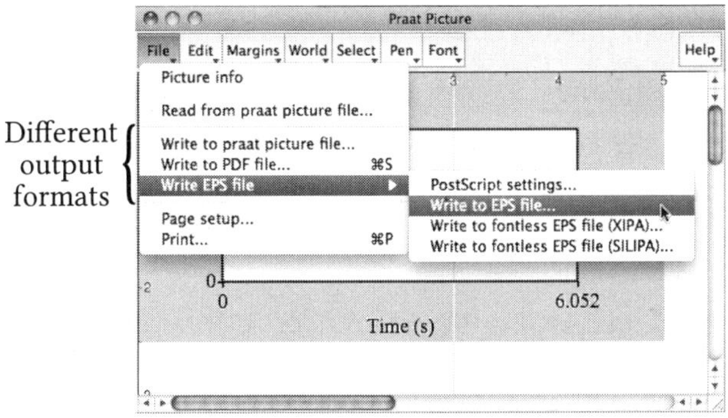

Figure 8.11 Saving the graphic

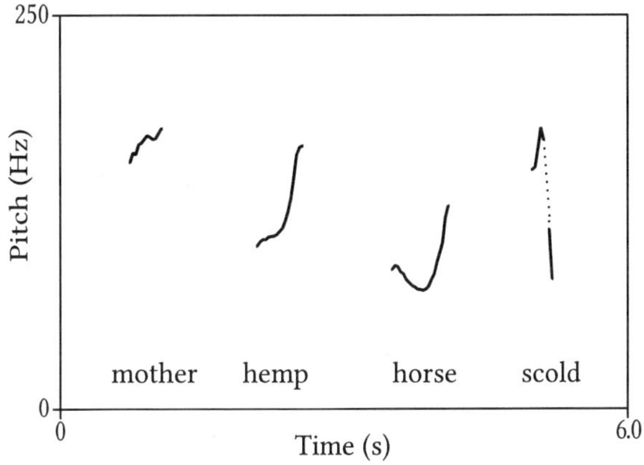

Figure 8.12 The final output of pitch analysis

Before leaving the discussion of tone, we will examine one other case: that of Busan Korean. In §5.5.1 it was remarked that Korean has a limited set of vowel length distinctions, only in the first syllable of the word. There is a concomitant of such vowel length that is realized as pitch in some dialects of Korean. Thus, the examples in (8.2), repeated from (5.6), show differences in pitch as well as vowel length in Busan Korean. In each case the first member of the pair has a short vowel and a high tone (˥) and the second has a long vowel and a rising tone (˩˥). According to Y.-H. Chung (2006), "monosyllables with a short vowel are high-toned and those with a long vowel are rising-toned."

(8.2) **Busan Korean pitch accent**

High Tone			**Rising Tone**		
[mal˥]	말	'horse'	[mal˧˥]	말	'language'
[pam˥]	밤	'night'	[pam˧˥]	밤	'chestnut'
[nun˥]	눈	'eye'	[nun˧˥]	눈	'snow'

The pitch track exhibiting the differences in tone in the words for 'snow' and 'eye' is shown in Fig. 8.13. In this case, the subject marker -*i* has been appended to each form, creating a two-syllable form. As a consequence of this, tone is distributed over the two syllables. In the case of 'eye' the result is a long high level tone, but in the case of 'snow' the rising tone is distributed over the two syllables, resulting in a low/mid level tone followed by a high level tone. This demonstrates the complex nature of contour tones.

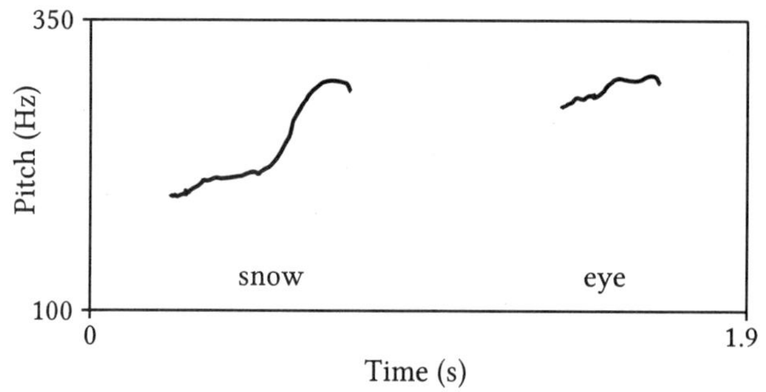

Figure 8.13 Korean 눈-이 'snow (SUBJ)' and 'eye (SUBJ)'

For many speakers of Korean there is no pitch difference in such words, so it depends on the dialect whether pitch is a significant factor.

8.2 Stress

In some languages a variation in pitch or intensity or vowel length may be associated with a certain prominence within the word. Each word is assigned a single, most prominent syllable to which all other syllables are subordinate. This may or may not be applied consistently to a particular position within the word. In such cases, the phenomenon is referred to as *stress* (강세).

There are different kinds of stress systems. In some systems, stress is completely regular and predictable. As an example, in French stress is always placed on the last syllable of a word, no matter how short or long the word is. In Hungarian, it is placed on the first syllable of the word. In Polish, it is usually placed on the second syllable from the end (penultimate). In all these cases, the placement of stress is regular and predictable. Because of this, the placement of stress in these languages is a very useful indicator of the boundaries of words. For instance, if you are listening to a sentence in spoken French you can tell that each time you hear a stressed syllable, the word is ending and the next word is beginning. The same strategy works for the other languages mentioned above and many others. This type of stress placement is often referred to as *demarcative* stress, since it *demarcates* the limits of words.

However, this is not true for all languages. Some languages, particularly those that use tone, may not make very much use of stress at all. In Cantonese, for example, stress plays a very marginal role. On the other hand, languages like English and Russian have *variable* stress, which moves about in the word and must be learned as a lexical class.

Stress should be viewed as a relative property, one that may have degrees such as primary and secondary or no stress at all. Typically, there is only a single *primary* stress per word, but there may be several secondary stresses depending on the length of the word.

We will begin with an example from French. In French, stress appears on the *final* syllable of the word, no matter how long it is, as indicated in (8.3) by the raised stroke [ˈ].

(8.3) **French stress**

a. table	[ˈtabl]	‘table’
b. secours	[søˈkuʁ]	‘aid’
c. dépendance	[depɑ̃ˈdɑ̃s]	‘dependence’
d. indépendance	[ɛ̃depɑ̃ˈdɑ̃s]	‘independence’

Thus, the placement of stress is a good indicator of the word boundaries. In Finnish, main stress is always on the first syllable of the word, as shown in (8.4). Again, this serves to indicate word boundaries.

(8.4) **Finnish stress**

a.	ˈkala	'fish (nom. sg.)'
b.	ˈjokainen	'every'
c.	ˈlimonaati	'lemonade (nom. sg.)'
d.	ˈpsykologia	'psychology (nom. sg.)'
e.	ˈilmoittautuminen	'registering'

However, this is not the only function of stress. In some languages, stress may be used to indicate differences in word meaning, much like with tone except that there is only one main, prominent syllable in each word. In Russian, for example, stress is relatively mobile and the placement of stress can affect the meaning of words that are otherwise identical, as in (8.5).

(8.5) **Russian stress 1**

a.	ˈmuka	'torment'	muˈka	'flour'
b.	ˈzamok	'castle'	zaˈmok	'lock'
c.	ˈatlas	'atlas'	atˈlas	'satin'
d.	ˈstoit	'be worth'	stoˈit	'stand'

As these examples demonstrate, the placement of stress can indicate a different word with a completely different meaning. It may also indicate a different grammatical category of the same word, as indicated by the examples in (8.6).

(8.6) **Russian stress 2**

a.	ˈruki	'hand (NP)'	ruˈki	'hand (GS)'
b.	ˈzemli	'lands, soils (pl.)'	zemˈli	'land, soil (gen.)'
c.	ˈsrezatʲ	'cut off (PERF)'	sreˈzatʲ	'cut off (IMPERF)'

Stress marking of this kind is not demarcative as in French or Finnish, but *lexical* in that it can signal a different meaning. Lexical stress is also found in English, which we will see in Ch. 12.

8.2.1 Acoustic Correlates of Stress

Before going any further into the analysis of stress, we should first examine the physical properties of stress to clarify exactly what it is that we are investigating.

Stress in language may be correlated with one or more of the following phonetic properties:[1]

1. Pitch (Fundamental Frequency)
2. Intensity or Loudness (Amplitude)
3. Vowel Length (Duration)

Stress can be measured acoustically using various instruments and software, resulting in the analysis of forms such as the related words, *hostile* and *hostility*, in Fig. 8.14.

This representation provides a number of pieces of information concerning stress placement. At the top, the waveform indicates the greater intensity of the stressed syllable. In the middle, the pitch track shows the higher pitch. Finally, at the bottom, the spectrogram indicates the greater length of the stressed syllable, as well as any effects on vowel quality. Clearly, English displays all three properties as correlates of stress, although other languages may only use a subset of these properties.

8.2.2 Analyzing Stress

Since stress is manifested as a rise in pitch, greater intensity or greater vowel length, the analysis of stress must make use of various aspects of acoustic analysis, including the waveform, spectrogram, and pitch track, as shown in Fig. 8.14.

---

1 There may also be other, secondary effects, but these are dependent on the main properties. For example, in English an unstressed vowel often appears as schwa, e.g. *satan* [ˈseɪʔn̩] versus *satanic* [səˈtʰænɪk].

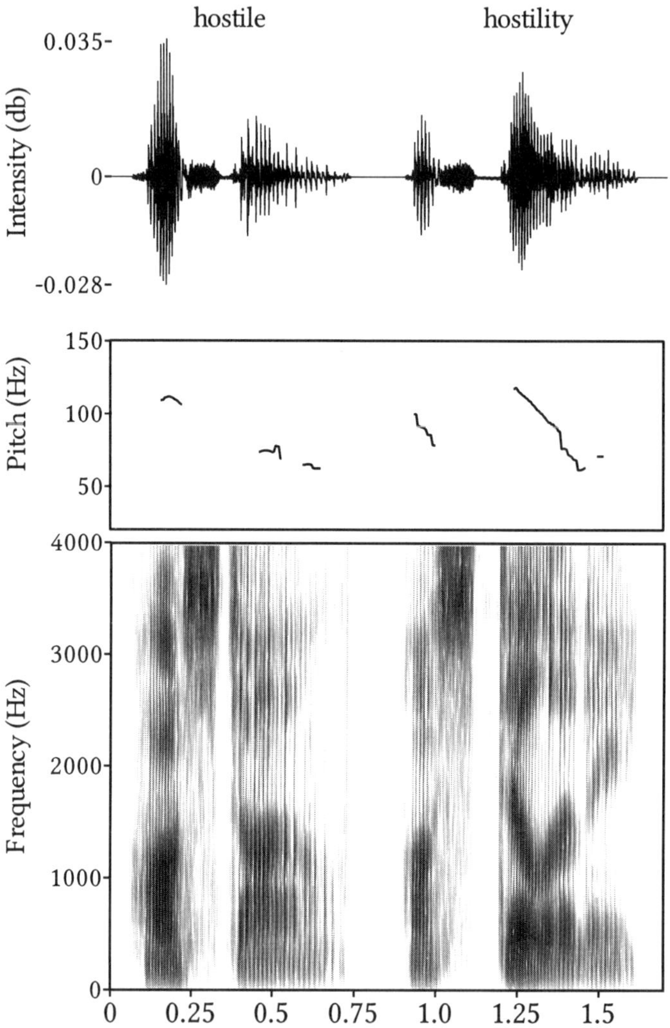

Figure 8.14 Acoustic correlates of stress

Obviously, the analysis will be similar to that of tone, discussed in §8.1, but it will involve additional windows to indicate the waveform and the spectrogram. We proceed as in (8.7).

(8.7) 1. Digitize the sound recording using Audacity.
2. Open the sound file in Praat.
3. Select the file and Edit.
4. In the Edit window, select Spectrum: Show spectrogram and Pitch: Show pitch.
5. This will provide a window that looks like Fig. 8.15.

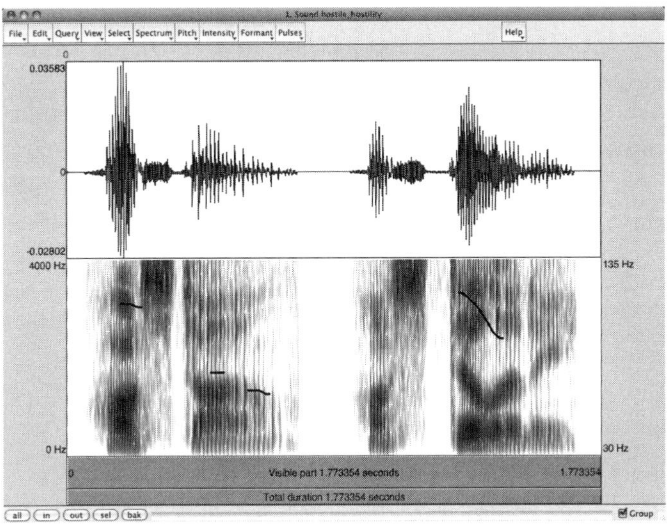

Figure 8.15 Stress Analysis Window

Notice that the pitch analysis is overlain on the spectrogram and may be difficult to see. The frequencies indicated on the left side of the window apply to the spectrogram and those on the right side apply to the pitch. The two objects are treated as separate entities in spite of their appearance, and when you export them to the Praat objects list they will be treated as separate objects, although they may be difficult to distinguish clearly when overlapping in this fashion.

6. To export the spectrogram go to **Spectrum** and choose *Extract visible spectrogram.*

7. Then go to **Pitch** and choose *Extract visible pitch contour.*

8. Now, close the **Edit** window and return to the Praat objects list, which should look something like in Fig. 8.16.

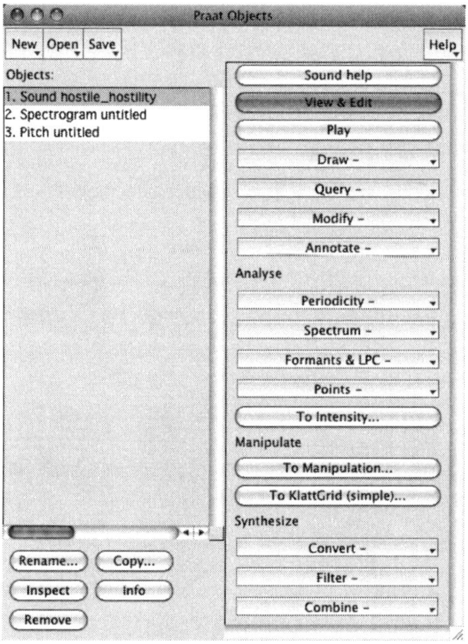

Figure 8.16 Praat Objects Window

Now we can build a composite graphic of the data. In order to do this we must build separate graphics of each part, step by step. The graphics may appear in any order, but for our purpose here we will follow the order in Fig. 8.14 for the words *hostile* and *hostility.*

9. To include the waveform, we go to the Praat picture window and, using the mouse, select a portion of the window where we want to place the waveform.

10. Then, click on the sound in the Praat object window and when the **Sound: Draw** window pops up, press OK. This will place the waveform in the selected portion of the Praat picture window.

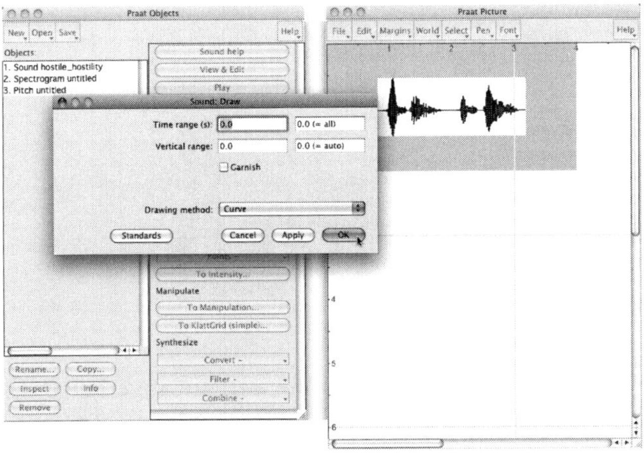

11. Now, select the next section of the Praat picture window where you will place the pitch track and follow the same procedure. The result should look like the following.

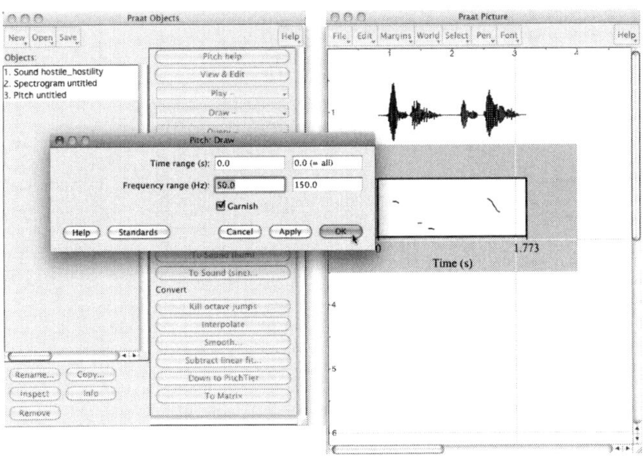

12. Select the final section of the Praat picture window where you will place the spectrogram and follow the same procedure. The result should look like the following.

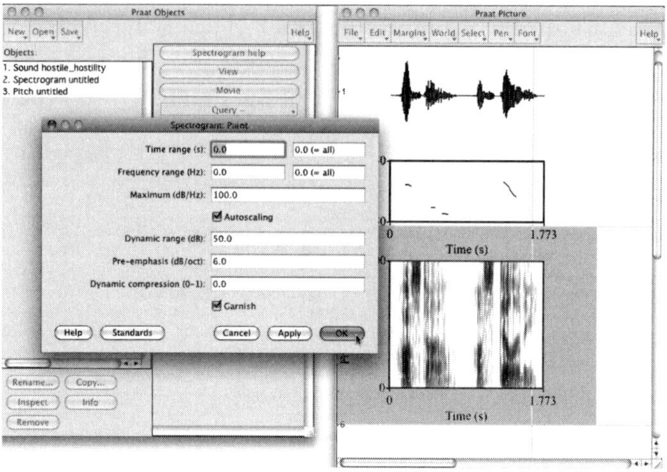

Now that all the parts of the graphic are put together in the Praat picture window, in order to export the picture to a suitable graphic format, we must select the entire graphic and follow the same procedure as we did for the tone example in §8.1.2, as exemplified in Fig. 8.17.

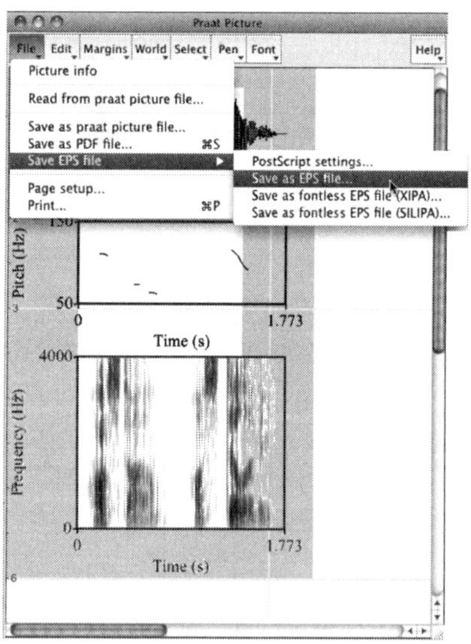

Figure 8.17 Exporting the graphic

The output is as in Fig. 8.14 above, showing waveform, pitch track, and spectrogram. This is the normal procedure for investigating stress assignment, which may take any or all of these elements into account, depending on the language.

We will study English stress in much more detail in Chapter 12. Instead, we now move on to *pitch accent*, another category in the prosodic typology of languages.

8.3 Pitch Accent

In some languages, a pitch-related phenomenon exists that lies somewhere in between tone and stress. Only a single prominent syllable surfaces in each word, but this syllable acts as a cue or anchor for a change in tonal pattern within the word. This is referred to as *pitch accent*, a term coined by the American linguist and intonation specialist, Dwight Bolinger (Bolinger, 1958). Linguists disagree on whether pitch accent systems are closer to tone systems or to stress systems. Haraguchi (1988: 123) provides a typology of prosodic systems, illustrated in Fig. 8.18, that distinguishes between accentual and non-accentual classes. In this context, accent refers to a single, prominent unit within a word. The former groups together stress and pitch accent, while the latter includes tone systems and unaccented systems.

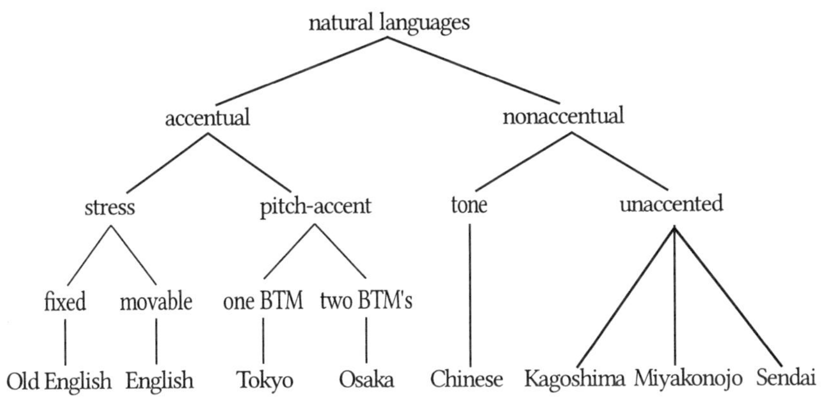

Figure 8.18 Prosodic typology (Haraguchi, 1988:123)

Pitch accent is a property of languages like Japanese, Serbo-Croatian and perhaps some varieties of Korean, as well. In the Tsuruoka dialect of Japanese, for instance, pitch contrasts exist as shown in (8.8), adapted from Haraguchi (1988: 125).

(8.8)	a. Unaccented	•••	sakana (to)	'fish (and)'
	b. Initial	•́••	kabuto (to)	'helmet (and)'
	c. Medial	••́•	kokoro (to)	'heart (and)'
	d. Final	•••́	atama	'head'
		•••́	atamato	'head and'

As one can see, there is an pitch difference between forms designated as *unaccented*, *initial*, *medial*, and *final* accent, but this is not a property of individual syllables; rather, it is a property of the phonological phrase as a whole, as is clearly shown by the case of (8.8d), where the final accent migrates to the appended postposition *to* 'and'. This distinguishes pitch accent systems from tone systems, where the tone is a property of a specific syllable.

The acoustic analysis of pitch accent is very much like that of tone (§8.1.2) and of stress (§8.2.2), and so we will not repeat the procedure here, but it should now be clear how to proceed. The most challenging aspect of such systems is determining their status. One must be careful to establish the nature of the system and to distinguish it from tone on the one hand, and stress on the other.

The interaction of tone and stress

It is also possible for tone and stress to interact, as is quite common in Standard Chinese. For example, the word *kuàizi* 'chopstick' has a falling tone on the first syllable and no tone on the second. The second is described as having neutral tone, much as an unstressed syllable in English would be described as having a concomitant reduction of its vowel. This is due to a rule of Standard Chinese phonology which produces unstressed syllables in certain environments, including with certain affixes and grammatical markers.

8.4 Intonation

Intonation (억양) is the variation of pitch over units larger than the word, typically the phrase or sentence. Intonation may serve a variety of functions including the indication of various grammatical categories, and the demarcation of boundaries. The actual realization of intonation in a particular language may vary from its realization in another language, but all languages make some use of intonation.

8.4.1 Analyzing Intonation

The analysis of intonation is very much like the analysis of tone, except that it spans larger units than tone. Furthermore, intonation in a stress-type language will tend to have longer stretches of more or less flat or gliding pitch than in a tone language, exemplified by the earlier example from Cantonese in Fig. 8.1. Compare this with the intonation pattern of the English sentence in Fig. 8.19.

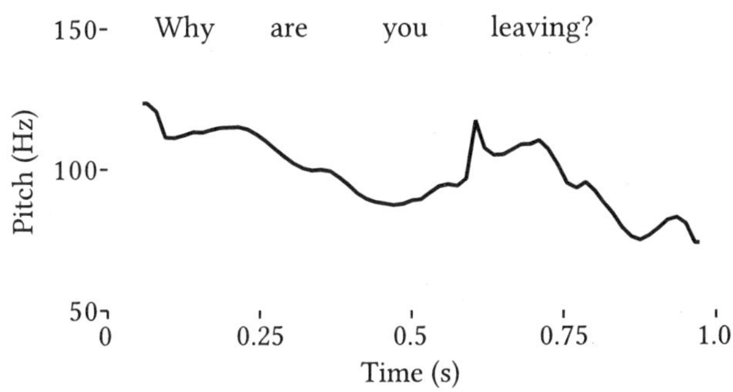

Figure 8.19 Pitch analysis of a sentence

Notice that this utterance appears to have two main peaks: one at the beginning, on the word *why*, and a second on the stressed syllable of the verb, *léaving*. Furthermore, the intonation gradually declines toward the end of the sentence, beginning around 125 Hz and ending around 75 Hz. This is typical of a wh-question type of sentence in English.[2]

[2] Wh-questions employ an interrogative word such as *who*, *how*, *why*, whereas yes-no questions merely seek confirmation or denial.

Obviously, the analysis of such an utterance will be similar to that of tone, discussed in §8.1.2, but will involve more information in the pitch analysis window, since a sentence will typically be longer than a single word or syllable. It will also employ the **autocorrelation** setting for analysis. We proceed as in (8.9).

(8.9) 1. Digitize the sound recording using Audacity.

2. Open the sound file in Praat.

3. Select the file and **Edit**.

4. In the **Edit** window, select *Pitch: Show pitch.*

5. This will give you a window that looks like this:

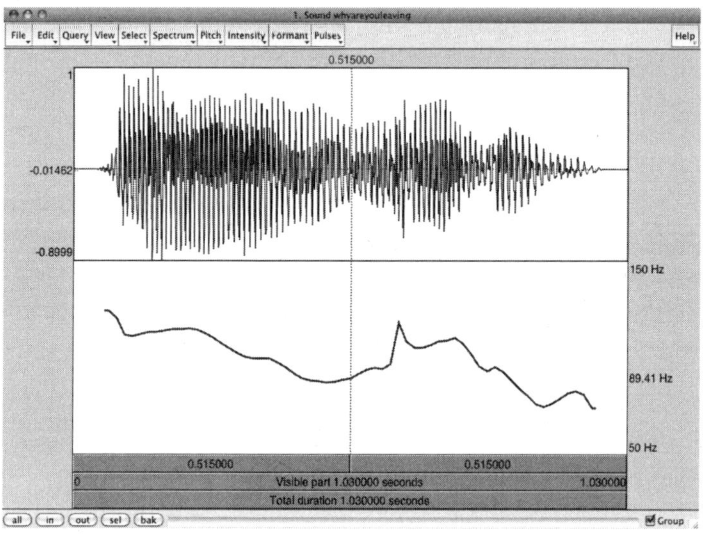

6. To export the pitchtrack go to Pitch and choose Extract visible pitch contour.

7. Now, close the Edit window and return to the Objects list.

Now we can build our composite graphic of the data. In order to do this we must build separate graphics of each part, step by step. The graphics may appear in any order, but for our purpose here we will follow the order in Fig. 8.14 for the words *hostile* and *hostility.*

8. To include the waveform, we go to the Praat picture window and, using the mouse, select a portion of the window where we want to place the waveform.
9. Then, click on the Sound in the Praat object window and when the Sound: Draw window pops up, press OK. This will place the waveform in the selected portion of the Praat picture window:

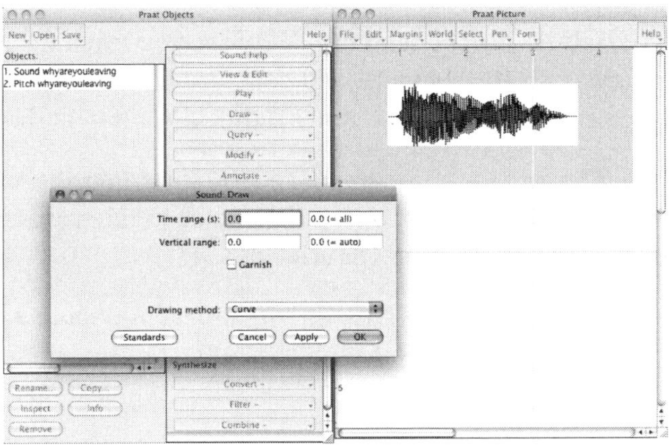

10. Now, select the next section of the Praat picture window where you will place the pitch track and follow the same procedure. The result should look like:

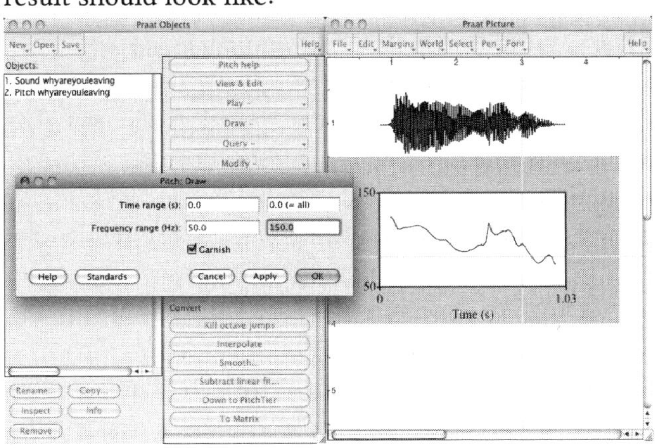

This is all that we require for an intonation analysis, so now we select the entire graphic and follow the same procedure as we did for the tone example in §8.1.2, and as exemplified in Fig. 8.17. The output is as in Fig. 8.19, showing just the pitch track for 'Why are you leaving?'. This is the usual procedure for investigating intonation. We will study the specific properties of English intonation more closely in Chapter 12.

Exercises

1. Record yourself saying the sentence 'Why are you leaving?' Perform a pitch analysis on the sentence and compare it with Fig. 8.19 from §8.4.1. Are they the same or different? If they are different, how?

2. Record the Korean words for *night* and *chestnut* (밤) the way you would normally say them and analyze the pitch in the words. Is there a difference in the two words? Describe it.

3. Does stress exist in Korean? Discuss the issues, providing examples to support your arguments. Note any difficulties you encounter in addressing this question.

Further Reading

Recommended additional readings for this chapter come from several sources. For general phonetic description, Ladefoged & Johnson (2010) and Lieberman & Blumstein (1988) are excellent. Jones (1918) is older but focuses on English phonetics and is worth reading. For detailed discussion of vowels, Ladefoged & Maddieson (1990) contains a wealth of information. For discussion of Prosodic Phonology, Firth (1948) is an early work from the London School. Crystal (1969) is a quite detailed examination of English prosody. Bolinger (1986) contains a lot of important observations on English intonation, as does Ladd (1996).

Keywords: Contour tone, demarcative stress, fundamental frequency, intonation, pitch accent, pitch track, prosody, stress placement.

Part III

The Sounds of English

Chapter 9

English Vowels

We have examined the articulatory and acoustic properties of vowels in general in Chapter 5. Now we will take a closer look at the features of the English vowel system in greater detail, including dialectal differences in the vowel inventory.

English vowels can be presented in the form of a chart such as that in (9.1). In this vowel chart, only a subset of the vowels, basically those required for standard varieties of English, are included for clarity of presentation.

(9.1) **Vowel inventory for English**

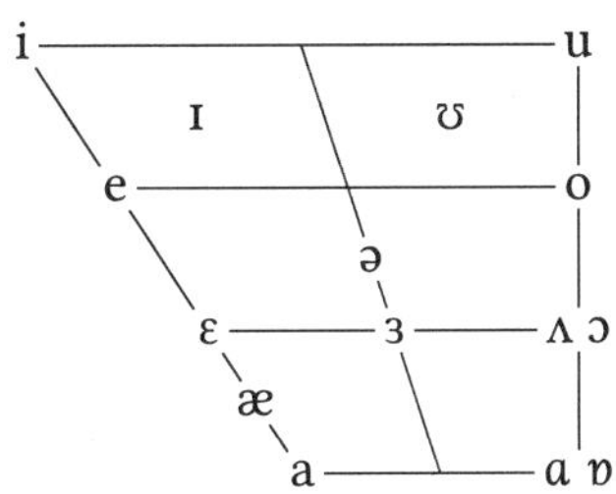

It should be noted at the outset that not all of these vowels can be found in one specific dialect of English and some of them are only found in a single dialect, although they all exist in at least one major variety of English. We will examine each of these vowels in this chapter.

9.1 The Vowels of English

In what follows, we will make a detailed examination of English vowels to come to a better understanding of their properties and shared attributes and the variation that exists within the language with respect to the vowels.

9.1.1 Vowel Length in English

In English, there are several kinds of vowel length, which may lead to confusion. First of all, there is *phonetic vowel length*, which is the result of either an open syllable or a voiced consonant appearing in the coda of the syllable. Thus, there is a phonetic difference in duration in the pairs of words in (9.2).

(9.2) **English vowel length 1**

beat	[bit]	bean	[biːn]
suit	[sut]	soothe	[suːð]
kit	[kʰɪt]	kid	[kʰɪːd]

In addition to phonetic vowel length as described above, many phonologists treat the distinction between English lax vowels, such as [ɪ] and [ʊ], and English tense vowels, such as [i] and [u], as a difference in length. Thus, words like *bit* [bɪt] or *soot* [sʊt] are described as having short vowels, and words such as *beat* [biːt] or *suit* [suːt] are considered long vowels. This type of length may be described as *phonological vowel length* (9.3).[1]

(9.3) **English vowel length 2**

bit	/bit/	beat	/biːt/
soot	/sut/	suit	/suːt/

It is important to keep these two notions of vowel length separate, as they have different properties and are intended for different purposes.

[1] Note the use of square brackets, [ ], in (9.2) to indicate phonetic length and the use of slashes, / /, in (9.3) to indicate phonological length.

9.1.2 The Short Vowels

The separation of English vowels into short and long equates roughly with the traditional distinction of lax and tense, as discussed in §5.5.2 above. English lax vowels are typically shorter than the corresponding tense vowels, but also differ in quality, as shown in Fig. 9.1 for [ɪ] and [i]. We begin with an examination of the short vowels since they are simpler to describe, but contrasting examples of long vowels will be provided where this may be useful. There are short vowels at all vowel heights and in both front and back quadrants, as shown in (9.4).

(9.4) **The English short vowels**

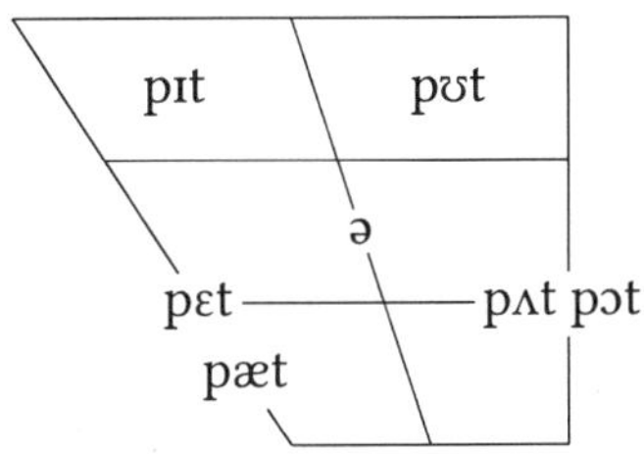

Short vowels may be stressed, but they have a restriction on them that they cannot stand alone, without a final consonant or second syllable, as a full word of English. This is said to be due to a phonological constraint on the size of the *minimal word* that requires either a long vowel (*tea* [tiː]), a diphthong (*tie* [tʰaɪ]), a closed syllable (*it* [ɪt]), or more than one syllable (*bitter* [bɪtɹ̩] for a free-standing word of English.

9.1.2.1 The Vowel [ɪ]

The high front lax vowel, [ɪ], appears in numerous environments, after any consonant or cluster of consonants and before most consonants. As noted above, it cannot stand alone as a word.

It presents some difficulties for Korean learners, since Korean does not make a contrastive distinction between [ɪ] and [i], but English does. Words such as *bit*, *pill*, and *mitt* contrast lexically with words such as *beat*, *peel*, and *meat* in English, so they must be pronounced differently. Compare the spectrograms of the vowels in *bit* and *beat* in Fig. 9.1.

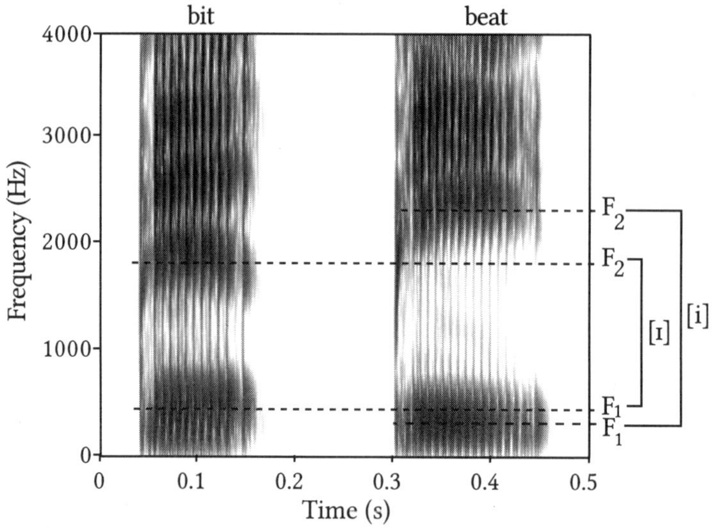

Figure 9.1 Spectrogram of *bit* and *beat*

Notice that the formants of the two words are distinctly different. The vowel of the word *bit* has an F_1 at approximately 700 Hz and an F_2 at around 1850 Hz, while the vowel of the word *beat* has an F_1 at around 350 Hz and an F_2 at around 2200 Hz. This clearly demonstrates that the quality of the two vowels is different. Notice also that the quantity of the two vowels is different: the vowel of *bit* is about 120ms, while the vowel of *beat* is around 170ms, approximately 50% longer.

Examples of corresponding pairs of long and short high front vowels include those in (9.5).

(9.5) **English Long and Short High Front Vowel Pairs**

eat	it	beat	bit	deep	dip	feet	fit
heat	hit	jeep	gyp	keen	kin	lean	Lynn
keel	kill	meat	mitt	meal	mill	neat	nit
kneel	nil	neep	nip	queen	Quinn	reap	rip
reek	rick	seek	sick	seep	sip	ream	rim
seat	sit	teak	tick	team	Tim	week	wick
sheet	shit	weal	will	teal	till	seal	sill

9.1.2.2 The Vowel [ʊ]

The high back lax vowel, [ʊ], also appears in a number of environments, although fewer than [ɪ] but, again, it cannot stand alone as a word.

It also presents some difficulties for Korean learners, since Korean does not make a contrastive distinction between [ʊ] and [u], as English does. Words such as *soot, foot,* and *hood* contrast with words like *suit, food,* and *who'd* in English, so they must be pronounced differently. Compare the spectrograms of the vowels in *soot* and *suit* in Fig. 9.2.

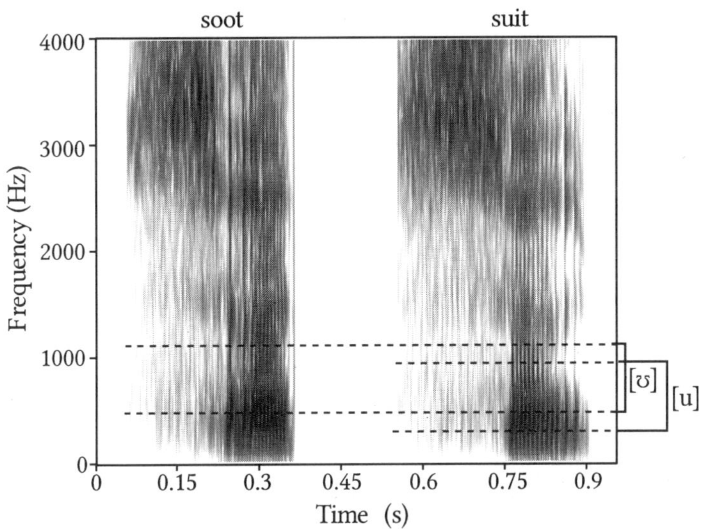

Figure 9.2 Spectrogram of *soot* and *suit*

Notice that, while there is variation in the formants of [ʊ] and [u], it is more subtle than with [ɪ] and [i]. The length difference is, however, clear, again approximately 100ms for [ʊ] and around 130ms for [u].

Corresponding pairs of long and short high back vowels are much less common that those in the front, but include the examples in (9.6).

(9.6) **English Long and Short High Back Vowel Pairs**

suit	soot	tuque	took	Luke	look	who'd	hood
cooed	could	food	foot	kook	cook	shoot	shook

9.1.2.3 The Vowel [ɛ]

The mid front lax vowel, [ɛ], also appears in a number of environments and also presents certain challenges for Korean learners, in this case contrasting with both [eɪ] and [æ]. Since the former is a diphthong, Korean speakers often treat it as two monophthongs effectively distinguishing it from the others. But the contrast of [ɛ] and [æ] may be quite challenging for learners.

Although Korean does have a putative contrast between [ɛ] and [æ], represented in Hangul by < ㅔ> versus < ㅐ>, this distinction does not form part of the inventory for most speakers nowadays. Hence, the English contrast of [ɛ] and [æ] is quite difficult for Korean learners of English. Words like *pet*, *men*, and *head* contrast lexically with words like *pat*, *man*, and *had*, so they must be pronounced differently. Compare the spectrograms of the vowels in *men* and *man* in Fig. 9.3.

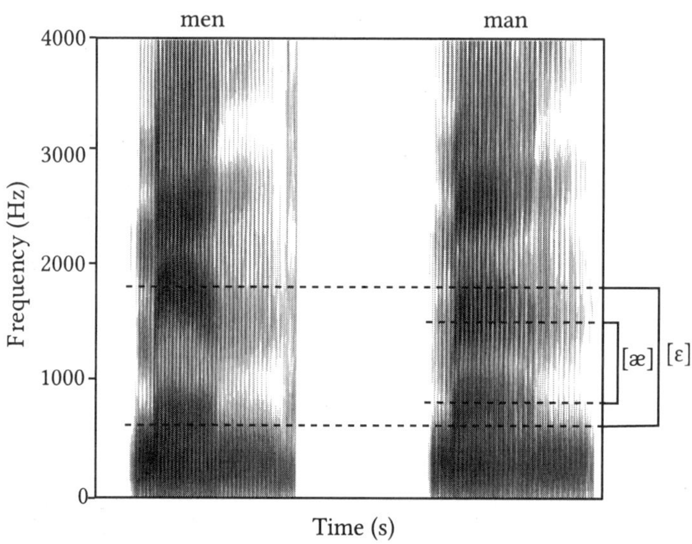

Figure 9.3 Spectrogram of *men* and *man*

Corresponding pairs of short mid front and low front vowels are quite common and include the examples in (9.7).

(9.7) **English Short Mid and Low Front Vowel Pairs**

bed	bad	bet	bat	beg	bag	bend	band
dead	dad	deb	dab	head	had	hem	ham
gem	jam	ketch	catch	ken	can	leg	lag
men	man	met	mat	net	gnat	neck	knack
peck	pack	pet	pat	pep	pap	wreck	rack
set	sat	shell	shall	ten	tan	wren	ran

9.1.2.4 The Vowel [æ]

The English vowel [æ] is a low front unrounded lax vowel with formants similar to, but distinct from those of [ɛ], as shown in the spectrogram in Fig. 9.3 and exemplified by the minimal pairs in (9.7). Since the contrast between these two vowels, and the difficulty this minimal contrast presents for Korean learners, has already been discussed, there is little to add here concerning this vowel other than to note that it is a contrastive lexical vowel of English and therefore it is important to learn how to pronounce it accurately in order to avoid confusion.

It should be noted that some dialects of English, such as Scottish English and Welsh English, substitute the low front unrounded vowel [a] for [æ] in words such as *cat* and *bad*.

9.1.2.5 The Vowel [ɔ]

The mid back lax rounded vowel, [ɔ], occurs in all dialects of English, although there is some variation concerning its relationship to the low back vowels.

In Canadian English, [ɔ] is the only vowel in the lower back quadrant of the IPA vowel chart, and words such as *cot* and *caught* are pronounced the same, as shown in Fig. 9.4.

This is not true in some varieties of American English however, where the two vowels are lexically distinct. American dialects may be divided into those where the merger of [ɑ] and [ɔ] is complete or substantially underway versus those where there is no substantial indication of merger. These are indicated in the map in Fig. 9.6.

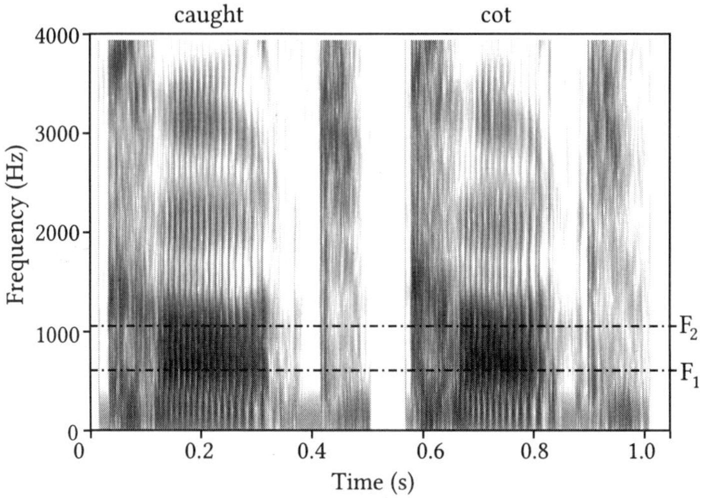

Figure 9.4 Canadian English *caught* [ɔ] and *cot* [ɔ]

The difference in the first two formants of these vowels in American English dialects is shown in the spectrograms of the words *caught* and *cot* in Fig. 9.5.

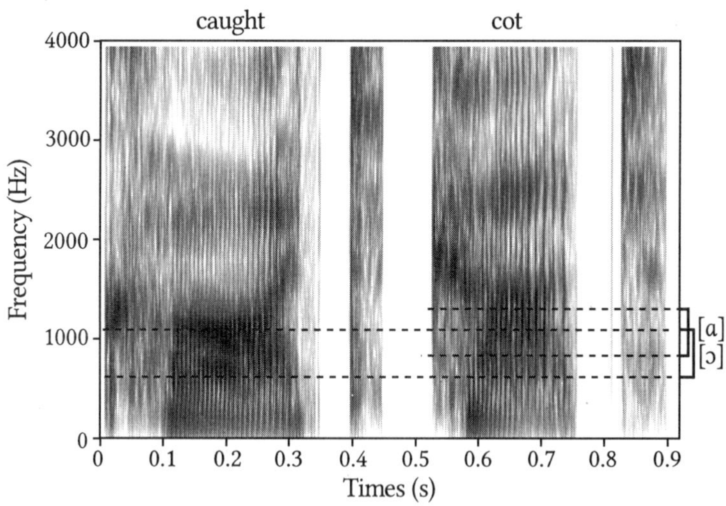

Figure 9.5 American English *caught* [ɔ] and *cot* [ɑ]

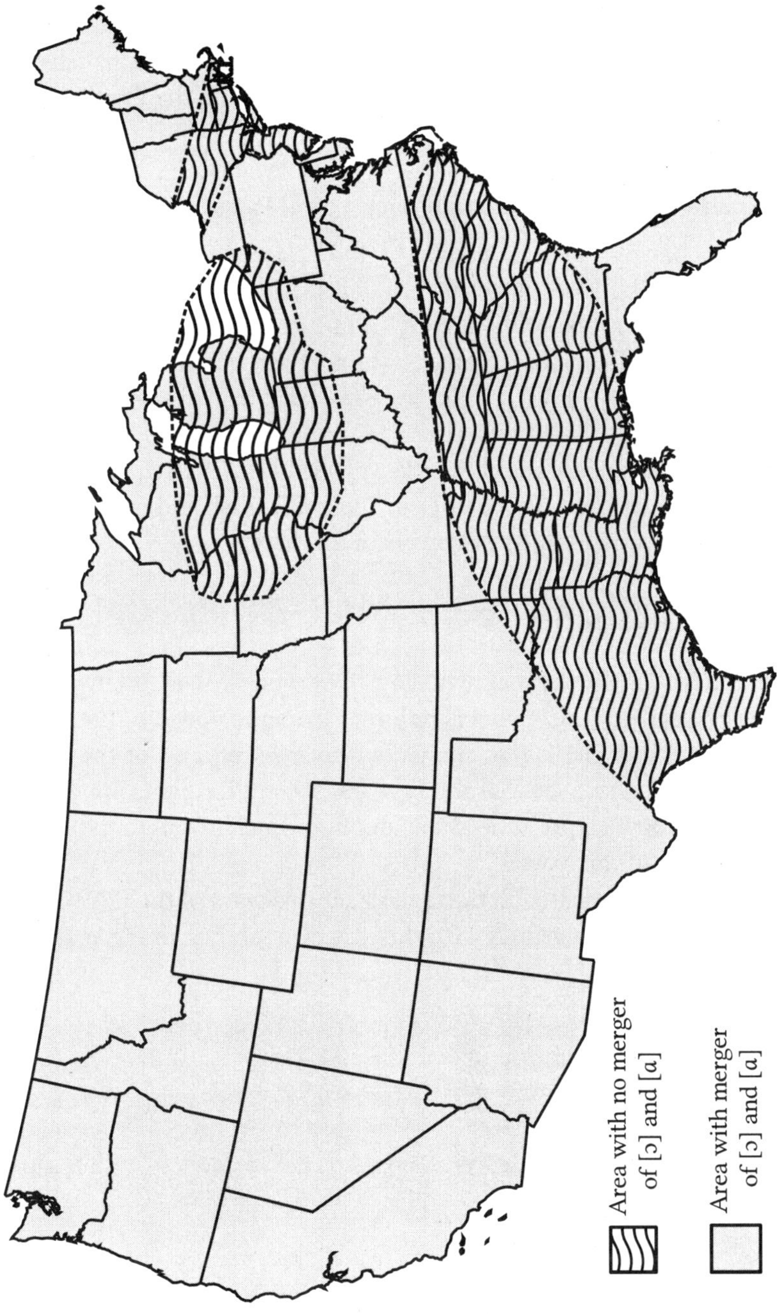

Figure 9.6 The *cot-caught* merger

Minimal pairs that illustrate the lexical distinction in certain dialects of American English include those in (9.8). In each pair, the first has [ɑ] and the second has [ɔ].

(9.8) **American English Non-High Back Vowel Pairs**

body	bawdy	bot	bought	clod	clawed	collar	caller
cock	caulk	chock	chalk	don	dawn	fond	fawned
holler	hauler	knotty	naughty	nod	gnawed	not	naught
odd	awed	pod	pawed	pond	pawned	rot	wrought
sod	sawed	stock	stalk	tot	taught	wok	walk

The lower back quadrant of the IPA vowel chart is, perhaps, the area of greatest diversity among varieties of spoken English and each dialect has its own type and number of vowels in this area.

9.1.2.6 The Vowel [ɒ]

In Standard British English, there is a low back round vowel, [ɒ] in words such as *cod, sod,* etc. This vowel is different from the vowel of the same words in American English, as shown by the spectrograms of the word *sod* in Fig. 9.7. You can see that the first and second formants are closer together in the British pronunciation, and F_2 is much lower, in part, due to the rounding of this vowel.

The vowel [ɒ] is located in the lower back quadrant of the IPA vowel chart, below [ɔ], and contrasts with this vowel, as shown in Fig. 9.14.

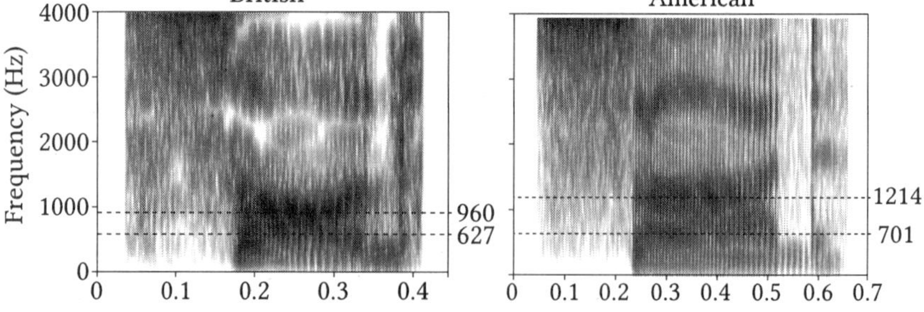

Figure 9.7 British [ɒ] and American [ɔ] in *sod*

9.1.2.7 The Vowel [ʌ]

The mid back lax unrounded vowel, [ʌ], occurs in a wide range of contexts and must be considered a contrastive vowel of English. In the dialects of Northern England (see the map in Fig. 9.8), [ʌ] is replaced in all contexts by the high back lax rounded vowel, [ʊ], resulting in a merger of the two vowels. In this context, word pairs like *put*/*putt* or *look*/*luck* are homonymous.

Figure 9.8 ʌ-ʊ Merger in Northern English dialects

While [ʌ] and [ə] are very similar phonetically, and occur in complementary distribution in English, they are acoustically distinct and serve different functions phonologically. The acoustic differences are shown by the first vowels of the words *button* and *baton* in Fig. 9.9.

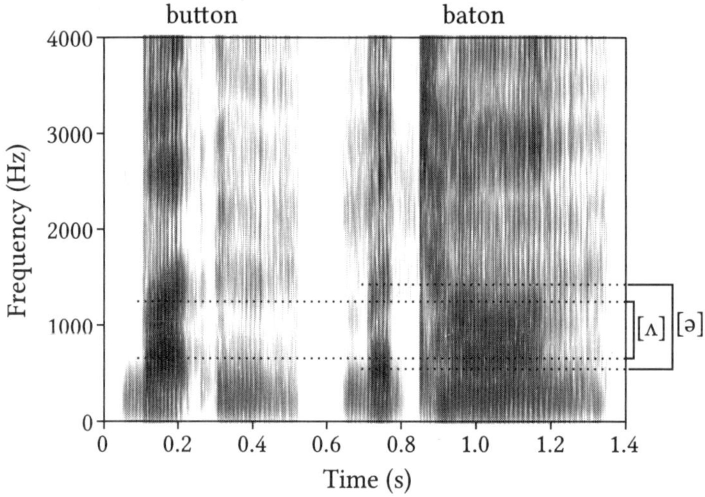

Figure 9.9 Spectrogram of *button* [ˈbʌtn̩] and *baton* [bəˈtʰɔn]

The most obvious difference between the two vowels is in F_2, which is an indicator of backness, as we have already discussed. What the spectrogram shows is that [ə] is significantly further forward, more a central vowel, than [ʌ]. This is consistent with the view that [ə] is a central vowel. If we examine a vowel plot of the two vowels (Fig. 9.10), we can confirm that [ə] is further forward and slightly higher than [ʌ], which is clearly in the region of a mid back vowel.

9.1.2.8 Schwa [ə]

Note that schwa, [ə], included in the table of short vowels and shown in Figs. 9.9 and 9.10, does not have a contrastive function in English. However, it is very frequent as the *reduced form* of vowels in the ab-

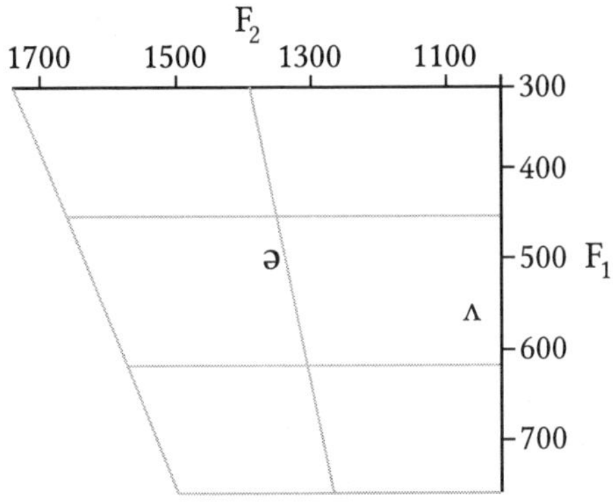

Figure 9.10 Vowel plot of [ʌ] and [ə]

sence of stress:[2] compare, for example, the second vowels in *declaration* [ˌdɛkləˈɹeɪʃn̩] and *declarative* [dəˈkʰlæɹətɪv] or the first vowels in *banana* [bəˈnænə] and *bandana* [ˌbænˈdænə].

The presence versus absence of stress is a major factor in the appearance of schwa, which, given the pervasiveness of stress, is thus the most frequently occurring vowel in English, despite its non-lexical status.

9.1.3 The Long Vowels

The English long vowels may be equated with tense vowels, as discussed in §5.5.2 and shown in (9.9). They share the property of greater duration with the diphthongs, to be discussed in §9.2.

(9.9) **The English long vowels**

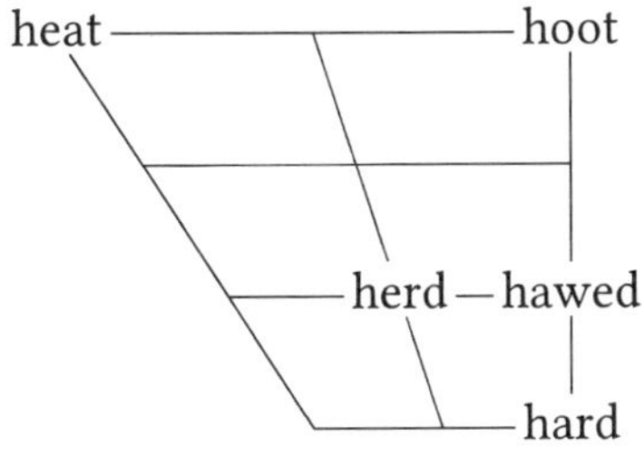

2 For more detailed discussion of stress and vowel reduction, see Ch. 12.

Unlike short vowels, long vowels may stand alone as a word, for instance *awe* [ɔ:] or *to* [tu:]. The open mid vowel, [ɜ:], occurs only in non-rhotic varieties of English and the [ɑ:] does not appear in all varieties either. We will examine each of the long vowels in the following.

9.1.3.1 The Vowel [i:]

The high front tense vowel, [i:], appears widely in English, after any consonant or cluster of consonants and before most consonants and it is able to stand alone as a word, as noted above. As shown by the spectrogram in Fig. 9.1, [i:] is considerably longer than [ɪ], discussed in §9.1.2.1 above, and is somewhat higher, as indicated by its F_1 and somewhat further forward, as shown by its higher F_2. The numerous minimal pairs provided in (9.5) demonstrate that [i:] and [ɪ] are contrastive, unlike in Korean where they are purely allophonic variants.

A further property of [i:] is its frequent co-occurrence with [j] when it is followed by another vowel, for instance when the definite article, *the*, precedes a word beginning with a vowel. In such cases, the [i:] leads immediately into the semivowel [j], as shown in Fig. 9.11. The same thing occurs with words such as *re-organize, de-activate*, etc.

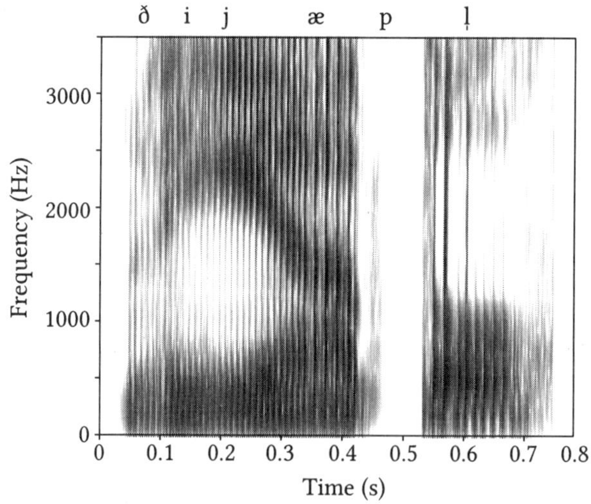

Figure 9.11 Spectrogram of *the apple* showing the semivowel [j]

9.1.3.2 The Vowel [uː]

The high back tense vowel, [uː], also appears widely in English, after any consonant or cluster of consonants and before most consonants, and it is able to stand alone as a word. As shown in the spectrogram in Fig. 9.2, [uː] is longer than [ʊ], which was discussed in §9.1.2.2, and is also slightly higher, as indicated by its F_1, as well as further back, as shown by its higher F_2. This corresponds with its placement in the IPA vowel chart (see page 52). Minimal pairs, as provided in (9.6), although not as numerous as for the high front vowels, are sufficient to demonstrate that [uː] and [ʊ] are contrastive, unlike in Korean where they are purely allophonic variants.

[uː] also frequently co-occurs with the semivowel [w] when followed by another vowel, as shown in Fig. 9.12 where the word *suicide* demonstrates the transition from [uː] to [ɪ].

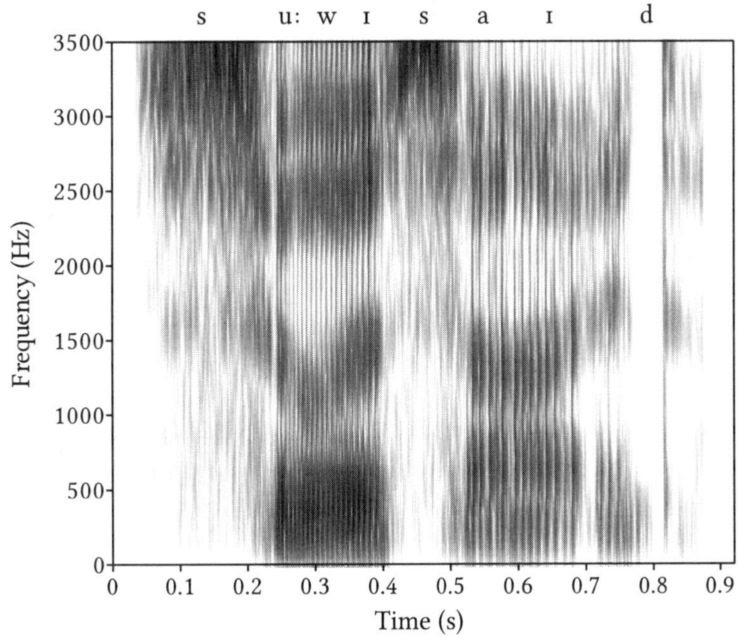

Figure 9.12 Spectrogram of *suicide* showing the semivowel [w]

9.1.3.3 The Vowel [ɔː]

The long mid back tense vowel, [ɔː], appears in some varieties of English in words such as *law, raw, saw,* etc. Its acoustic properties are basically the same as those of short [ɔ], discussed in 9.1.2.5, except for the fact that this vowel is long.

Note that the distinction between [ɔː] and [ɑː] does not exist in Canadian English, just as with the short varieties of these vowels discussed in §9.1.2.5.

9.1.3.4 The Vowel [ɑː]

The low back unrounded vowel, [ɑː], appears in both Standard British English and in some varieties of American English, where it is used to distinguish between words such as *ant* and *aunt*, as shown in Fig. 9.13. This distinction is not encountered in Canadian English or in some other varieties, where both of these words are pronounced with the same vowel, [æ], as [ænt].

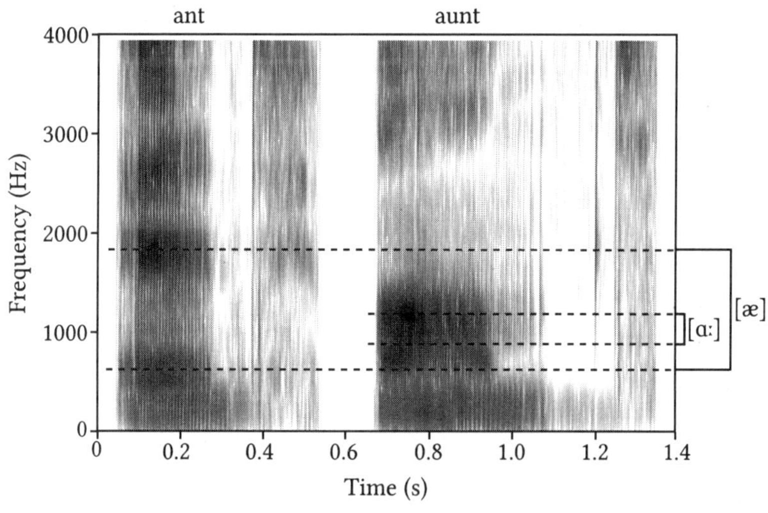

Figure 9.13 *ant* [ænt] and *aunt* [ant]

9.1.3.5 The Vowel [ɜː]

The mid central long vowel, [ɜː], occurs only in non-rhotic dialects, such as Standard British English and is the result of the absence of the r-sound in the coda of words such as *bird, burr, worse,* etc. The vowel is slightly lower than schwa, as indicated in the IPA vowel chart, and is longer.

In rhotic varieties, this vowel is realized as a rhotacized variant, [ɝ] or [ɚ] in unstressed position, reflecting the presence of [ɹ] in the coda of syllables in such dialects.

9.1.3.6 The Lower Back Quadrant

The English vowels in the lower back quadrant of the IPA vowel chart present the greatest variation among English vowels. As already stated in §9.1.3.3, Canadian English has only a single round vowel in this region, whereas other varieties may have two or three vowels in the same area. Figure 9.14 provide the vowels of this area for both Standard British and American varieties. Both speakers are adult males in the vowel plots.

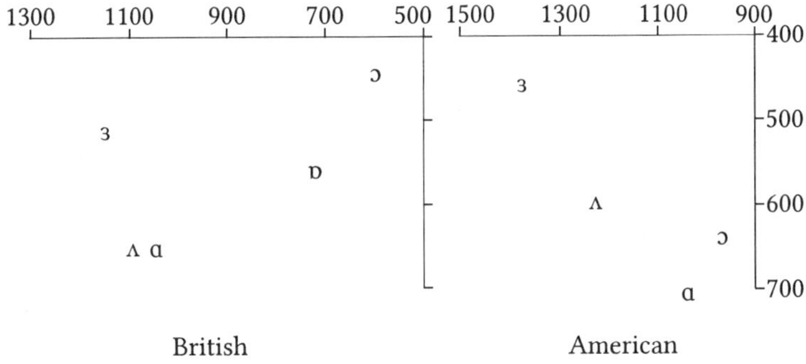

Figure 9.14 English lower back quadrant vowels

In the charts in Fig. 9.14, the placement of vowels in the lower back quadrant diverges in both the number of vowels and in their position between British and American speakers of English.

9.1.4 Acoustic Properties of English Vowels

English vowels can be studied in terms of both their quality and quantity. With respect to quality, the first three formants (F_1-F_3) provide a picture of the variation, as indicted in Table 9.1 from Peterson & Barney (1952).

		i	ɪ	ɛ	æ	ɑ	ɔ	ʊ	u	ʌ	ɜ
Fundamental	M	136	135	130	127	124	129	137	141	130	133
frequencies (Hz)	W	235	232	223	210	212	216	232	231	221	218
	Ch	272	269	260	251	256	263	276	274	261	261
Formant											
frequencies (Hz)	M	270	390	530	660	730	570	440	300	640	490
F_1	W	310	430	610	860	850	590	470	370	760	500
	Ch	370	530	690	1010	1030	680	560	430	850	560
	M	2290	1990	1840	1720	1090	840	1020	870	1190	1350
F_2	W	2790	2480	2330	2050	1220	920	1160	950	1400	1640
	Ch	3200	2730	2610	2320	1370	1060	1410	1170	1590	1820
	M	3010	2550	2480	2410	2440	2410	2240	2240	2390	1690
F_3	W	3310	3070	2990	2850	2810	2710	2680	2670	2780	1960
	Ch	3730	3600	3570	3320	3170	3180	3310	3260	3360	2160
Formant	L_1	-4	-3	-2	-1	-1	0	-1	-3	-1	-5
amplitudes (db)	L_2	-24	-23	-17	-12	-5	-7	-12	-19	-10	-15
	L_3	-28	-27	-24	-22	-28	-34	-34	-43	-27	-20

Table 9.1 Averages of the first three formants of American English vowels, from Peterson & Barney (1952)

As can be seen from this table (9.1), where M=adult male, W=adult female, and Ch=child, the formants range systematically within specific parameters. As we might expect, the range for children is generally higher than for adults, and that for women is higher than for men. We can clarify the relationship between the vowels of men, women and children by presenting the data from Table 9.1 in the form of a vowel plot (Fig. 9.15). Here we can clearly see the consistent differences, where the children's vowels are the lowest and most leftward within each set and the men's are the highest and most rightward. Plotting the results and linking the vowels according to gender shows the nature of the variation clearly, as in Fig. 9.16.

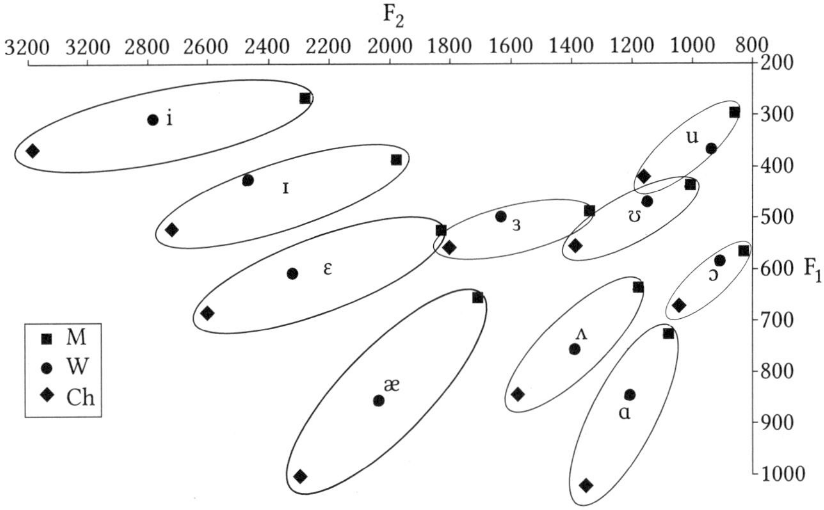

Figure 9.15 Plot of the vowels in Table 9.1

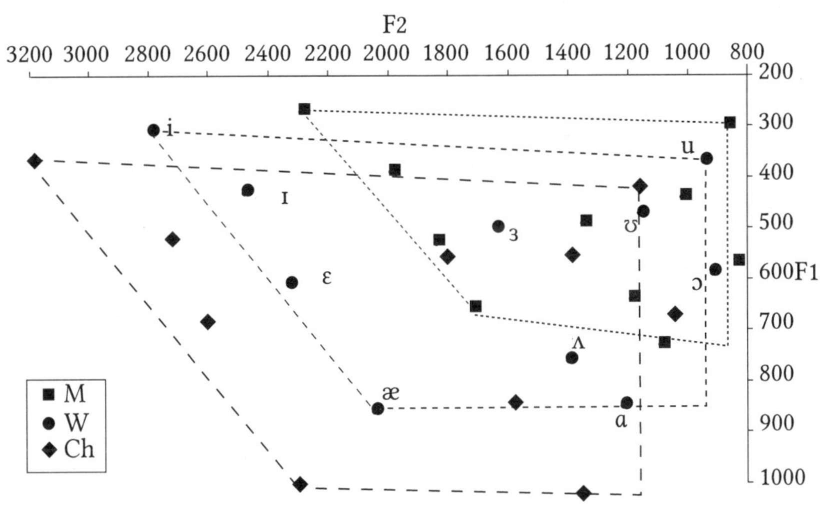

Figure 9.16 Vowel charts of Table 9.1 by gender

In these charts, we can see the overall vowel configurations for men, women and children, showing the greater range of formants for children and the much more restricted range of male speakers, with the range for women lying somewhere between these two extremes.

9.2 English Diphthongs

In addition to short and long vowels, English also has a number of diphthongs of different types. There are several types of diphthongs, with either [ɪ], as in Fig. 9.17 or [ʊ], as in Fig. 9.18, as the second member. Words with ɪ-final diphthongs include *bay* [beɪ], *buy* [baɪ], and *boy* [bɔɪ].

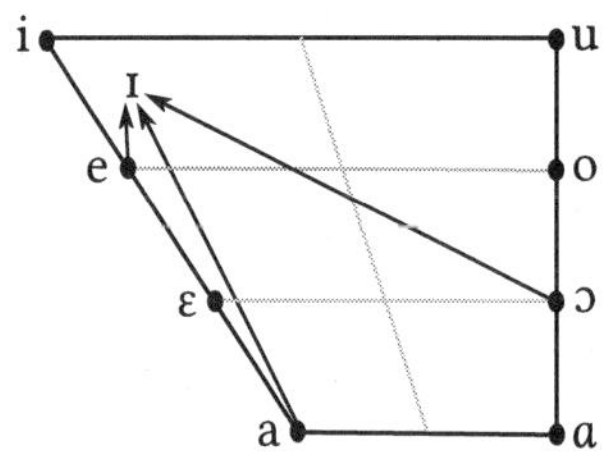

Figure 9.17 ɪ-final diphthongs

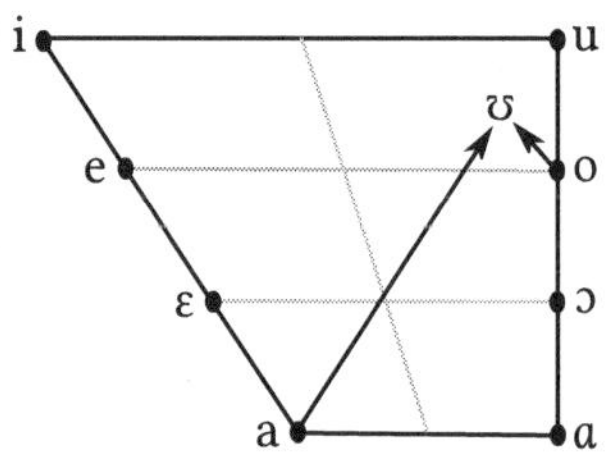

Figure 9.18 ʊ-final diphthongs

Words with ʊ-final diphthongs include *bow* [baʊ] 'bend the head or body forward' and *bow* [boʊ] 'a knot tied with two loops' or 'a weapon for shooting arrows.' Notice that the spelling of these two words is identical but the pronunciation is different.

There is also a third type of diphthong found only in non-rhotic varieties of English, shown in Fig. 9.19. This third type of diphthong ends with [ə] and arises from the loss of the [ɹ] at the end of the syllable in such dialects.

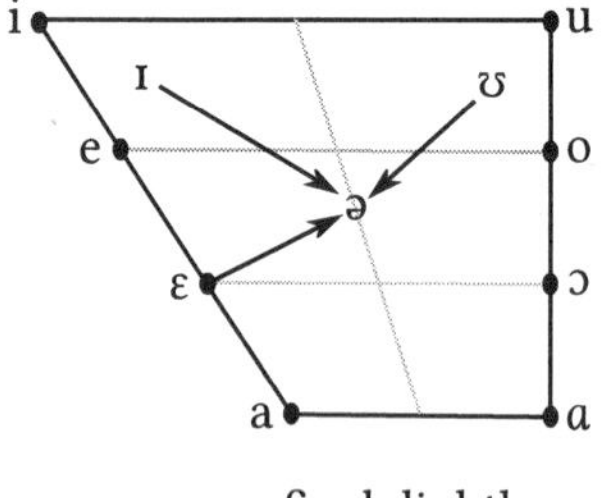

Figure 9.19 ə-final diphthongs

In words which normally have a final [ɹ] in rhotic dialects, the range of diphthongs is somewhat different for non-rhotic varieties. In such dialects, final [ɹ] is realized as [ə] when at the end of a phrase or when followed by a consonant in the next word, as shown in (9.10).

(9.10)

Word	Rhotic	Non-rhotic	With -ing
fear	[fiːɹ]	[fiːə]	[fiːɹɪŋ]
bear	[bɛɹ]	[bɛə]	[bɛɹɪŋ]
lure	[lʊɹ]	[lʊə]	[lʊɹɪŋ]

While there is a difference between rhotic and non-rhotic dialects with respect to [ɹ]-final forms, when a vowel-initial suffix such as *-ing* is added, the final [ɹ] of the base moves into the beginning of the next syllable, where it is pronounced in all dialects. Consequently, the diphthong in the non-rhotic varieties disappears in this context.

A final thing to note about diphthongs is that because they have *two* vowels elements, they act like long vowels and may occur alone in words, such as *eye* [aɪ], *owe* [oʊ], *ow* [aʊ], etc.

In addition to diphthongs, in some languages there are *triphthongs*, i.e., vowels with three vocalic elements. Due to its non-rhotic nature, RP is often claimed to possess triphthongs such as /aɪə/ 'ire' and /aʊə/ 'hour', although not all phoneticians agree with this analysis, which depends on these words being treated as monosyllabic.[3] Daniel Jones has this to say about these forms (Jones, 1914: 56):

> The groups *aiə*, *auə* are not true triphthongs; i and u are less sonorous than a, ɑ and ə, and therefore the a, ɑ and ə belong to different syllables. When the second element of these groups is lowered they approach nearer to true triphthongs, but they never become true triphthongs. In their extreme forms they become diphthongs (aə, ɑə) or single vowels (aː, ɑː). It is however convenient to call the groups *aiə*, *auə* triphthongs, because they are often treated in poetry as forming only one syllable.

[3] For arguments against the treatment of such forms as triphthongs, see John Wells' comments at: http://phonetic-blog.blogspot.com/2009/12/triphthongs-anyone.html.

9.2.1 Acoustic Properties of English Diphthongs

English diphthongs are invariably of the falling type, i.e., the first part of the diphthong is the most prominent and the second part, the off-glide, consists of a high vowel, either front or back, sometimes represented as a semivowel.

If we examine a spectrogram of an English diphthong, we can see the two distinct vowel qualities and the gliding formant between them, as illustrated in Fig. 9.20. Note that one cannot measure a diphthong at only one point in the formant like a vowel, since the frequency is gradually changing from one point to the next.

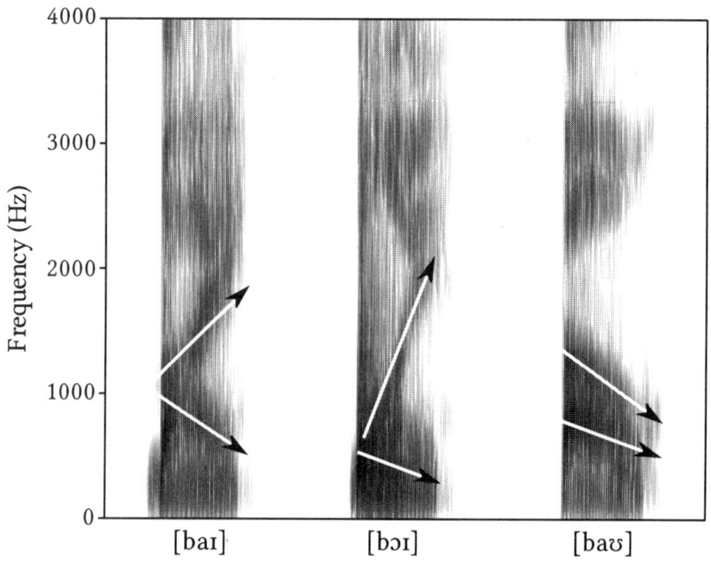

Figure 9.20 F_1 and F_2 of some English diphthongs

9.3 Syllabic Sonorants in English

In English syllabic sonorant consonants are quite common. The nasals, [m] and [n], and the liquids, [l] and [ɹ], can all be syllabic in the appropriate context. Forms such as those in (9.11) demonstrate the difference between non-syllabic and syllabic sonorant consonants in English.

(9.11) **English syllabic sonorants**

Non-syllabic		**Syllabic**	
resume	[rəˈzuːm]	bosom	[ˈbuːzm̩]
bassoon	[bəˈsuːn]	basin	[ˈbeɪsn̩]
rebel$_V$	[ɹəˈbɛɫ]	rebel$_N$	[ˈɹɛbl̩]
compare	[kəmˈpɛɹ]	camper	[ˈkʰæmpɹ̩]

Syllabic sonorant consonants are almost never stressed and they may fluctuate between being syllabic and non-syllabic, based on the context, as illustrated in (9.12).

(9.12) **Variation in syllabicity of sonorants**

Non-syllabic		**Syllabic**	
lightning	[ˈlaɪtnɪŋ]	lighten	[ˈlaɪʔn̩]
metrify	[ˈmɛtɹəfaɪ]	meter	[ˈmitɹ̩]
simplify	[ˈsɪmpləfaɪ]	simple	[ˈsɪmpl̩]

This demonstrates the potential variability in syllabification for sonorant consonants in English. The physical differences are clearly shown in the spectrogram of the words *lightning* and *lighten* in Fig. 9.21.

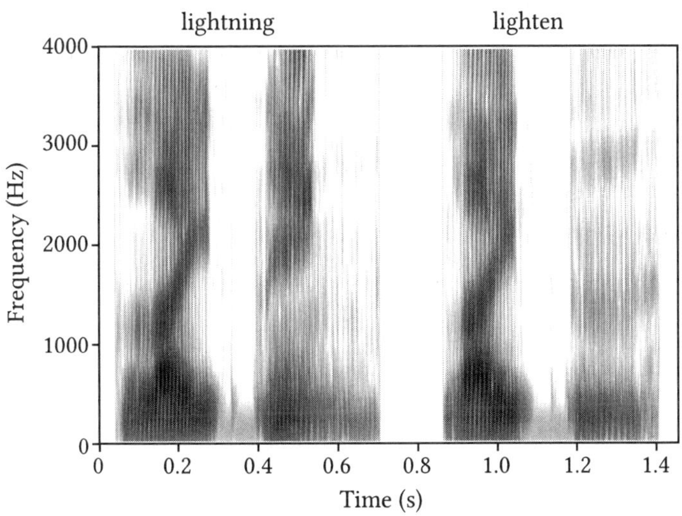

Figure 9.21 [n] in *lightning* and *lighten*

There is a common reduction in colloquial English of the *-ing* verb suffix from [ɪŋ] to [n̩], often represented in writing as -n'. Thus, *writing* becomes *writin'*, *singing* becomes *singin'*, etc. This ending is reduced to a syllabic alveolar nasal because there is no syllabic velar nasal available in English.

9.3.1 Acoustic Properties of English Syllabic Sonorants

Syllabic sonorants are similar to non-syllabic sonorants in their spectrographic profile, except that the formants are somewhat more intense and, therefore, darker. This indicates the syllabic nature of such segments. Examples of this are provided in Fig. 9.22, where the syllabic sonorant follows the fricatives [s] or [z] in order to clearly indicate the boundaries of the sounds.

All of these examples involve a syllabic sonorant in an unstressed syllable. Syllabic sonorants in English do not usually occur in stressed syllables, although there are a few exceptions. One example of this involves the Latinate root *-fer*, found in words like *defer*, *refer*, *confer*, etc. We will discuss this further in §11.2.2.

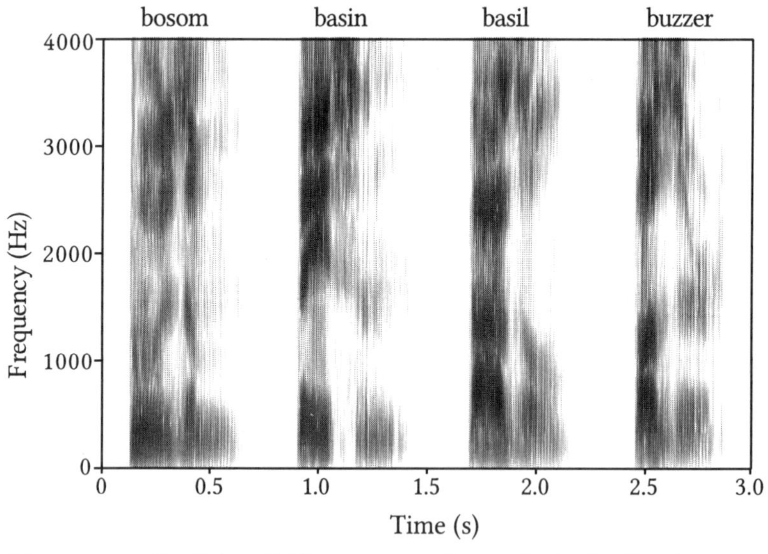

Figure 9.22 English syllabic sonorants: *bosom*, *basin*, *basil* and *buzzer*

Exercises

1. Provide examples of five English words containing one of the short vowels.
2. Provide examples of five English words containing one of the long vowels.
3. Provide examples of five English words containing diphthongs. How are these words pronounced by Korean speakers? Explain why.
4. Considering the discussion of triphthongs on page 177, find the phonetic transcription of the English words *fire* and *buyer* from three different sources and compare the results, especially considering the number of syllables.

Further Reading

Recommended additional readings for this chapter come from several sources. For general phonetic description, Ladefoged & Johnson (2010) and Lieberman & Blumstein (1988) are excellent. Jones (1918) is older but focusses on English phonetics and is worth reading. For detailed discussion of vowels, Ladefoged & Maddieson (1990) contains a wealth of information.

For discussion of Prosodic Phonology, Firth (1948) is an early work from the London School. Crystal (1969) is a quite detailed examination of English prosody. Bolinger (1986) contains a lot of important observations on English intonation, as does Ladd (1996).

Keywords: non-rhotic dialects, lax vowel, long vowel, syllabic sonorant, triphthong, vowel length.

Chapter 10

English Obstruents

We can divide English consonants into two subgroups, *obstruents* and *sonorants*. An obstruent is a consonant that is formed by obstructing the airflow, causing increased air pressure in the vocal tract. Sonorants, to be discussed in the next chapter, involve no turbulent airflow in the vocal tract, and include the nasals, liquids and semivowels.

In this chapter we will examine the properties of the English obstruent consonants, which include the plosives, fricatives and affricates, as shown in Table 10.1.

Plosives	vl.	p			t		k	(ʔ)
	vd.	b			d		g	
Fricatives	vl.		f	θ	s	ʃ		h
	vd.		v	ð	z	ʒ		
Affricates	vl.					ʧ		
	vd.					ʤ		

Table 10.1 The English obstruents

Obstruents involve either a total closure of the vocal tract or a partial closure, i.e., a stricture causing friction. They may be subdivided into *plosive*, which involves a complete closure followed by an *explosive* release of air, *fricative*, with only limited closure, i.e., a sufficient degree of closure to cause friction, and *affricate*, with a total closure followed by a fricative-style release. Obstruents are prototypically voiceless, although voiced obstruents also occur and, in English, form contrasting pairs with the voiceless obstruents.

10.1 English Plosives

Plosives create an interruption in the flow of air through the oral cavity, in effect shutting off the airflow momentarily, much like putting your finger over the end of a water hose stops the flow of water. Also like a hose, when you release the closure the flow bursts out initially. This latter part of the articulation is often referred to as the *release phase* or *burst* and is the source of the term *plosive*.

The English plosives consist of voiced and voiceless pairs of consonants at the labial, alveolar, and velar points of articulation, as well as the glottal stop, which has a special status to be discussed in §10.1.4. We will examine the plosives according to their place of articulation and voicing in the following sections.

10.1.1 Labial Plosives

The labial plosives, /p/ and /b/, may have several different realizations in English, depending on the position where they occur. When voiceless /p/ is at the beginning of a stressed syllable, as in *paper*, *peas*, or *popular*, it is fairly strongly aspirated, symbolized by [p^h]. Aspiration is clear in Fig. 10.1 in the time range 0.5–0.9s, appearing as high-intensity noise in the frequency range of 2,500–5,000 Hz.

The presence of aspiration in plosives in initial position is a crucial aspect of English phonetics. The example of the word *peas* pronounced by a native speaker of English clearly shows the aspiration in the spectrogram in Fig. 10.1, from 0.05–0.9s. Its absence in this position, as in the pronunciation of the /p/ in the word *peas* as spoken by a French speaker in Fig. 10.2 (0–0.6s), clearly marks the individual as a non-native speaker of English.

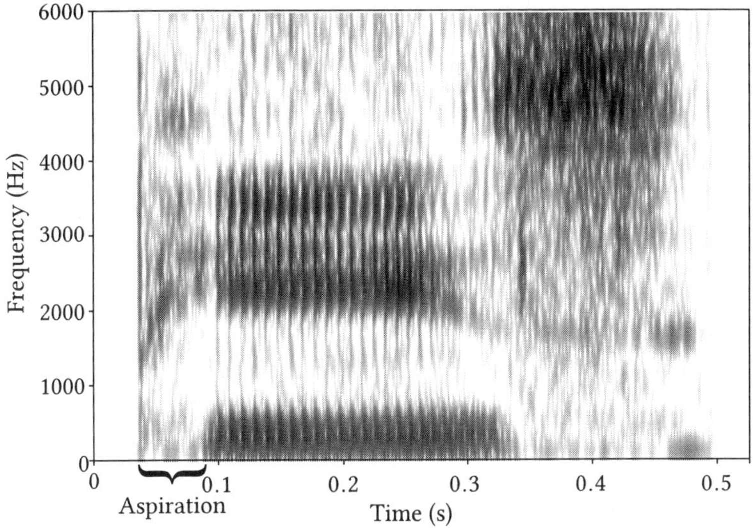

Figure 10.1 *peas* spoken by a native English speaker

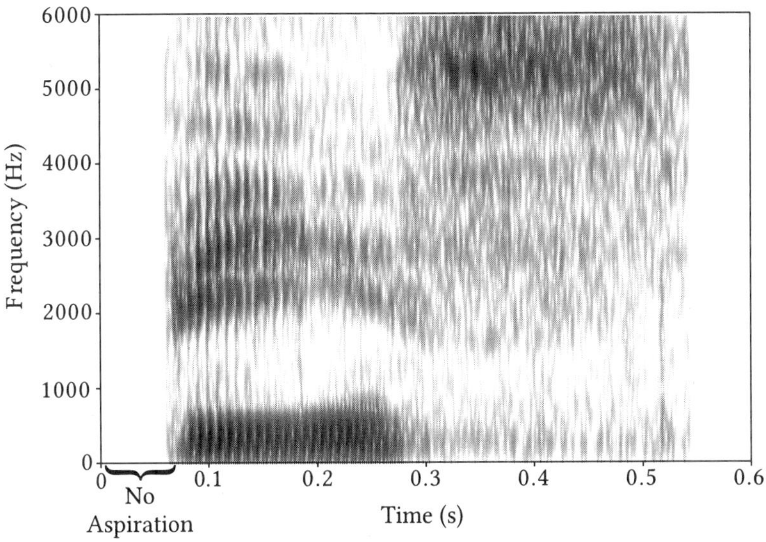

Figure 10.2 *peas* as pronounced by a French speaker

However, the English voiceless bilabial plosive is not always aspirated. For instance, after [s] at the beginning of the syllable, it has a rather different articulation, as shown in Fig. 10.3.

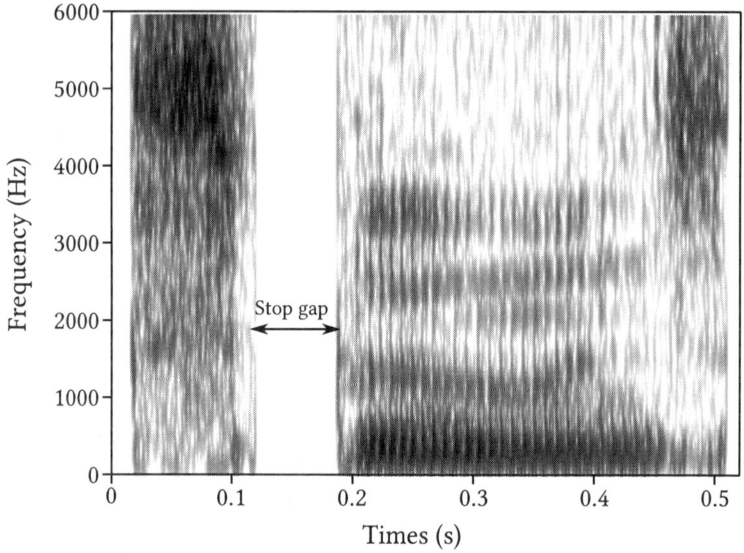

Figure 10.3 English *spoons*

Notice especially the gap (referred to as a *stop gap*) from approximately 140–210ms, signaling the [p] and the near total absence of turbulence following this until the vowel begins at 230ms. This is the typical profile of an English voiceless plosive following [s].

In addition to these two forms of the English /p/, there is a third variety that appears at the end of the syllable, referred to as unreleased [p˺]. Examine the word *scoop* in Fig. 10.4. Note that from 300ms in the spectrogram, there is basically nothing, i.e., the plosive is unreleased and therefore provides no information on the spectrogram.

English also has a voiced bilabial plosive, [b]. Voicing of plosives is not strong in English, as demonstrated in the spectrogram of the word, *Bob*, in Fig. 10.5. Compare the voicing of the English [b] with that of the French speaker saying the same word in Fig. 10.6. Note that the stop gap is much larger in the French pronunciation (English 70ms, French 120ms)

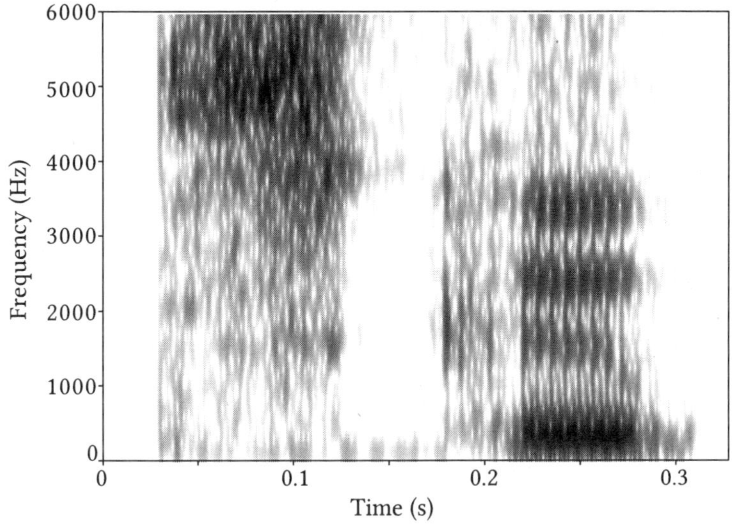

Figure 10.4 English *scoop*

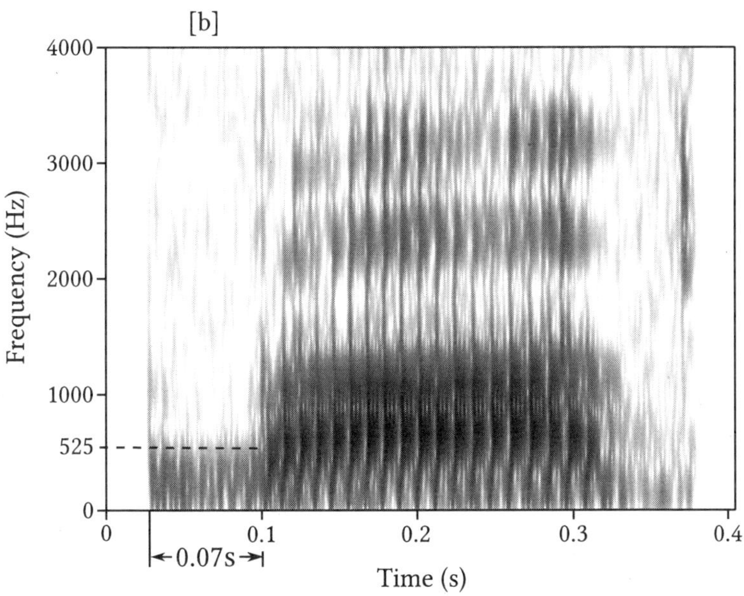

Figure 10.5 English speaker's pronunciation of *Bob*

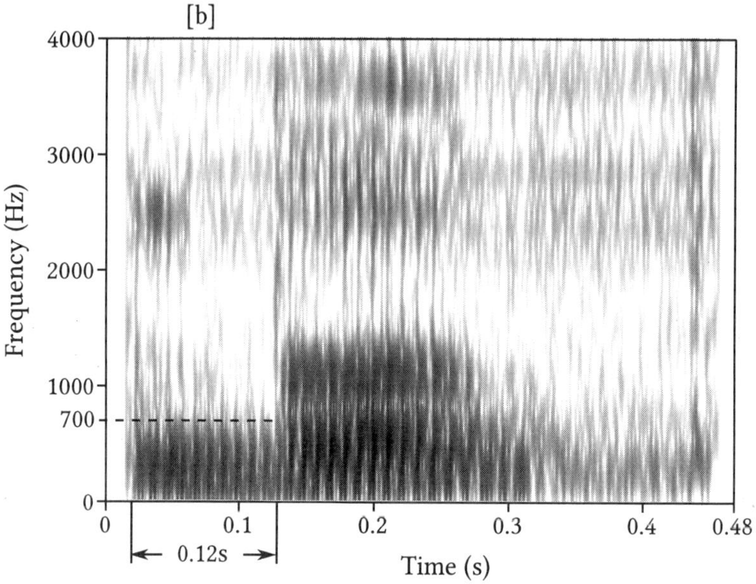

Figure 10.6 French speaker's pronunciation of *Bob*

and the voicing bar is higher (English 525Hz, French 700Hz). In general, English voicing of obstruents is weak compared with other languages where voicing is an important distinctive feature. For English, aspiration is a more significant marker of the distinction between voiced and voiceless obstruents than voicing.

10.1.2 Alveolar Plosives

Like the labial plosives, English has contrastive voicing among the alveolar plosives, /t/ versus /d/. Like voiceless /p/, voiceless /t/ in initial position is aspirated, [t^h]. This aspiration is indicated in Fig. 10.7 from 0.26–0.8s. The same comments concerning aspiration of the [p^h] hold for [t^h]. Similarly, /t/ following [s] is unaspirated, [t], as in Fig. 10.8 for the word *store*.

Note the absence of aspiration on the [t] in *store*, just as with the [p] in *spoons*, due to the preceding [s]. The stop gap is from 150–182ms, followed by a very brief burst and then the vowel. If you compare this with the aspiration in 10.7 it is easy to see the difference in aspiration.

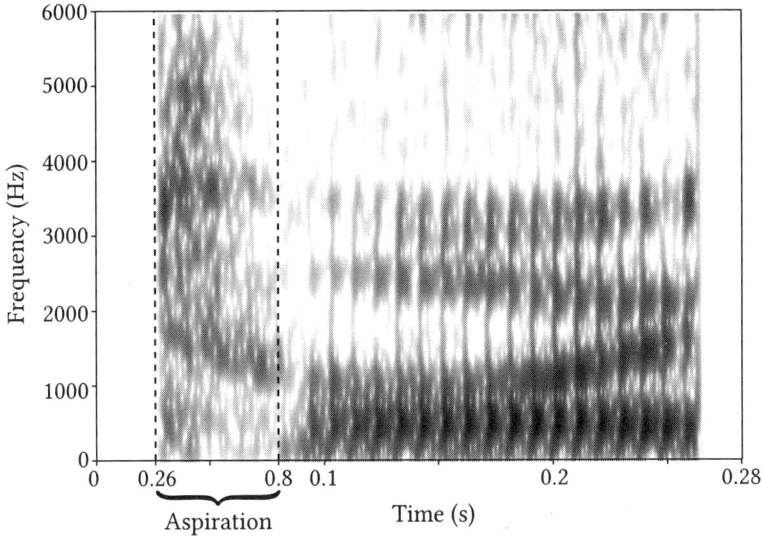

Figure 10.7 English *toy* [tʰɔɪ]

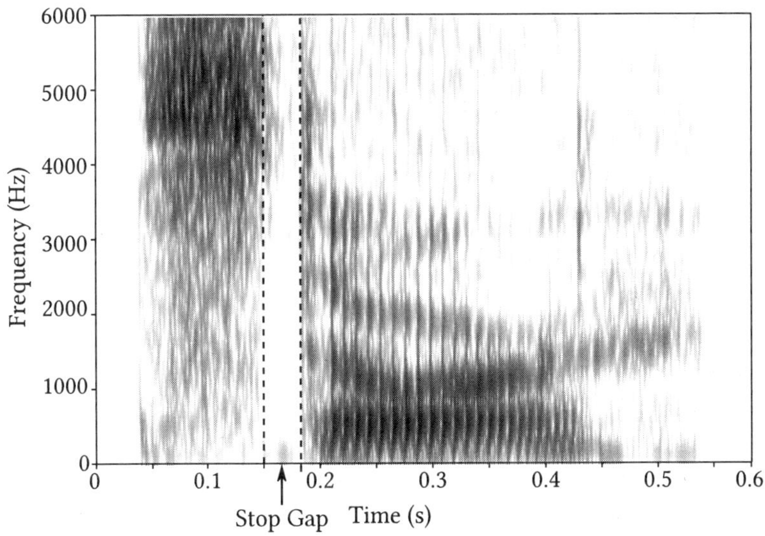

Figure 10.8 English *store* [stɔɹ]

As with the voiceless bilabial, there is also an unreleased version of /t/, which appears at the end of the syllable. It is represented as [t̚] and is shown in Fig. 10.9 from 0.23s.

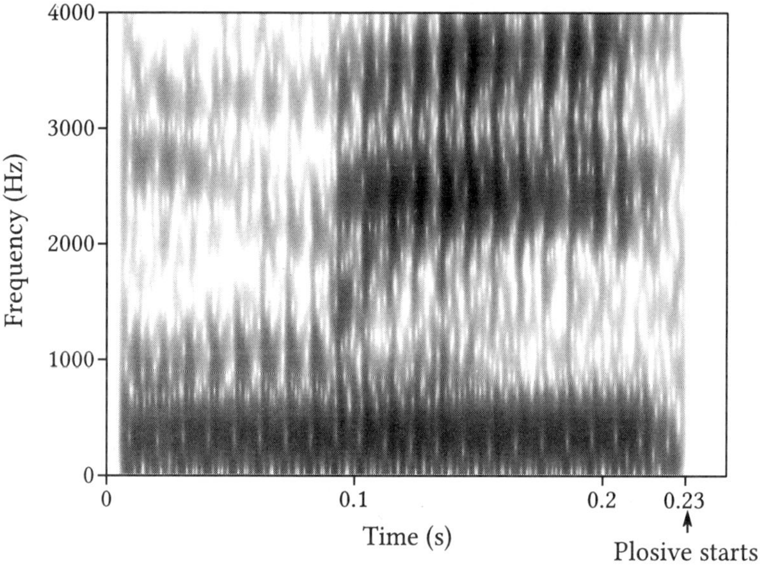

Figure 10.9 English *meet* [miːt̚]

In addition to these three phonetic realizations of /t/, shared by nearly all varieties of English, there are also other variants that appear in only certain dialects. These include the glottal stop, [ʔ], commonly found in British English varieties, and the alveolar flap, [ɾ], found in North American dialects. Since these are not strictly alveolar plosives, they will be discussed further in their relevant sections later.[1]

Before leaving the alveolar plosives, we should examine the voiced alveolar plosive, /d/. As with English /b/, /d/ is not strongly voiced and is much less voiced than, for instance, the French /d/. An example of English [d] is shown in Fig. 10.10, the word *dude*.

As one can readily see, the voicing, and the plosive overall, is very

[1] See §10.1.4 for discussion of the glottal stop and §11.2 on the alveolar flap.

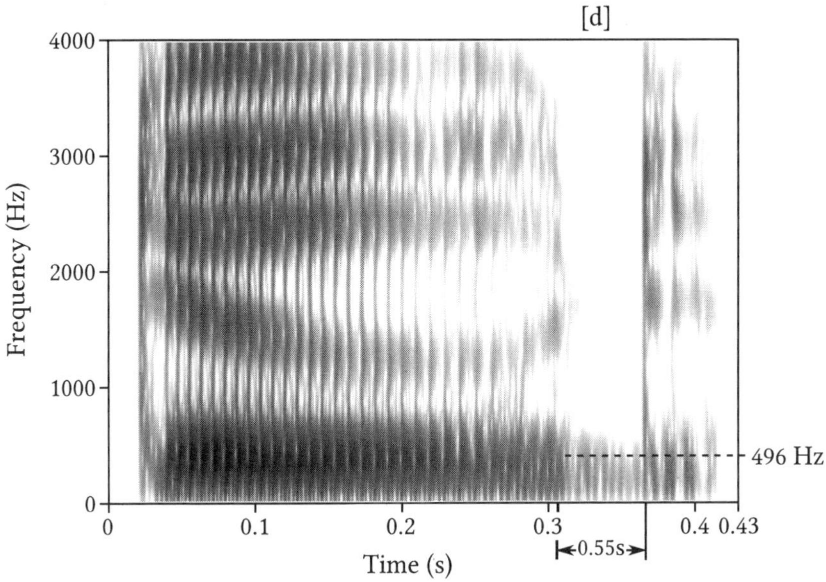

Figure 10.10 *dude* [du:d]

brief. Compare the initial [d] in Fig. 10.10 with the final [d]. The final [d] is about 55ms long and its voicing bar reaches approximately 500Hz, much like [b] discussed earlier.

The voiced alveolar plosive may also appear as a flap [ɾ] in intervocalic position in North American varieties of English, just as with the voiceless alveolar plosive, as shown in Fig. 10.11. Notice that the two words, *metal* and *medal*, are pronounced exactly the same in this North American accent, whereas in a British accent the medial consonants would be quite different. In this way, one can see that intervocalic flapping neutralizes an important contrastive distinction.

10.1.3 Velar Plosives

The velar plosives, voiceless /k/ and voiced /g/, appear in the same varieties as the bilabial plosives. In word- or syllable-initial stressed position, the voiceless velar plosive is aspirated, [kʰ], as shown in the spectrogram of the word *call* in Fig. 10.12.

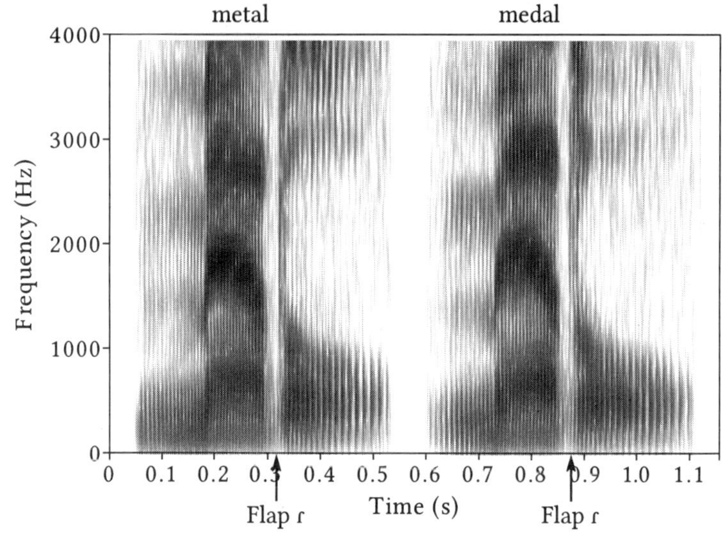

Figure 10.11 Flapping of [t] and [d] in North American English

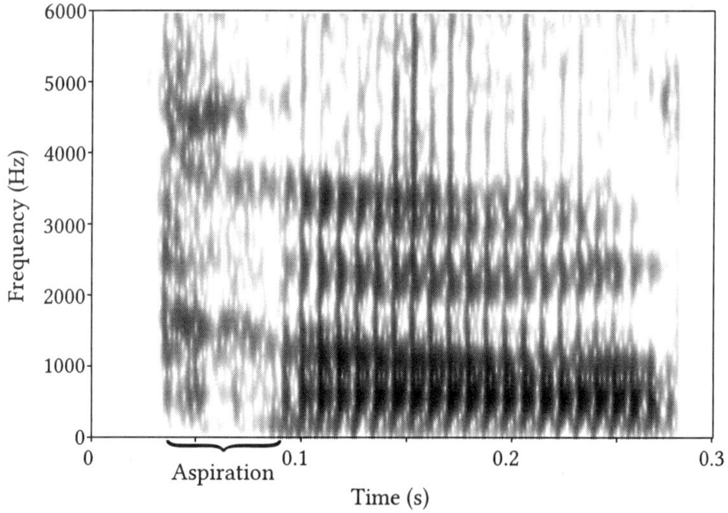

Figure 10.12 Voiceless aspirated velar plosive in *call* [kʰɔɫ]

When preceded by [s], it has the same properties as the other plosives discussed so far, as shown by the spectrogram of *scoop* provided in Fig. 10.4. Note the brief aspiration, from 190–215ms, much less than that for Fig. 10.12 above, where aspiration ranges from approximately 40–90ms.

There is also an unreleased version of the voiceless velar plosive, [k˺], found at the end of the syllable, as in the word *snack* illustrated in Fig. 10.13. The velar pinch at the end of the vowel [æ] indicates that the following sound is a velar and the gap marks it as a stop. The absence of a voicing bar tells us that it is a voiceless stop.

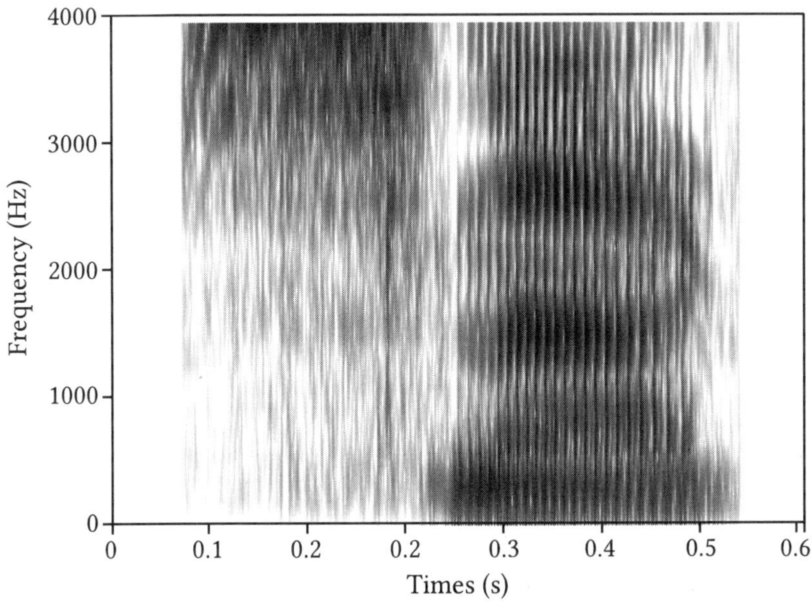

Figure 10.13 Unreleased [k˺] in *snack*

As with the other voiced plosives discussed above, English [g] is not strongly voiced, as is made clear by the [g] in the word *goal* in Fig. 10.14, where the voicing of the [g] lasts less than 50ms, but the velar pinch is quite clear.

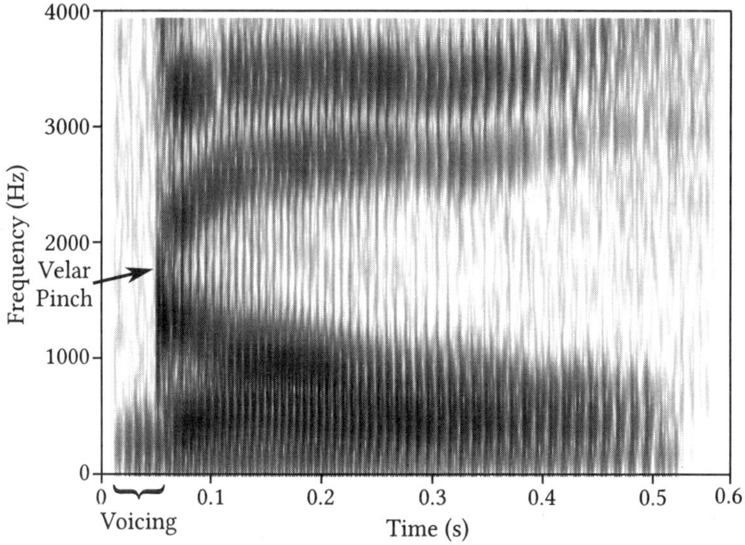

Figure 10.14 [g] in *goal*

10.1.4 Glottal Stop

One final consonant remains to be examined here. It is distinct from the others in that it does not serve a contrastive function in English, but acts as an allophonic variant of /t/ in some dialects and as a concomitant of other sounds as well.

One special property of the glottal stop is that its phonation type is invariably voiceless since, when producing the sound the vocal cords are held tightly together, preventing vibration. Furthermore, it cannot be described as a plosive, since it does not involve the same type of release phase as the other plosives. The glottal stop allophone of /t/ occurs in London English, for instance, in words such as *little*, as shown in Fig. 10.15.

Glottal stop is realized as an interruption in the flow of sound. It occurs in some varieties of British English as *preglottalization* on consonants at the end of the syllable. As Wells (1982:260) puts it:

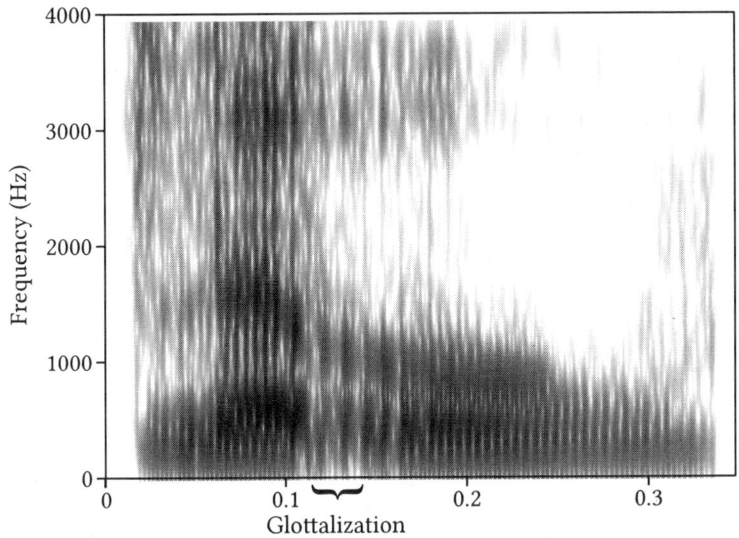

Figure 10.15 London English *little* [lɪʔoʊ]

> The voiceless plosives /p,t,k/, and also the affricate /ʧ/, are in England often preceded in certain syllable-final environments by a glottal stop [ʔ]. Either this is a new, twentieth-century phenomenon, or else no phonetician had previously noticed it. Because the [ʔ] is inserted before the oral closure is effected, and thus masks the approach phase of the oral plosive, it is referred to as Preglottalization, or Glottal Reinforcement.

Wells goes on to give examples of this, such as those in (10.1).

(10.1) a. quite good [kwaɪʔt gʊːd]
b. look down [lʊʔk daʊn]
c. happen [hæʔpn̩]

The final use of glottal stop appears in North American English, and is similar to the case of (10.1c). It applies to forms having a syllabic alveolar nasal preceded by a voiceless alveolar plosive. Thus, words like *button*, *cotton*, and *kitten* show preglottalization, but those such as *sud-*

den, *happen*, *bottom*, *little*, or *butter* do not. This confirms that it only happens with syllabic alveolar nasals preceded by voiceless alveolar plosives. A spectrogram of the word *button*, [bʌʔn̩], is provided in Fig. 10.16, illustrating the facts of alveolar nasal preglottalization. It clearly shows the glottal stop before the syllabic alveolar nasal, [n̩].

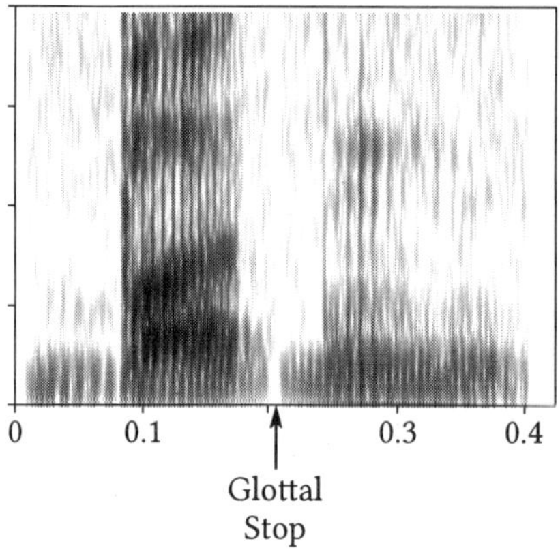

Figure 10.16 *button*

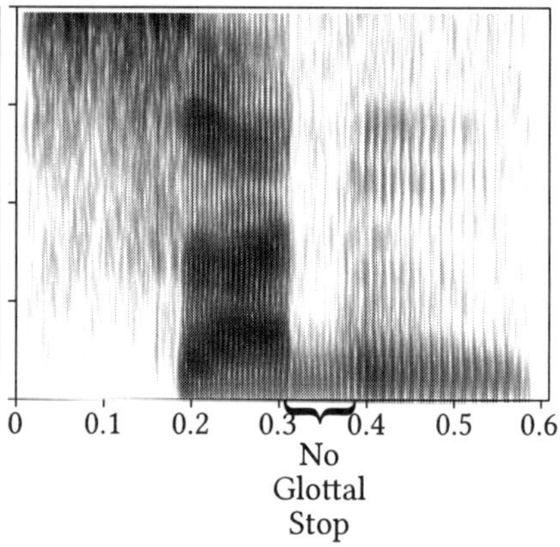

Figure 10.17 *sudden*

Fig. 10.17 demonstrates that glottalization does not appear in forms such as *sudden*, which do not have a voiceless alveolar plosive.

10.2 English Fricatives

The English fricatives include [f, θ, s, ʃ, h, v, ð, z, ʒ]. This is a rather large set of fricatives typologically, and we find very few languages with so many contrastive fricatives. Korean, by contrast, has only two, or three, depending on the dialect: [s, s', h].

10.2.1 Labiodental Fricatives

English has two contrastive labiodental fricatives, the voiceless [f] and the voiced [v]. They exhibit the typical properties of such fricatives, including high frequency turbulence concentrated above 4,000 Hz.

The voiceless variant, [f], exhibits no substantial voicing bar. The initial voiceless labiodental fricative is exemplified by words such as *fox*, *file*, and *frame*, while *tough*, *half*, and *stuff* all end with [f]. Intervocalically, [f] can be found in words such as *siphon*, *sniffle*, and *safer*, as shown by the spectrographic profile of [f] in Fig. 10.18.

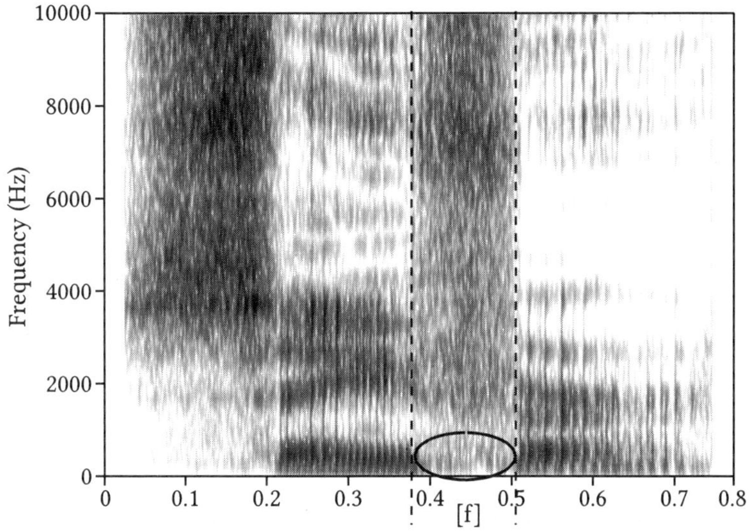

Figure 10.18 Voiceless labiodental fricative [f] in *safer*

The voiced labiodental fricative, [v], also exhibits high frequency turbulence concentrated above 4,000 Hz, as well as a substantial voicing bar occupying the lower 400 Hz. Words beginning with the voiced labiodental fricative, [v], include *vie*, *valve*, and *view*, while words ending with [v] include *halve*, *live*, and *cove*. Intervocalic [v] occurs in words such as *hover*, *waver*, and *savor*. The analysis of *savor* is given in Fig. 10.19.

10.2.2 Interdental Fricatives

Interdental fricatives are not common in the languages of the world, but English has both voiceless and voiced variants. Their frequency profile

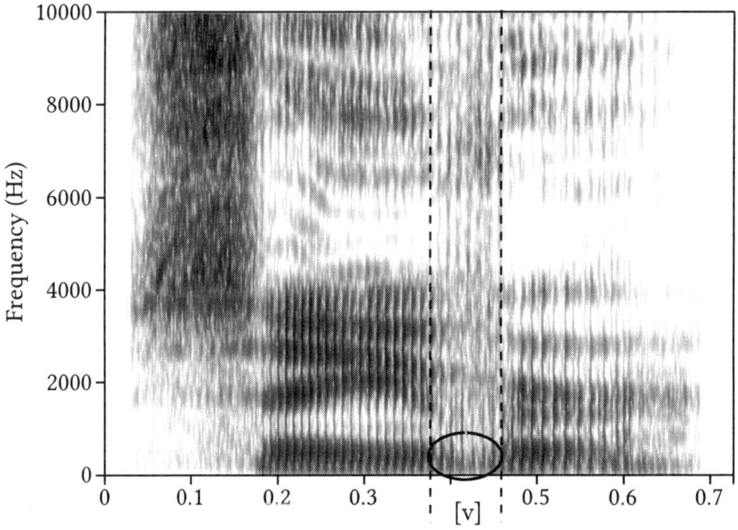

Figure 10.19 Voiced labiodental fricative [v] in *savor*

begins around 2,000Hz, with a lower intensity than alveolar fricatives, to be discussed in the next section. These fricatives are a common source of difficulty for non-native speakers, often resulting in substitution by similar, more common sounds.

The voiceless interdental fricative, [θ], is found as the first sound in words such as *think*, *thigh*, and *thought*, as well as the last sound of words such as *both*, *path*, and *with*. Between vowels, it may be found in words such as *catheter*, *ether*, and *pathetic*. The voiceless interdental fricative is exemplified by the spectrogram of the word *toothy* in Fig. 10.20.

The voiced interdental fricative, [ð], occurs as the first sound in words such as *though*, *that*, and *they* and as the last sound in words such as *bathe*, *betroth*, and *soothe*. It occurs as the consonant in the middle of words such as *bother*, *either*, and *smoothie*, which is represented in the spectrogram in Fig. 10.21.

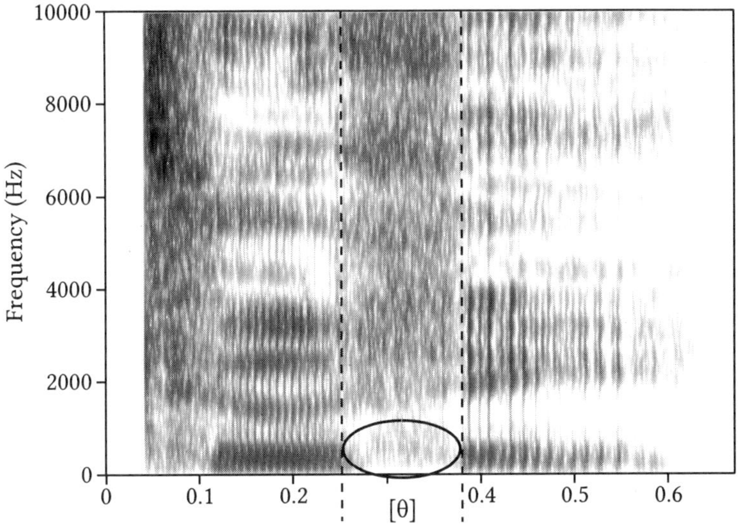

Figure 10.20 Voiceless interdental fricative [θ] in *toothy*

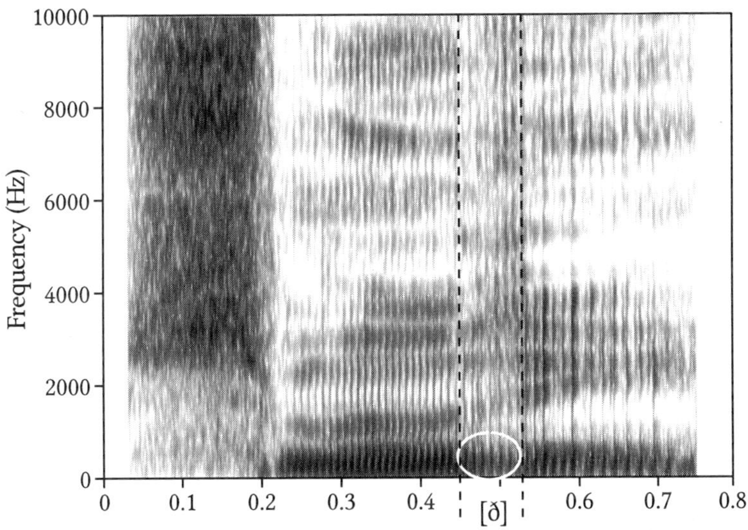

Figure 10.21 Voiced interdental fricative, [ð], in *smoothie*

10.2.3 Alveolar Fricatives

English also has alveolar fricatives, [s] and [z], perhaps the most common fricatives crosslinguistically. While Korean also has alveolar fricatives, it does not have the same voiceless/voiced distinction as English alveolar fricatives.

The voiceless alveolar fricative can be found initially in words like *cease*, *science*, and *sorrow*, while words such as *bus*, *pace*, and *toss* provide examples of final [s]. Intervocalically, [s] can be found in words like *castle*, *passage*, and *racer*.

As can be seen from the spectrogram of the word *faces* in Fig. 10.22, the bulk of the turbulence in [s] occurs above 3500Hz and continues strongly up to and beyond 10,000Hz. There is no significant voicing bar.

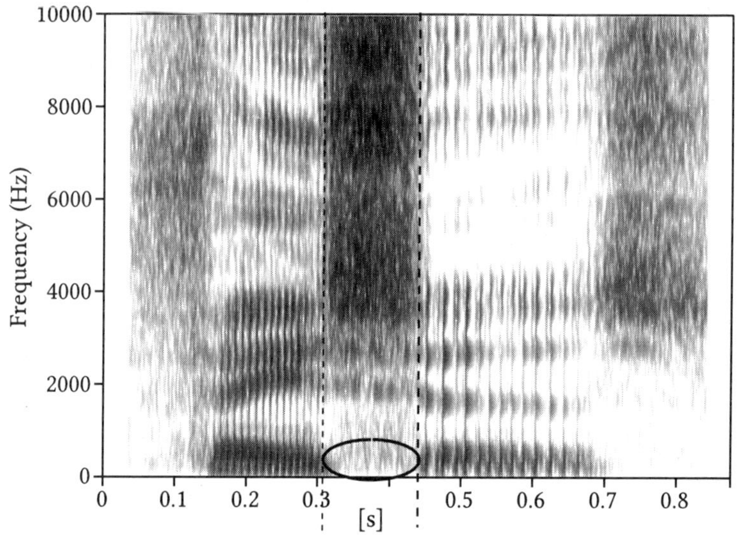

Figure 10.22 Voiceless alveolar fricative [s] in *faces*

With respect to the voiced alveolar fricative, [z], the range of turbulence and intensity is the same as for [s], but there is a concomitant voicing bar signaling the voicing of [z], as shown on the spectrogram of the middle consonant of the word *phases* in Fig. 10.23.

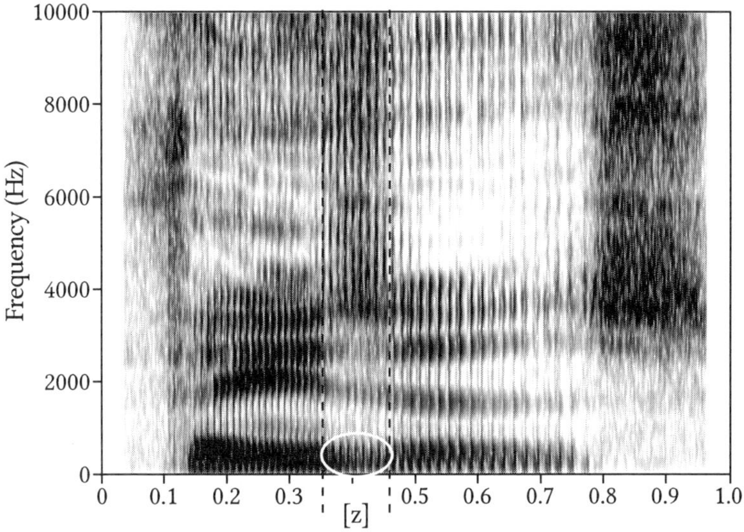

Figure 10.23 Voiced alveolar fricative [z] in *phases*

[z] is found initially in words like *zither*, *zone*, and *xylophone*, and finally in words like *hose*, *fez*, and *days*. Word-internally, it may be found in words like *basil*, *laser*, and *buzzer*.

10.2.4 Alveo-Palatal Fricatives

English has both voiceless and voiced alveopalatal fricatives, [ʃ] and [ʒ]. The frequency range of the turbulence for both of these fricatives is from 2000 up to 10,000 Hz, as can be readily seen in Figs 10.24 and 10.25. Their intensity is high.

The voiceless alveopalatal fricative (Fig. 10.24) may be found initially in words such as *champagne*, *shake*, and *sure*. It may be found at the end of words like *cache*, *fish*, and *wash* and intervocalically in *motion*, *tissue*, and *washer*. [ʃ] may also arise due to a process referred to as Yod-coalescence, by which an [s] followed by a palatalizing vowel results in a palatal, as in some speakers' pronunciation of words like *capsule* [kʰæpʃu:ɫ] or *suit* [ʃu:t].

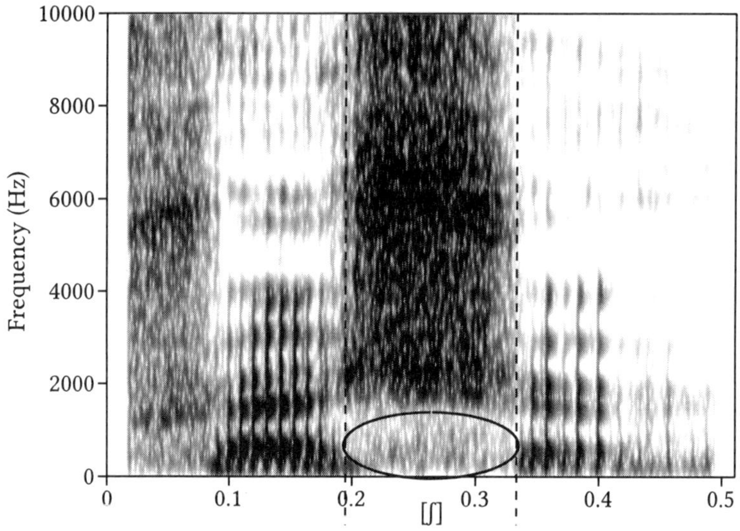

Figure 10.24 Voiceless alveopalatal fricative [ʃ] in *pressure*

The voiced alveopalatal fricative, [ʒ], exhibits an obvious voicing bar, as shown in Fig. 10.25. Examples of initial [ʒ] are extremely rare and found only in obviously foreign borrowings, such as *genre* or *gendarme*. Similarly, final [ʒ] is also rare, although slightly more common than in initial position. Examples include *garage*, *rouge*, *loge*, and *luge*.

[ʒ] is most commonly encountered in intervocalic position, in words such as *fusion*, *pleasure*, and *usual*, as well as forms palatalized by Yod-coalescence, e.g., *because you* ... [bəkʰʌʒuː], *use your* ... [juːʒuːɹ], etc.

10.2.5 Glottal Fricative

The remaining contrastive English fricative is the voiceless glottal fricative, [h], exemplified by the word *haven*, shown in Fig. 10.26. There is no voicing bar for [h] and its turbulence appears to be strongest in the low range, around 1,000 Hz.

[h] is found initially in words such as *have*, *help*, and *holiday*. It is never encountered finally, in spite of its presence in orthographic forms such as *Sarah*, *fellah*, etc.

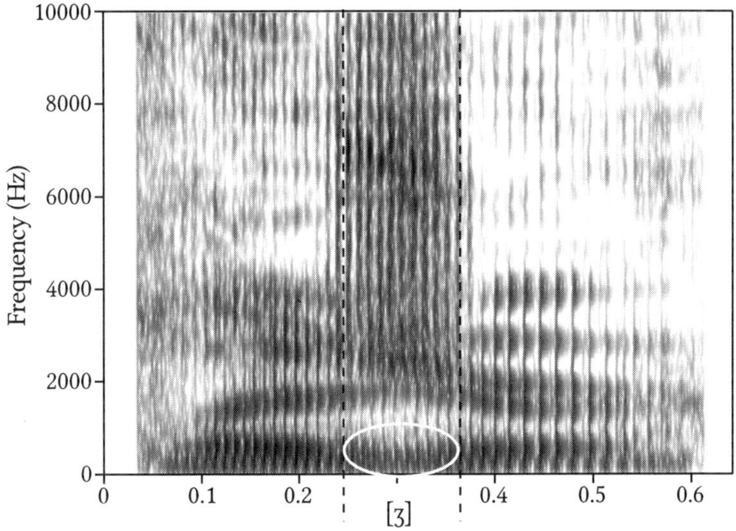

Figure 10.25 Voiced alveopalatal fricative [ʒ] in *pleasure*

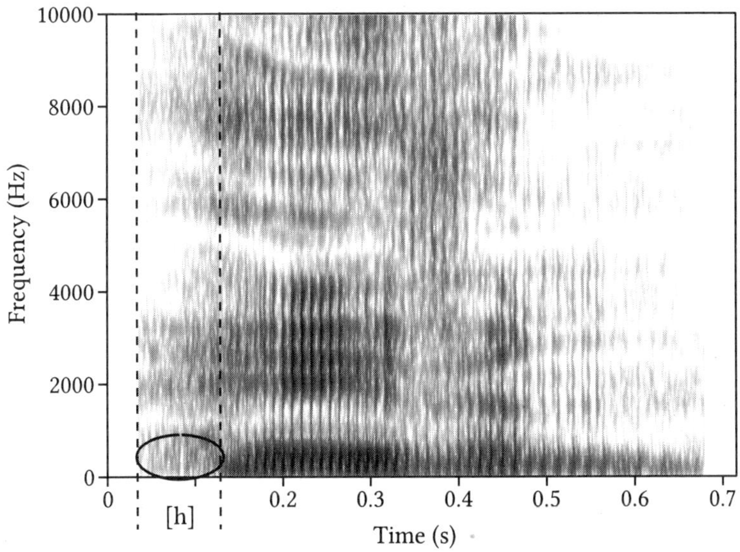

Figure 10.26 Voiceless glottal fricative [h] in *haven*

[h] is usually considered to be voiceless in English, but may exhibit a certain degree of voicing between vowels. This is often attributed to what is known as *glottal transparency*, i.e. the ability of certain phonetic properties to continue through glottal sounds. An example of this is provided in Fig. 10.27, for the word *behave*.

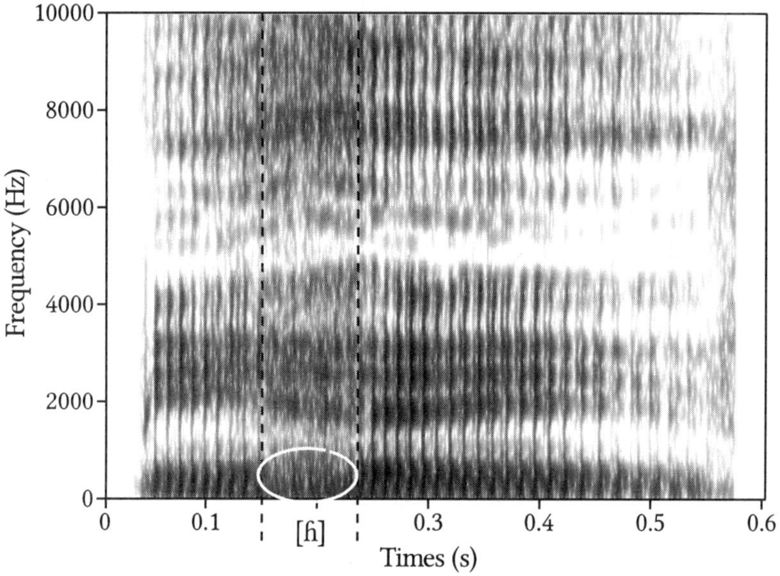

Figure 10.27 Voiced glottal fricative [ɦ] in *behave*

10.2.6 Sibilants

The final topic to address in the discussion of fricatives is that of sibilants (치찰음) versus non-sibilants. This property has significance in English because of the rules for forming the plural and other morphemes involving a suffix with the shape /-s/ or /-z/. In such cases, words ending with certain fricatives behave differently with respect to epenthesis from those ending with other fricatives. The traditional account of this relies on the notion of *sibilant*.

Sibilants are usually considered to involve a turbulent airstream that strikes an obstacle, such as the teeth, whereas non-sibilants result from turbulence that is generated at the site of the constriction. Sibilants tend to be louder than their non-sibilant counterparts, and most of their acoustic energy occurs at higher frequencies. [s] has acoustic energy starting at around 3,500 Hz, and reaching as high as 10,000 Hz. [ʃ] has most of its acoustic energy around 4,000 Hz, extending up to 8,000 Hz. The English sibilants include [s, ʃ, z, ʒ], shown in Table 10.2.

Fricative	Frequency Range (Hz)	Intensity	Sibilant	Voicing Bar
f	5000 and above	low	no	no
v	5000 and above	low	no	yes
θ	2,500 and above	low	no	no
ð	2,500 and above	low	no	yes
s	3,500 and above	high	yes	no
z	3,500 and above	high	yes	yes
ʃ	2,000 and above	high	yes	no
ʒ	2,000 and above	high	yes	yes
h	750–3000	low	no	no

Table 10.2 Properties of English fricatives

Most importantly, sibilants require the insertion of a neutral vowel when a morpheme ending in the sibilant is followed by a morpheme beginning with a sibilant, e.g. *wish-es* [wɪʃəz], *rose-s* [ɹoʊzəz], etc.

10.3 English Affricates

As discussed in §6.3.3, affricates are complex segments consisting of a plosive component with a fricative component. The English affricates include both voiceless, [ʧ], and voiced, [ʤ], alveopalatal affricates.

The voiceless alveopalatal affricate may occur initially, as in *chip, church, chalk,* or medially, as in *butcher, lecher, macho,* or finally, as in *catch, such, itch.*

Fig. 10.28 illustrates the voiceless alveopalatal affricate, [ʧ], in the word *lecher.* Acoustically, this affricated exhibits the stop gap associated with [t], followed immediately by the turbulent airflow of the fricative [ʃ]. The frequency range of the latter is similar to that of the alveopalatal fricative. Furthermore, it behaves as a sibilant for the purposes of the plural and other rules of similar form.

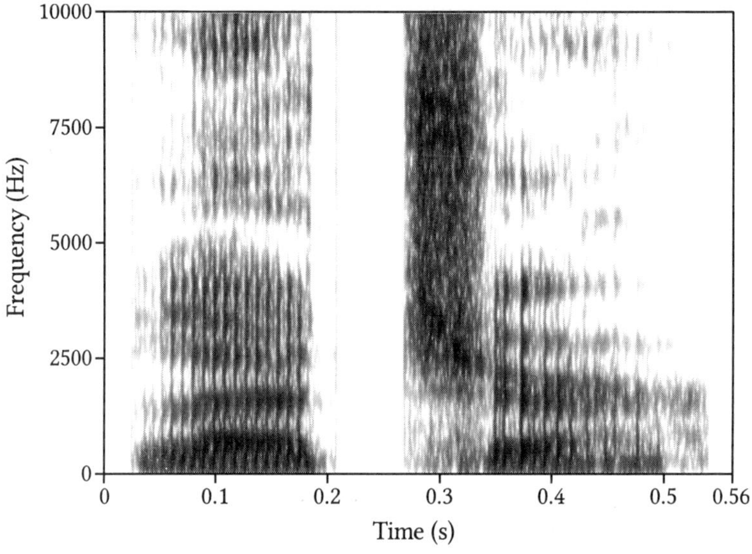

Figure 10.28 Voiceless alveopalatal affricate [ʧ] in *lecher*

Just as with the voiceless alveopalatal affricate, the voiced alveopalatal affricate may occur initially, as in *jam, jump, giant,* or medially, as in *badger, major, wager,* or finally, as in *badge, cage, ridge.*

Fig. 10.29 provides an example of the voiced variant, [ʤ], in the word *ledger,* where a dark voicing bar is clearly visible from 0.2–0.33s. Note that the voicing bar spans both the plosive and fricative components of the affricate. Similar to the voiceless alveopalatal affricate, it exhibits the stop gap associated with [d], followed immediately by the turbulent airflow of the fricative [ʒ]. The frequency range of the latter is similar to that of the voiced alveopalatal fricative and it behaves as a sibilant for the purposes of the plural and other rules of similar form.

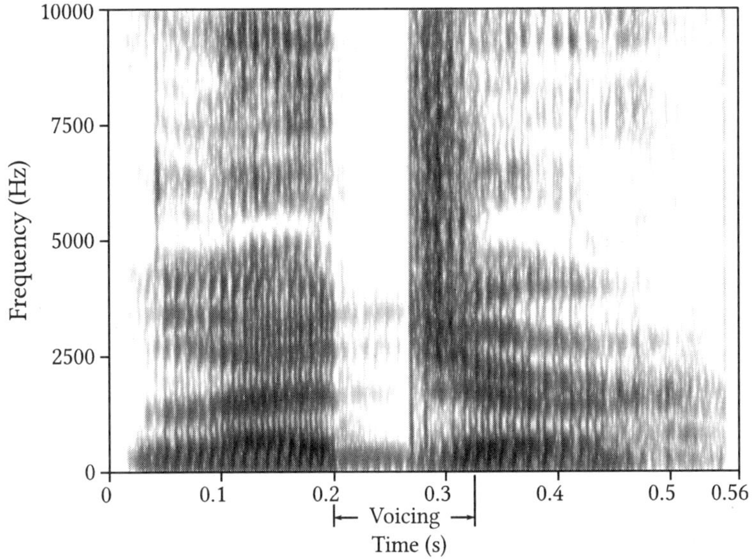

Figure 10.29 Voiced alveopalatal affricate [ʤ] in *ledger*

The Nature of Affricates

An interesting issue associated with affricates is that of their status as distinct, individual segments. The IPA represents affricates using two consonant symbols conjoined and it may seem that they should be treated as a sequence, but there is good evidence from aspiration that they do not involve a sequence.

When aspiration is associated with the voiceless alveopalatal affricate, [tʃʰ], as in the word *chip*, the aspiration appears after the entire affricate, not after the plosive portion alone. Since English fricatives do not bear aspiration, we cannot treat the affricate as simply a sequence of plosive followed by fricative.

Exercises

1. Give examples of five words containing one of the English plosives in i) the beginning, ii) the middle, and iii) the end of the word.

2. Give examples of five words containing one of the English fricatives in i) the beginning, ii) the middle, and iii) the end of the word.

3. Analyze one English word containing a plosive in the middle, making a spectrogram and indicating the stop gap and any aspiration.

4. Analyze one English word with a fricative, indicating the high frequency markers of the fricative on your spectrogram.

Further Reading

Recommended additional readings for this chapter include Ladefoged & Johnson (2010), Ladefoged & Maddieson (1996), and Lieberman & Blumstein (1988) on the general description of sounds, as well as Jones (1918) on English phonetics and is worth reading. Ladefoged (2005) is a detailed study of consonants.

Keywords: alveolar flap, closure complete, glottal stop, preglottalization, sibilant.

Chapter 11

English Sonorants

The sonorant consonants make up one group of consonants within the English consonant system, along with the obstruents discussed in the previous chapter. The sonorant consonants include the nasals, liquids, and approximants.

There are three contrastive nasal sonorants, contrastive rhotic and lateral approximants, and labiovelar and palatal approximants, as shown in Table 11.1. In addition to these, the alveolar rhotic flap, the velarized lateral approximant and the voiceless labiovelar approximant/fricative are included in the table for completeness, since they will be discussed in this chapter.

Nasals		m	n		ŋ
Liquids:	rhotics		ɹ ɾ		
	laterals		l		ɫ
Semivowels		w		j	
		ʍ			

Table 11.1 The English Sonorants

We will begin our examination of sonorant consonants with the nasal sonorant consonants.

11.1 Nasal Stops

The first class of sonorant consonants we will examine is the nasals. Nasal consonants involve a closure somewhere in the oral cavity and the concomitant lowering of the velum to allow air to pass through the nasal cavity. Since they interrupt the flow of air in the oral cavity, they are often referred to as *nasal stops*, although they are not considered plosives, since the lowered velum does not permit the buildup of pressure necessary for a stop burst.

In English, there are three contrastive nasal stops, the bilabial nasal, [m], the alveolar nasal, [n], and the velar nasal, [ŋ], although other nasal consonants may arise due to assimilation to adjacent consonants. For instance, the nasal in the words *emphasis* or *invite* is often closer to a labiodental nasal [ɱ], since it anticipates the following labiodental fricative [f] or [v]. Nevertheless, this is not contrastive in English.

11.1.1 Acoustic Correlates of Nasals

The first thing to note about nasals is that they involve a heavy voicing bar, attesting to their inherent voicing. In addition, they have formants like vowels, although they are somewhat lighter, confirming their sonorant nature. The nasal is also less prominent on the waveform, although still more so than a plosive. Note that these properties appear in either the beginning or end of the syllable.

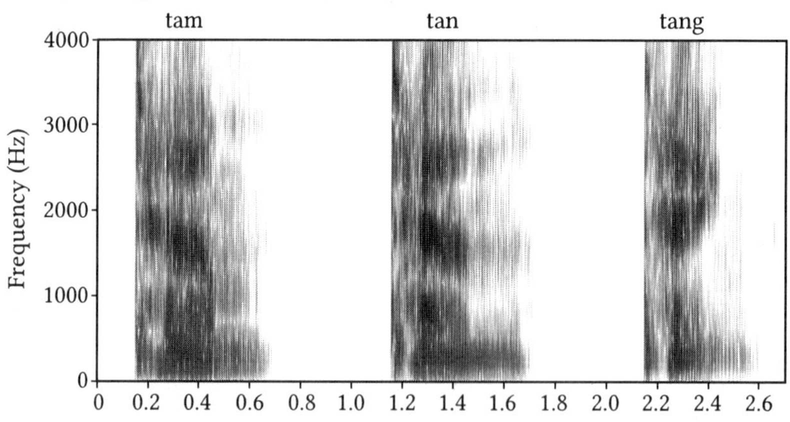

Figure 11.1 Examples of final nasals in *tam*, *tan*, and *tang*

The individual place of articulation of the nasal is indicated by the adjacent vowel formants, just as for the obstruents, as shown in Fig. 11.1. Note that the [m] shows a fairly level F_1 with a downward sloping F_2, wheareas [n] shows a relatively level profile for both F_1 and F_2, and [ŋ] shows an upward direction for F_2 and a downward direction for F_3, i.e., the velar pinch.

Nasals may be devoiced when following the voiceless fricative [s] at the beginning of the syllable, as in *smoke* or *snack*. This appears in the spectrogram as a reduction in the intensity of the formants for the nasal, as shown in Fig. 11.2. What is clear from Fig. 11.2 is that nasals following [s], in this case the [m] at 290–320ms and the [n] at 1125–1150ms, respectively, are extremely short and show only a faint trace of a voicing bar and virtually no indication of higher formants, supporting the claim that they are devoiced in this environment.

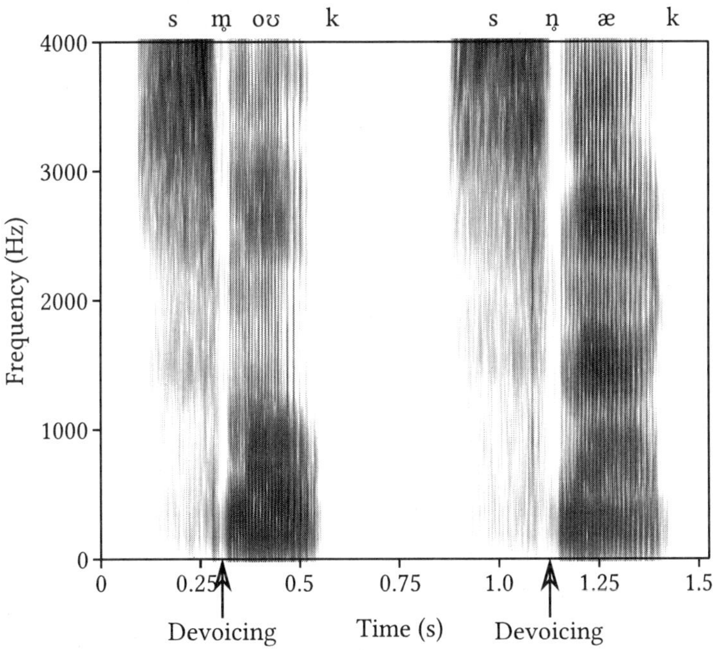

Figure 11.2 Nasal devoicing in *smoke* [sm̥oʊk] and *snack* [sn̥æk]

11.1.2 Syllabic Nasals

In English, nasals may also appear as the head of the syllable, just like a vowel. In this case, they show similar properties to vowels, including movement in their formants to reflect adjacent consonants. Since these segments have already been discussed in §9.3, we will only present an example of the special status of syllabic nasals here. For further discussion of syllabic sonorants, please refer to §9.3.

Fig. 11.3 presents examples of syllabic [m̩] and [n̩] in English. The darkness of the formants indicates that these nasals are, in fact, syllabic here. The downward trend of F_2 at the end of the word *rhythm* reflects the labiality of the [m̩].

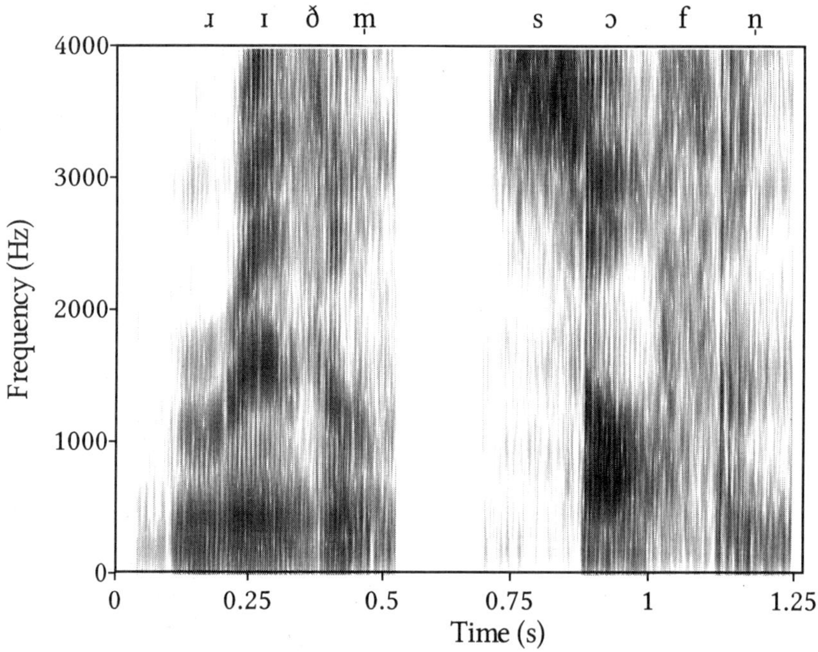

Figure 11.3 Syllabic nasals in *rhythm* and *soften*

This concludes our discussion of nasals in English. We will now move on to an examination of English rhotics.

11.2 Rhotics

Although there is only one /r/ phoneme in English, there are several different r-sounds. The first rhotic is the basic form, [ɹ], found in onsets and codas in standard North American English. It is a rather complex sound, made in several possible ways and is one of the last to be acquired by children due to this complexity. The age of full acquisition is considered to be around six years.

The most obvious acoustic characteristic of the basic English rhotic, [ɹ], is the very low F_2 and F_3 (F_3 is around 1600 Hz). This is a useful property for differentiating the two English liquids, [ɹ] and [l], since F_3 tends to be much higher.

The articulation of the English /r/ has been studied by a number of phoneticians. Zhou et al. (2007) examine the two most common means of producing the English [ɹ]: (i) as a retroflex or (ii) with a bunched tongue. MRI scans of speakers producing /r/ are provided in Fig. 11.4 for the retroflex [ɻ], and in Fig. 11.5 for the bunched [ɹ] (from Zhou et al., 2008:4467).

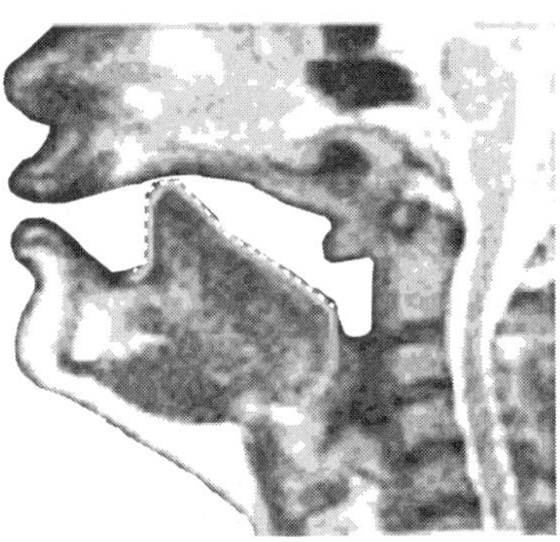

Figure 11.4 Retroflex [ɻ]

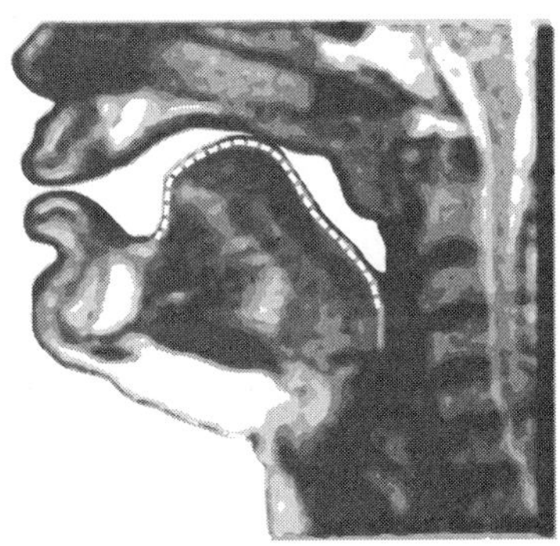

Figure 11.5 Bunched [ɹ]

The second rhotic variant in English is the voiceless alveolar rhotic variant, [ɹ̥]. This is usually found after voiceless obstruents, in particular the aspirated plosives of words like *pretty* [pʰɹ̥ɪɾi], *trip* [tʰɹ̥ɪp], *creek* [kʰɹ̥iːk]. Aspiration may be a contributing factor to the devoicing. An example of this devoicing can be seen in the word *trap*, analyzed in Fig. 11.6.

The third rhotic sound found in English is not connected to the contrastive /r/, but is, rather, associated with the alveolar plosives. This is the alveolar flap [ɾ], which is found in North American English when /t/ or /d/ occurs between a preceding stressed vowel and an immediately following syllabic segment, as in *auto, coda, butter, ladder.* Examples of each type of rhotic are provided in Fig. 11.6.

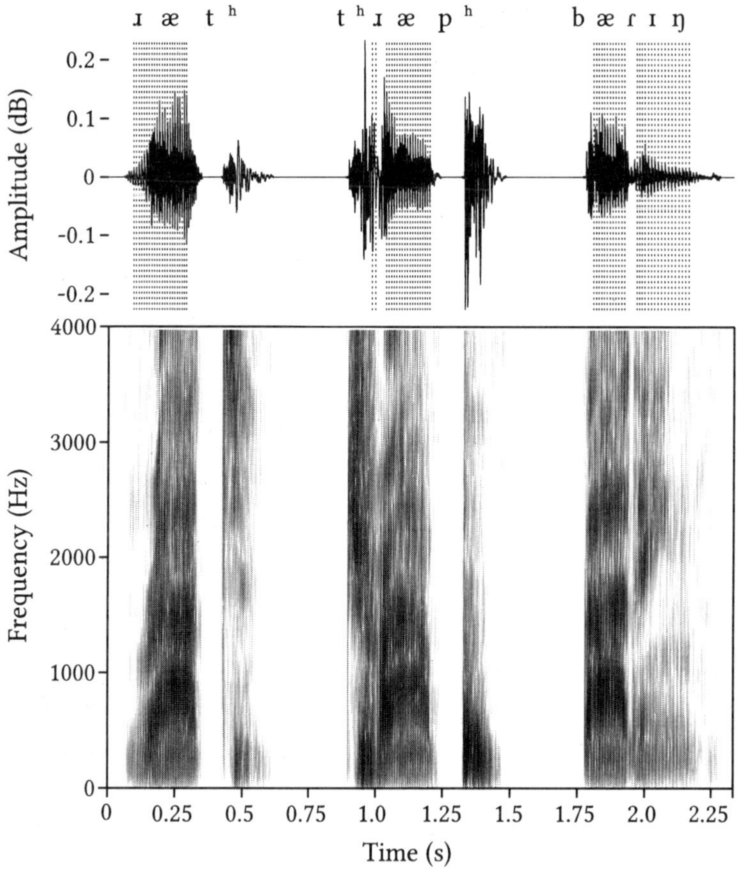

Figure 11.6 Rhotics in the words *rat, trap,* and *batting*

11.2.1 Acoustic Correlates of Rhotics

The basic alveolar rhotic approximant [ɹ] has average formant frequencies as provided in Table 11.2, taken from Dalston (1975). Note, in particular, the rather low F_3, as compared with that of the alveolar lateral approximant shown in Table 11.3 on page 222.

	F_1	F_2	F_3
Men	348	1061	1546
Women	350	1065	2078
Children	431	1503	2491

Table 11.2 Average formant frequencies for English [ɹ] (Dalston, 1975)

As noted above, the English /r/ is also subject to devoicing when following voiceless obstruents. This includes [s], at least for some speakers, as shown in Fig. 11.7 for the word *Sri Lanka*. Note that it is particularly rare for /r/ to follow [s] or any other sound besides the plosives and it is often pronounced as [ʃ] in such contexts. Nevertheless, it is clear from this spectrogram (from about 230–260ms) that the [ɹ̥] is both short (30ms) and has very weak voicing and formants.

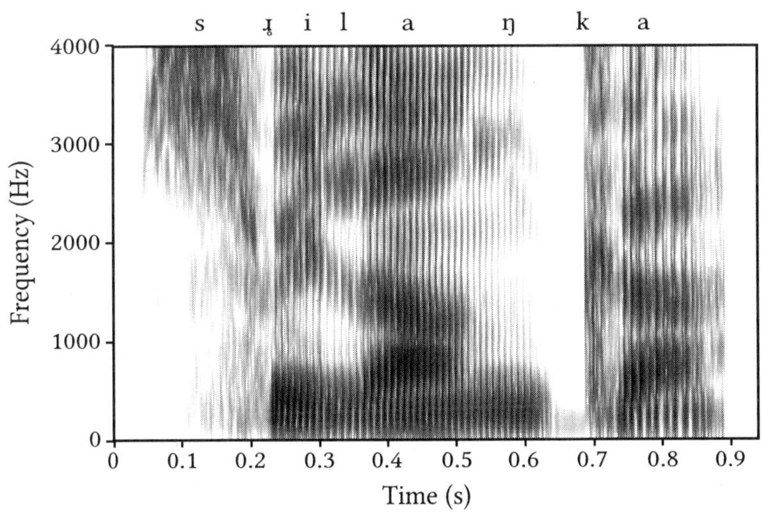

Figure 11.7 Devoicing of [ɹ] before [s] in *Sri Lanka*

11.2.2 Syllabic Rhotics

Just as with the nasals, it is possible to have syllabic rhotics in English. Such syllabic rhotics function as the head of a syllable, although they do not typically bear stress. As an example, the final [ɹ] in words like *racer* or *laser* is syllabic, as demonstrated by the spectrogram of the word *racer* in Fig. 11.8. In this case one can readily see the formants of the syllabic [ɹ̩] at the end of the word, showing an F_1 at 440 Hz and an F_2 at around 1500 Hz.

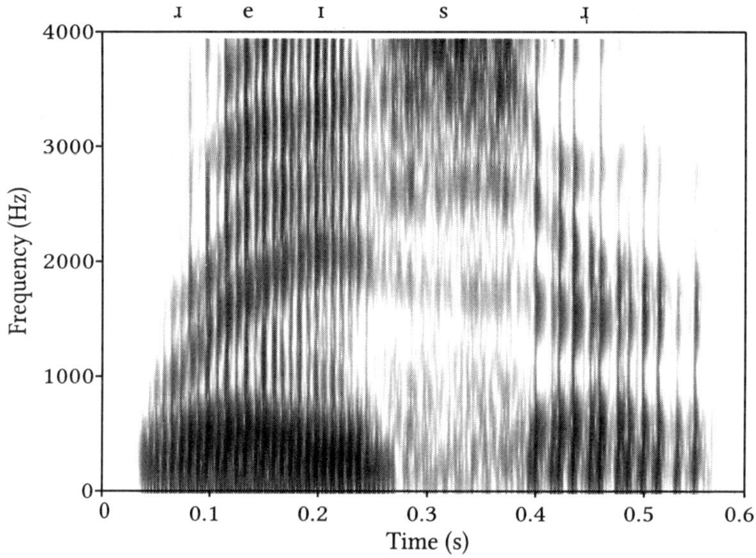

Figure 11.8 Syllabic [ɹ̩] in *racer*

While it is typically the case that syllabic rhotics and syllabic consonants, in general, are not stressed in English, there are cases of near-minimal pairs involving unstressed versus stressed syllabic rhotics in English. One such case is that of the words *differ* [ˈdɪfɹ̩] and *defer* [dɪˈfɹ̩], shown in Fig. 11.9.

Cases such as *defer* involve the Latinate root *-fer*, found in words like *defer, refer, confer*, etc. One possible explanation for the placement of

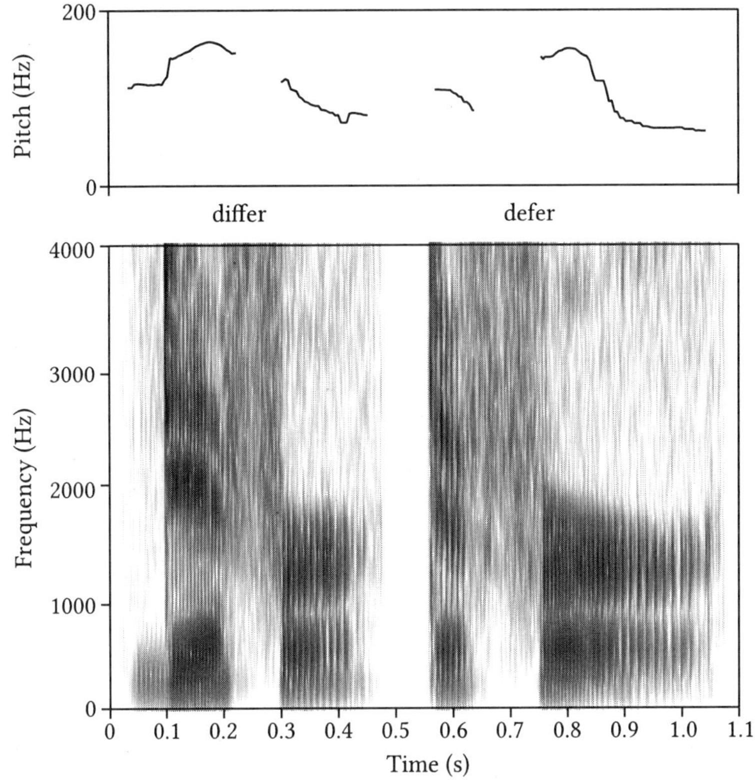

Figure 11.9 *differ* versus *defer*

stress in these forms is that the root, *-fer*, requires the stress, even though it is weak. Obviously, this is not a phonetic requirement and goes beyond the scope of discussion here, but this should be borne in mind when considering the placement of stress in English, which will be discussed in the next chapter.

11.2.3 Linking [ɹ] and Intrusive [ɹ]

In non-rhotic varieties of English, such as those found in certain parts of the United Kingdom (cf. the blank areas of Fig. 11.10), [ɹ] does not appear in the coda of a syllable, but when it moves from coda to onset it resurfaces as [ɹ], as in the examples in (11.1a).

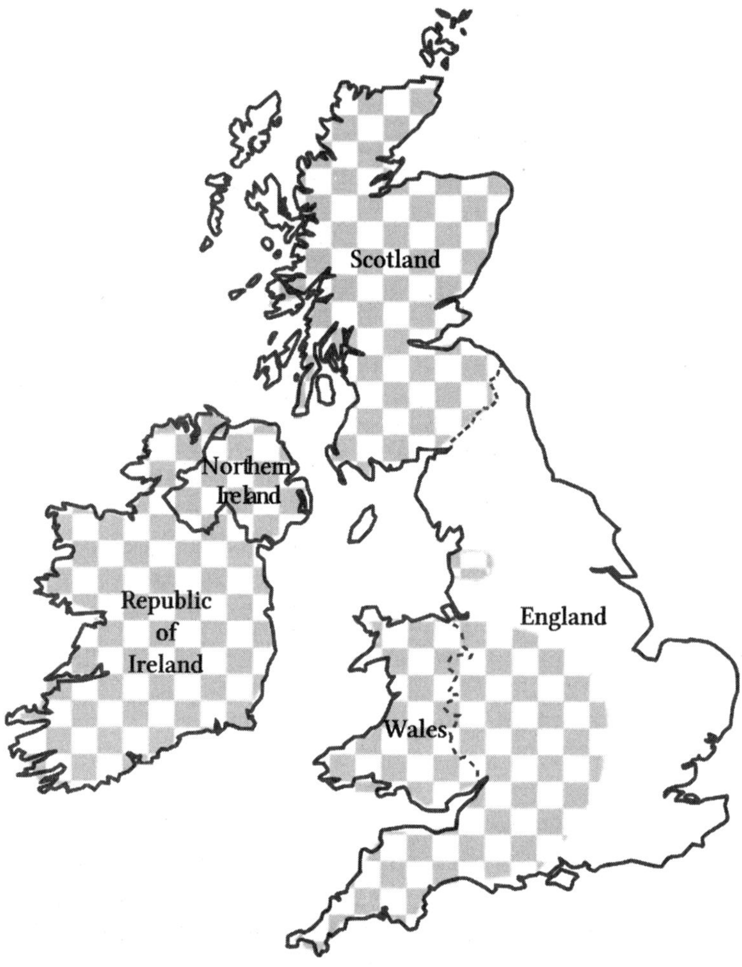

Figure 11.10 Rhotics in the United Kingdom

This process is often referred to as *linking r*. The application of this 'resurfacing' process may open up the possibility of [ɹ] appearing even in contexts where there is no underlying /r/ in the word, but where the environmental conditions are otherwise met. Examples of this include those in (11.1b).

(11.1) **Linking and Intrusive R**

a.	car	[kʰɑː]	car is	[kʰɑɹ ɪz]
	deer	[dijə]	deer is	[diɹ ɪz]
	lore	[lɔː]	lore is	[lɔɹ ɪz]
b.	Asia	[eɪʒə]	Asia is	[eɪʒəɹ ɪz]
	idea	[aidijə]	idea is	[aidijəɹ ɪz]
	law	[lɔː]	law is	[lɔɹ ɪz]

Cases like those in (11.1b) are referred to as instances of *Intrusive r*, i.e. an [ɹ] that is inserted in a context where there is no original, underlying [ɹ]. This occurs when the word ends with one of the vowels [ə], [ɑː], or [ɔː], as in *Asia, idea, law*, etc.

The [ɹ] in such cases is not different from the regular English [ɹ] except for the fact that it has no lexical origin in the words involved. It is clearly the result of the influence of the linking [ɹ] that arises in non-rhotic varieties.

11.2.4 The Northumbrian Burr

Before leaving the discussion of English rhotics, we should consider one last case: the very rare case of the *Northumbrian burr*. This is a rather distinctive rhotic found only in the most northeasterly region of England, referred to as Northumberland, as shown in the shaded region on the map in Fig. 11.12. The Northumbrian burr is no longer in general use among the local population, and only the older generation retain it.

According to Påhlsson (1972), the Northumbrian burr was usually pronounced as a voiced uvular fricative, often with accompanying lip-rounding ([ʁ(ʷ)]). In addition to appearing in syllable onsets, this uvular rhotic was also articulated in the coda, unlike the non-rhotic variant currently in use (see Fig. 11.11). This seems to suggest that those speakers who employed the Northumbrian burr regularly were rhotic speakers of English, albeit with a very special rhotic.

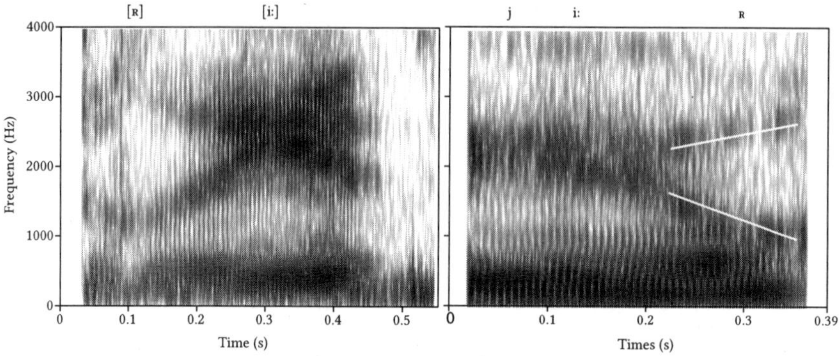

Figure 11.11 Northumbrian burr in onset and coda

The clearest effect of this uvular rhotic was on the surrounding vowels, where it *colored* their value distinctively.

We can see from the comparison of the Northumbrian and North American /r/'s in the word *period* in Fig. 11.13 that there is a significant difference in their formants and in their influence on the adjacent vowel. One clear difference is in the frequency of F_3, which is much higher in the uvular rhotic of Northumberland.[1] This difference in F_3 is similar to the results discussed in Alwan (1986), who assigns an average F_3 of 2400Hz for the Arabic uvular rhotic fricative, [ʁ].

Clearly, the Northumbrian burr is a very special kind of English rhotic and one that is fast disappearing from the language.

11.3 Laterals

Laterals are sonorant consonants that involve an airflow around one or both sides of the tongue. In English, there are two principal variants of the lateral consonant phonetically: one is found in the beginning of the syllable, [l], referred to as 'light l'; the other occurs at the end of the syllable, [ɫ], sometimes referred to as 'dark l' or 'velarized l'. [l] is a difficult sound to make as attested by its relatively late acquisition by children, the average age for complete mastery being around 6 years old.

[1] Note that in the American articulation, F_2 and F_3 are very close together.

Figure 11.12 The Northumbrian Burr

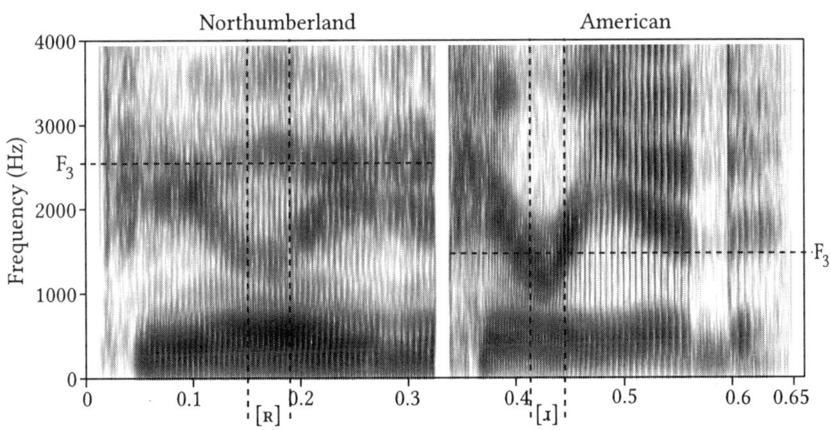

Figure 11.13 Rhotics in the word *period*

11.3.1 Acoustic Correlates of Laterals

The basic alveolar lateral approximant [l] has the average values for the first three formant frequencies for men, women and children, as provided in Table 11.3 from Dalston (1975).

	F_1	F_2	F_3
Men	344	1179	2523
Women	365	1340	2935
Children	412	1384	3541

Table 11.3 Average formant frequencies for [l] (fr. Dalston, 1975)

Examples of the two main variants of the English alveolar lateral are provided in Fig. 11.14. [l] has a formant frequency for F_1 of around 350 Hz and an F_2 of around 1100 Hz. The effects of velarization in the [l] in *tell* are indicated in the transition from the vowel [ɛ] to the following [ɫ], resembling that of a diphthong in many ways.

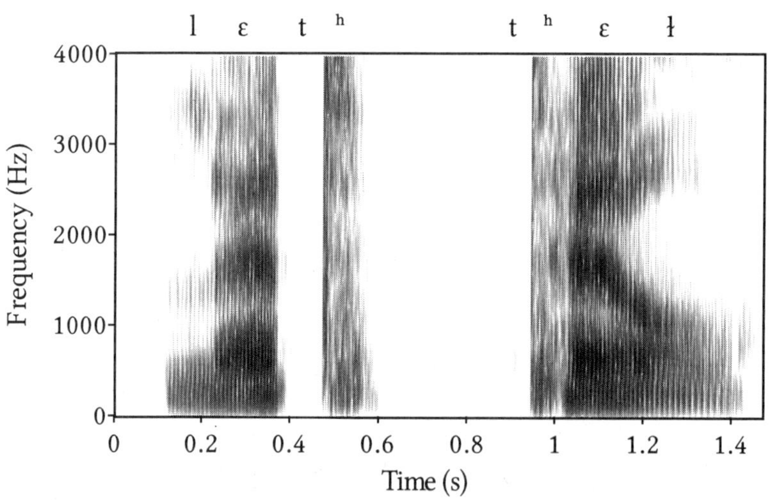

Figure 11.14 Examples of laterals in *let* and *tell*

In certain dialects, the velarized [ɫ] can be realized as strong velarization, i.e., [w]. Compare the last syllable in the spectrogram for *little* in

Fig. 11.15 with the analysis of the word *two* in Fig. 11.16. The [ɫ] appears to lose all of its lateral qualities and becomes a [w], as shown by the spectrogram of *little* spoken by a native of Norwich, England.

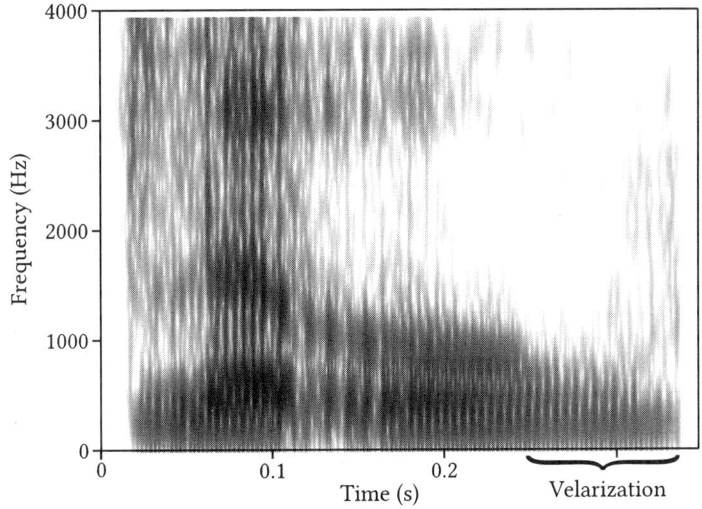

Figure 11.15 Spectrogram of *little*

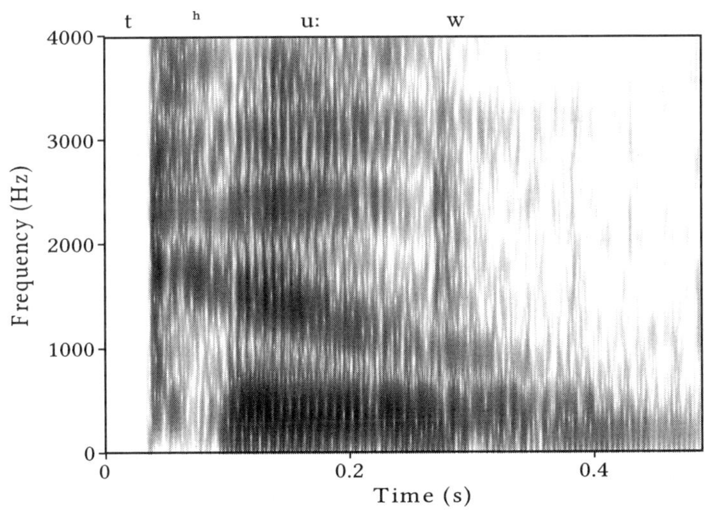

Figure 11.16 Spectrogram of *two*

The alveolar lateral approximant is subject to devoicing just as the nasals are and, in similar fashion, it appears as a short segment with little voicing and only very faint formants.

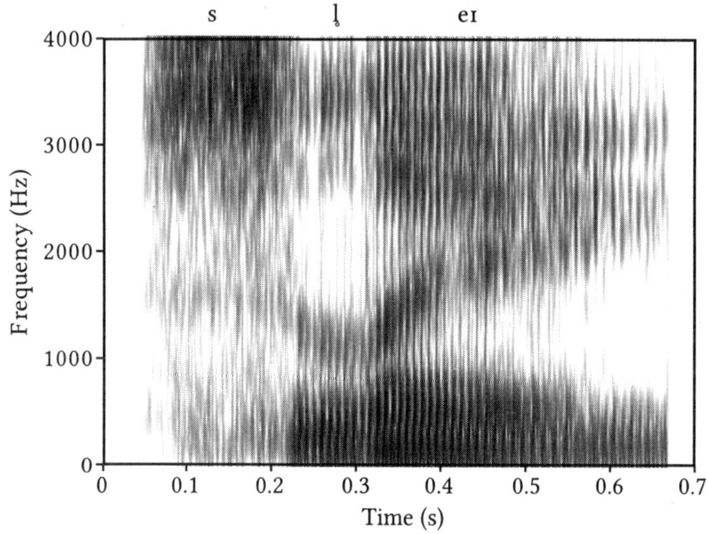

Figure 11.17 Devoicing of the alveolar lateral in *sleigh* [sl̥eɪ]

11.3.2 Syllabic Laterals

As discussed in §9.3, laterals may also act as the syllabic head of a syllable, like a vowel. In this case, they show similar properties to vowels, including greater intensity and movement in their formants to reflect adjacent consonants. Unlike vowels however, they do not usually bear stress. They may alternate between syllabic and non-syllabic forms, like the case of *simple* and *simplify* in (9.12).

Note the downward trend of the F_2 formant at the end of the word *basil* in the spectrogram in Fig. 11.18, reflecting the velarization of the lateral in this position. In general, laterals are velarized except in the onset of the syllable.

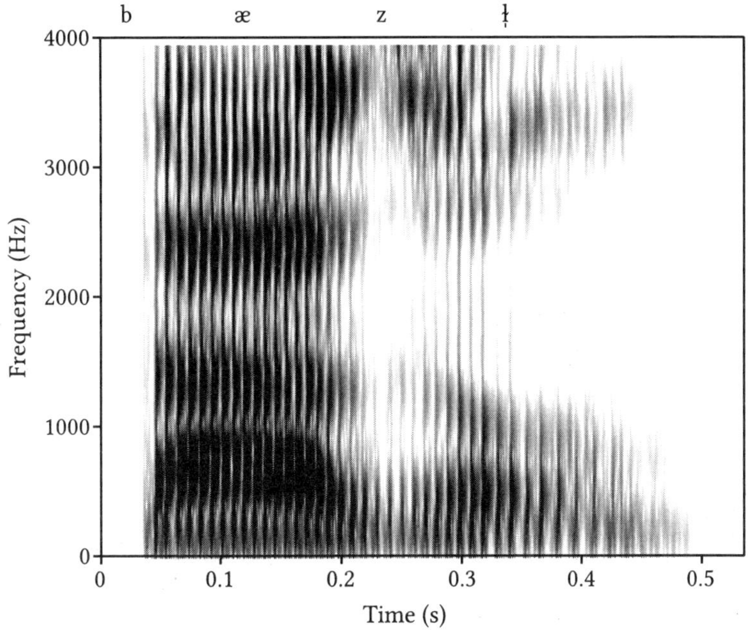

Figure 11.18 Spectrogram of syllabic [l] in *basil* [bæzɫ̩]

11.3.3 Intrusive [l]

Just as there is an intrusive [ɹ] in some varieties of English, so there is also the possibility of an intrusive [l] in a small number of cases. Wells (1982:344) has discussed the case of Bristol English intrusive [l] and Gick (1999, 2002a) have examined instances of intrusive [l] in American dialects. Both cases are much more restricted than intrusive [ɹ] and we will not discuss them further here.

11.4 Semivowels

English has two semivowels, [w] and [j], also referred to as *glides*. They are approximant consonants sharing many of the qualities of the vowels [u] and [i], respectively, hence their description as 'semi' vowels.

They may occur as single consonants at the beginning of words, as in *we* (Fig. 11.19) or *you* (Fig. 11.20) or they may occur along with certain consonants: compare, for instance, *cake* and *quake* (Fig. 11.21) where the latter has a [w] modifying the [k], often referred to as rounding or labialization. Similarly, *poor* and *pure* (Fig. 11.22) involve [j] combined with [p], as in *pure*. This is referred to as palatalization.

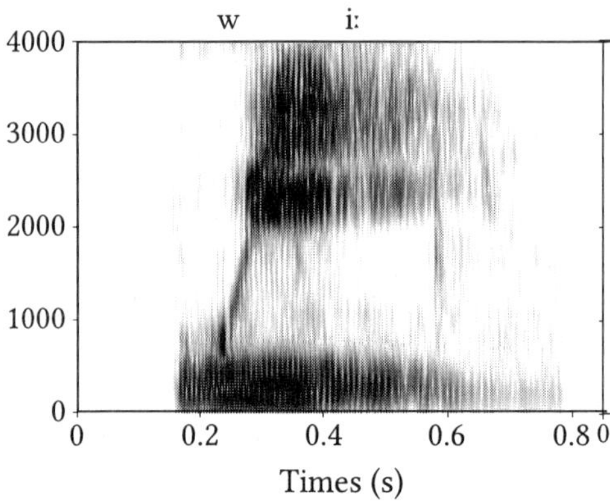

Figure 11.19 [w] in *we*

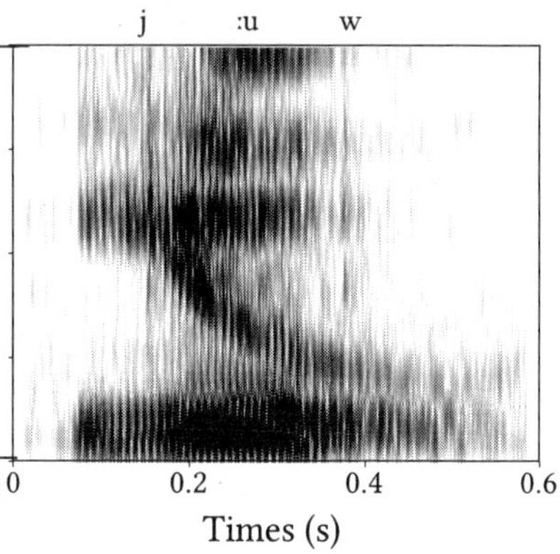

Figure 11.20 [j] in *you*

Semivowels are acquired early by children and typically pose no problems for second language learners, except perhaps in one special context. The semivowels may co-occur with their corresponding vowels in English, but not in Korean. Compare English *woos* and *ooze* (Fig. 11.23) or *yeast* and *east* (Fig. 11.24).

Note that the combination of [j] with [i] in English words like *yeast*, *year*, *yield*, etc. is particularly difficult for Korean speakers. Even though Korean has the palatal glide, [j], and the high front vowel, [i], this combination is prohibited in Korean and therefore, is not familiar to speakers. Compare the pronunciation of these words with the forms *east*, *ear*, *eel*. This difference poses a distinct problem for Korean learners of English, since this contrast does not exist in Korean.

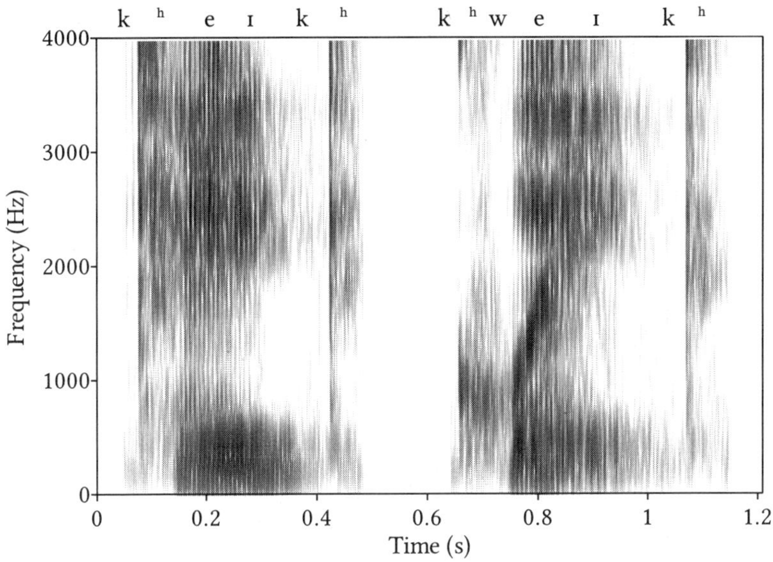

Figure 11.21 *Cake* versus *quake*

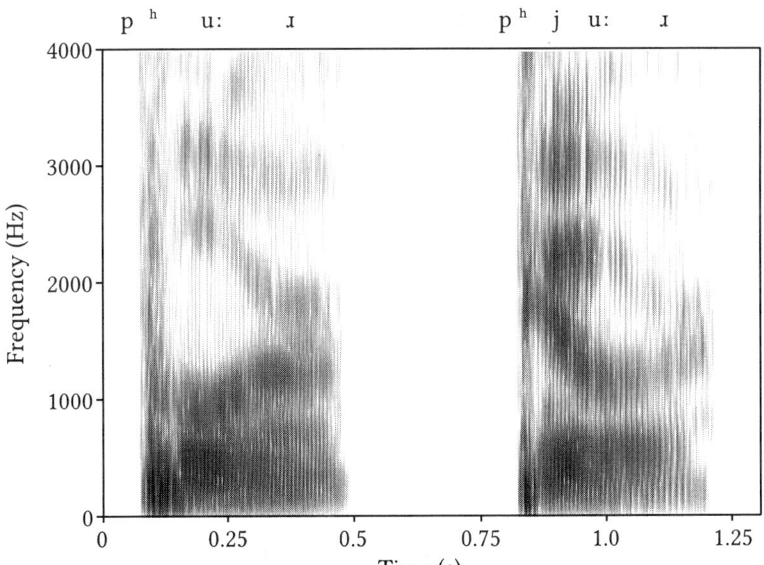

Figure 11.22 A comparison of *poor* and *pure*

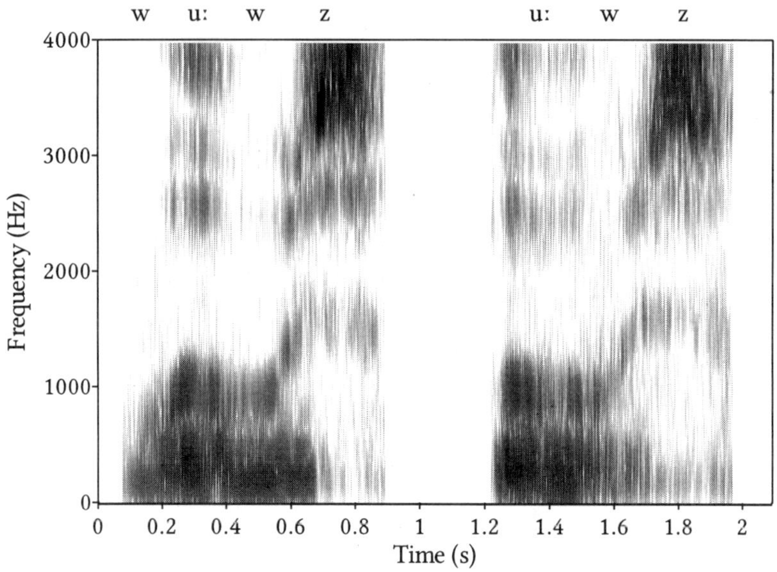

Figure 11.23 *Woos* versus *ooze*

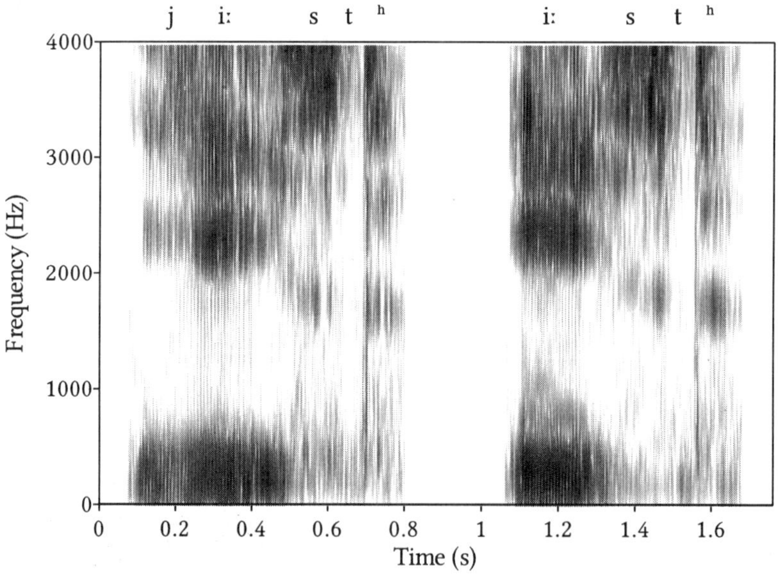

Figure 11.24 Spectrograms for *yeast* and *east*

11.4.1 [ʍ]

In addition to the two semivowels [j] and [w], there is a related sound in some varieties of English and in some individuals' idiolects as well. This is [ʍ], described in the IPA chart as a voiceless labiovelar fricative. It shares many features with [w] and is lexically contrastive for some speakers. Minkova (2004: 37) describes it this way:

> In the IPA the "inverted w" ([ʍ]) is used both for the voiceless rounded labiovelar approximant, and the corresponding fricative (Pullum & Ladusaw, 1986: 164). I follow Ladefoged & Maddieson (1996: 326) in treating /ʍ/ as a non-fricative, i.e. an approximant, in the dialects in English where it is contrastive. This makes it identical to the sound transcribed as a <w> with an under-ring ([w̥]);

As indicated by the quote above, there is some disagreement about the status of [ʍ], treated by some as a fricative with rounding and by others as a labiovelar approximant without voicing, a somewhat strange property for a sonorant.

This voiceless variant of [w], represented in the IPA by [ʍ], is found to occur in only a handful of forms, even in those dialects that have it. It is not widely attested but does distinguish certain minimal pairs such as *witch* and *which* in those dialects that have it, as indicated in Fig. 11.25.

Labov et al. (2006) note that the distribution of [ʍ] is quite limited in North America, with the greatest concentration of usage located in the Southeastern United States, as indicated on the map in Fig. 11.26.

11.4.2 Acoustic Correlates of Semivowels

As for the acoustic correlates of the semivowels, they share many properties with the corresponding vowels. For instance, Fig. 11.27 provides the formants for [w], from Dalston (1975) and the average formants for the English vowel [u] from Peterson & Barney (1952). The averages for [j] and [i] would be similar.

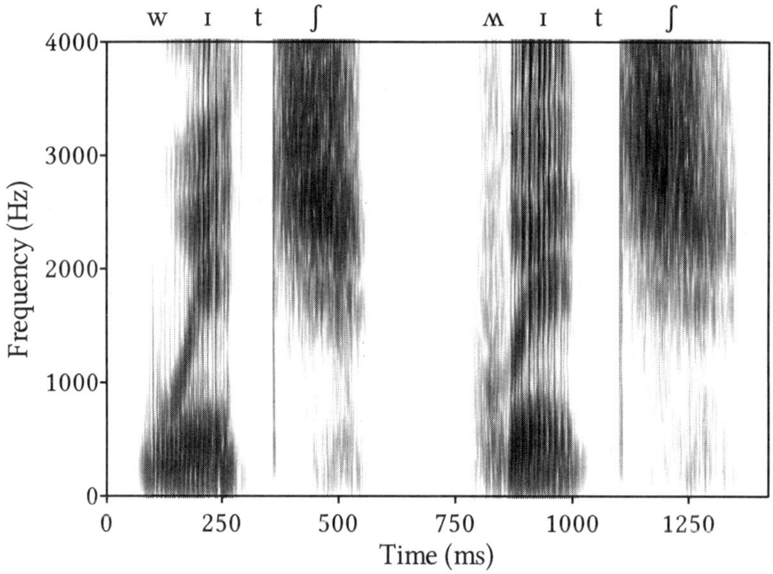

Figure 11.25 *witch* [w] versus *which* [ʍ]

	[w]				[u]		
	F_1	F_2	F_3		F_1	F_2	F_3
Men	336	732	2290	Men	300	870	2240
Women	337	799	2768	Women	370	950	2670
Children	402	1020	3547	Children	430	1170	3260

Figure 11.27 Average formant frequencies for English [w] from Dalston (1975) and [u] from Peterson & Barney (1952)

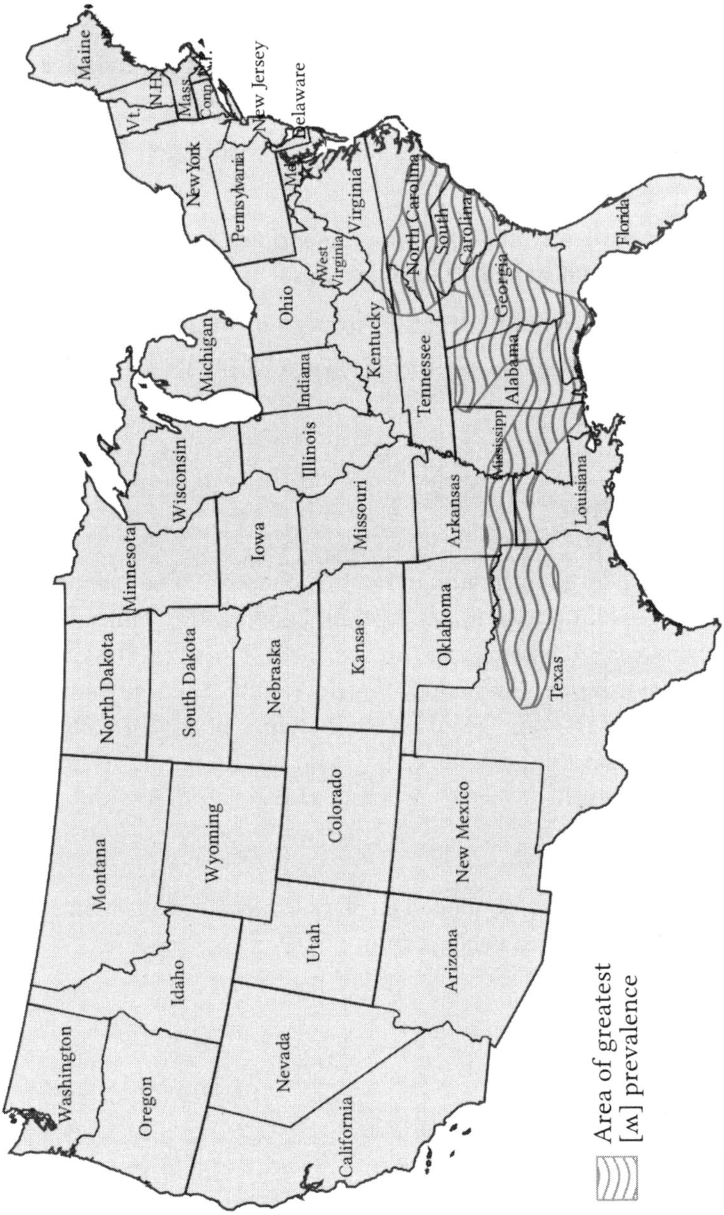

Figure 11.26 Greatest concentration of the distribution of [w]/[ʍ]

Exercises

1. Give examples of three words that contain each of the English sonorant consonants.
2. What properties distinguish sonorants from obstruents? Explain your answer with examples.
3. Analyze one word containing a nasal sonorant from Ex. 1, showing the properties that indicate that it is a nasal on the spectrogram.
4. Analyze a word from Ex. 1 that illustrates one of the English liquids. Indicate on the spectrogram the properties that mark the liquid.

Further Reading

Recommended additional readings for this chapter come from several sources. For general phonetic description, Ladefoged & Johnson (2010) and Lieberman & Blumstein (1988) are excellent. Jones (1918) is older but focuses on English phonetics and is worth reading. See also Peterson & Barney (1952) and Dalston (1975) for their studies of the formant frequencies of American English. See Gick (1999) on the nature of intrusive consonants in English.

Keywords: alveolar flap, bunched [ɹ], dark l, intrusive consonant, retroflex [ɽ], syllabic sonorant, velarization.

Chapter 12

English Stress

We will begin this chapter with a presentation of the characteristics of English stress assignment, followed by an examination of the various factors involved in the assignment of stress in English. After clarifying the various factors affecting the placement of stress, we will move on to a look at the phonetic analysis, measurement, and representation of stress in various contexts, including the nature of compound stress and the application of vowel reduction.

We will conclude with a brief examination of the main differences in stress placement between British and American English, which reflect the variation in stress placement in virtually all varieties of English.

12.1 English Stress Assignment

Examples of stress placement in English words show that stress is not always on the same syllable of the word and, thus, is not as simple as the cases of stress assignment in other languages like French or Finnish discussed in Ch. 8. English is more like Russian with respect to stress assignment, i.e. it involves a lexical component.

Primary stress may be found on the last syllable, the second syllable from the end, or the third syllable from the end of the word, as shown by the data in (12.1).

(12.1) **English stress**

'elephant	po'tato	kanga'roo
'cinema	ho'rizon	jambo'ree

This fluctuation in the position of primary stress doesn't mean that English stress is entirely unpredictable, but does show that it is not demarcative, in the sense discussed in Ch. 8. There may, however, be criteria that can help to explain how the placement of stress is determined in many cases.

English stress is typically calculated from the end of the word, counting syllables towards the beginning. The main stress may appear on the last syllable, which is called *final* or *ultimate* stress,[1] e.g., *kanga'roo, jambo'ree.* It may also appear on the second syllable from the end, referred to as *penultimate* stress, e.g., *po'tato, ho'rizon.* Otherwise, it is placed on the third syllable from the end, which is called *antepenultimate* stress, e.g., *'cinema, 'elephant.* Primary stress is almost always on one of these three syllables.

In what follows, we will employ the concept of long and short vowels discussed in Ch. 9 to assist us in the characterization of stress assignment. We will approach the analysis of English stress from the perspective of three interacting domains:

1. Syllable structure
2. Syntactic category
3. Morphological structure

One or more of these domains may be relevant in any particular case, although syllable structure is almost always a factor in the determination of stress placement and should, therefore, be given priority. Syllable structure is the only one of these factors that is related to phonetics, the other two being non-phonetic in nature. Nevertheless, we will examine all of these criteria here for the sake of completeness in our analysis of stress assignment in English.

[1] Cf. §8.2 for further discussion of the terms used here relating to stress.

12.1.1 Syllable Structure

Stress assignment in English relies heavily on syllable structure or, more accurately, syllable weight. In such cases, heavy syllables win over light syllables, as shown by the examples in (12.2).

(12.2)	**Penultimate**	**Antepenultimate**
	Korea	cucumber
	secretion	scenery
	potato	violence
	relation	latency
	apartment	quantity
	prediction	emperor
	disaster	custody

In *Korea*, for example, the penultimate syllable is heavy due to the presence of a long vowel, [iː], so this syllable will receive the main stress. Similarly, *secretion* has a long vowel in the penultimate syllable and also bears the primary stress. Both *potato* and *relation* have diphthongs, [eɪ], also considered long, in their penultimate syllables, and therefore show primary stress on this syllable. The other words with penultimate stress in (12.2) contain consonants in the coda of that syllable, effectively closing off the syllable and making it phonologically heavy and phonetically longer.

In the case of antepenultimate stress assignment, one may encounter either i) a long vowel, as in *scenery* [ˈsiː.nə.ɹi], ii) a diphthong, as in *violence* [ˈvai.ə.ln̩s], or iii) a syllable closed by one or more consonants, as in *emperor* [ˈɛm.pə.ɹɹ̩]. In words like *camera* [ˈk^{h}æməɹə] or *cinema* [ˈsɪnəmə], where all three syllables are light, stress appears on the penultimate. This is due to the fact that the main stress must appear on one of the last three syllables in English, so if both the ultimate and penultimate syllables are not sufficiently heavy, stress must be assigned to the antepenultimate.

Syllabic consonants are fairly common in English, as discussed in §9.3, but they do not typically constitute a syllable heavy, so they are normally not stressed. This means that words like *ˈbottle*, *ˈbutton*, *ˈstrat-*

agem, *ˈhydrogen*, etc., usually exhibit stress on the penultimate or antepenultimate syllable, i.e. the one without the syllabic consonant.[2]

12.1.2 Non-phonetic Factors

As noted above, stress assignment may also be sensitive to non-phonetic information, especially in the case of lexically-based stress systems like English. We will briefly examine these factors here for the sake of completeness, before returning to the phonetic issue of measuring stress. The two non-phonetic aspects of stress assignment in English are i) syntactic category (noun, verb, etc.) and ii) morphological domain. We will begin with syntactic category.

Stress assignment is often different for related nouns and verbs in English, as demonstrated by the pairs of words in (12.3).

(12.3) **English noun/verb pairs**

Verb	**Noun**
conˈtract	ˈcontract
transˈfer	ˈtransfer
perˈmit	ˈpermit
proˈduce	ˈproduce

As we can see, stress is final in the case of these verbs, but penultimate for the related nouns. There is no reasonable phonetic explanation for this fact, since either syllable is capable of bearing stress according to this data, so the placement must be assumed to be a consequence of non-phonetic conditions on stress assignment.

Nouns typically have either penultimate or antepenultimate stress, e.g., *Koˈrea* versus *ˈCanada*, etc. Whether a noun's stress is penultimate or antepenultimate depends on syllable weight. If the penultimate is heavy, it receives stress; otherwise, stress is placed on the antepenultimate, as demonstrated in (12.2) above. However, there are exceptions, such as certain nouns with final stress, illustrated in (12.4).

[2] For certain exceptions to the absence of stress on syllabic sonorant consonants, see §11.2.2.

(12.4) **English nouns with final stress**

ca'noe	la'ment	de'gree	bal'loon	kanga'roo
Ju'ly	e'state	ra'vine	fricas'see	maga'zine

What do these nouns have in common? Their final syllable is heavy, containing either i) a long vowel, as in *degree* [də'gri:], ii) a diphthong, as in *July* [dʒə'lai], or iii) a closed syllable, as in *lament* [lə'mɛnt]. Also, in most cases, the preceding syllable(s) is weak. This result further confirms the priority of syllable weight over syntactic category.

Moving on to verbs and adjectives, one can readily see that many verbs and adjectives are stressed finally, as in (12.5). In all such cases, the form has a heavy final syllable, with either i) a long vowel, as in *concede* [kʰən'si:d], ii) a diphthong, as in *deny* [də'nai], or iii) at least two final consonants, as in *correct* [kʰə'ɹɛkt].

(12.5) **Verb and adjectives with final stress**

a. V:	de'ny	re'vise	con'cede	pro'duce	at'tempt	cor'rect
b. A:	di'vine	se'rene	ob'scene	a'live	im'mune	cor'rect

However, there are cases of verbs and adjectives, like those in (12.6), where stress appears before the final syllable.

(12.6) **Verb and adjectives without final stress**

a. V:	'listen	'bother	'profit	'register	'visit	'borrow
b. A:	'happy	'yellow	'simple	'beautiful	'solid	'silent

In all such cases, the final syllable must be considered too weak to bear the stress, due to syllable weight and other considerations.

The other non-phonetic criterion for stress assignment in English is morphological structure. Specifically, certain suffixes can affect the placement of stress, while others do not have such an effect: this is clearly a lexical feature, not a phonetic one.

The traditional term for those that have no effect on stress is *neutral* (12.7). Those that have an affect on stress placement are referred to as *non-neutral* (12.8).

(12.7) **English neutral suffixes**

ˈfriendly	ˈfriendli*ness*
ˈneighbor	ˈneighbor*hood*
ˈMendel	ˈMendel*ism*
ˈgangster	ˈgangster*dom*
exˈpression	exˈpression*less*

(12.8) **English non-neutral suffixes**

ˈconduct	conˈduc*ive*	ˌconducˈt*ivity*
ˈneutral	neuˈtral*ity*	ˌneutral*iˈzation*
ˈsolid	soˈlid*ify*	soˌlid*ifiˈcation*
ˈtotal	toˈtal*ity*	toˌtal*iˈtarian*
ˈsyntax	synˈtact*ic*	ˌsyntacˈt*ician*
ˈsense	senˈs*ation*	senˌ*sationaliˈzation*
ˈconstitute	ˌconstiˈtut*ion*	ˌconstiˌtut*ioˈnality*

A careful comparison of the data in (12.7) and (12.8) will confirm that it is not simply length or distance from the end of the word that decides the stress placement in all cases: *suffix type* is also important.

Suffixes such as *-ness, -hood, -ism, -less, -dom* are *neutral* with respect to the effect they have on the base to which they attach. On the other hand, suffixes such as *´-ive, ´-ity, ´-ic, ´-ian* change the stress of the base to which they attach, if possible and are, thus, *non-neutral.*

There is a special kind of non-neutral suffix that attracts the stress onto itself. This includes the suffixes *-ée, -ésque, -áire, -éer, -ése* and a few others.[3] They are typically referred to as *auto-stressing* suffixes and are exemplified in (12.9). Note that in all the cases in (12.9) there is a secondary stress two syllables before the main stress, as is common the case in longer English words.

[3] For a detailed study of the various types of suffixes found in English, see Marchand (1960).

(12.9) **Auto-stressing suffixes**

Base Form	**Auto-stressing**
emˈploy	ˌemploˈy*ee*
ˈpicture	ˌpictuˈr*esque*
ˈprivate	ˌprivaˈt*eer*
ˈquestion	ˌquestionˈn*aire*
ˈCongo	ˌCongoˈl*ese*

Non-neutral suffixes don't always affect the base to which they are attached. There are certain conditions under which the stress shift fails to apply, in particular, those in (12.10).

(12.10) **Absence of stress-shift**

a. the base may be too small to shift the stress:
ˈcon-ic ˈsan-ity ˈact-ive

b. the stress may already be on the syllable before the suffix:
oˈbese oˈbes-ity urˈbane urˈban-ity

c. the syllable before the suffix may be too weak to bear stress:
inˈtestine inˈtestin-al (cf. ˈadjective → adjecˈtiv-al)[4]
[ɪnˈtʰɛstn̩] [ɪntʰɛstənɫ̩]

Under any of these conditions we may encounter unexpected stress assignments, but we should remember that when requirements clash, they may be resolved in different ways, although usually it is syllable weight that takes precedence. Notice also that other conditioned changes associated with non-neutral suffixes, such as vowel changes ([kʰoʊn]/[ˈkʰɔnɪk], [ɹˈbeɪn]/[ɹˈbænɪti]), may still occur.

[4] Some speakers of British English manifest an alternative pronunciation for *intestinal* in which the penultimate vowel is a diphthong, [aɪ], and bears the main stress, i.e., [ɪntɛsˈtaɪnl̩].

12.1.3 Compound Words and Stress

Words consisting of two or more other words combined to form a new word are referred to as *compounds*. Compounds can be made from any major word class and the process is very productive in English, as shown by the examples in (12.11).

(12.11) **English compounds**

a. 2 members: greenhouse, blackboard, etc.
b. 3 members: airline attendant, newspaper reporter, etc.
c. 4 members: high-school sweetheart, airport security officer, etc.

Compounding may involve words of various syntactic categories, including nouns, verbs, or adjectives in different combinations. Table 12.1 provides examples of some of the most common combinations.[5]

2nd / 1st	**Adjective**	**Noun**	**Verb**
Adjective	bluegreen	greenhouse	whitewash
Noun	headstrong	mailman	spoonfeed
Verb	dropdead	pickpocket	sleepwalk

Table 12.1 English compounds by category

Orthography is not a good indicator of compounding, since compounds may involve a single orthographic form, as in *greenhouse, blackboard*, etc., may be joined by a hyphen, as in *middle-aged, blue-green*, etc., or may be separated by a space, such as *lawn tennis, high school*, etc. A more reliable indicator of compound status is stress placement, as we will see in (12.12).

It is important to recognize the difference in stress patterns between a compound and a syntactic phrase in English. The stress patterns are distinct in the two cases, as exemplified by the data in (12.12).

[5] Prepositions/particles may also participate in compounding, e.g. *bystander, inbreed, outsource.*

(12.12) **Syntactic Phrase vs. Compound**

Syntactic Phrase	**Compound**
a ˈblack ˈboard	a ˈblackˌboard
a ˈgreen ˈhouse	a ˈgreenˌhouse
a ˈblack ˈbird	a ˈblackˌbird
a ˈhouse, ˈboat, and ...	a ˈhouseˌboat

In the case of syntactic phrases, each separate word has its own primary stress, whereas with a compound, there is only one primary stress for the entire construction, with other stressed syllables bearing secondary stress. This is the main phonetic difference between syntactic phrases and compounds.

In a compound, the result of compounding two or more words together would be that there are two or more primary stresses with a single word, but words may have only a single primary stress, although they may have several, less prominent, secondary stresses. For this reason, additional primary stresses in a compound must be reduced to secondary stresses by some principle of the grammar. The usual stress pattern for compounds with two members in English is that the stress of the first element retains the primary stress.

Even with larger compounds the same generalization holds: there can be only one primary stress in a word, all other stressed syllables must be reduced to secondary stress by the Compound Stress rule (12.13).

(12.13) ***Compound Stress Rule***

a. In a compound there may be only one primary stress, on the first member of the compound.

b. Reduce all other primary stresses to secondary stress.

There are some exceptions to the Compound Stress Rule, e.g. ˌ*apple* ˈ*pie*, but we will not examine these in detail here. We will assume that the principle applies in the vast majority of the cases. Fig. 12.10 shows the exceptional stress pattern of *apple pie*, confirming its irregular nature.

12.2 Acoustic Correlates of Stress in English

We know move on to the examination of the acoustic correlates of stress in English. In §8.2.1 we discussed the general properties of stress in language. These properties included the following:

1. Pitch/Fundamental Frequency
2. Intensity or Amplitude
3. Duration

With respect to English, all of these properties are involved in the measurement of stress. Stress can be measured and analyzed acoustically using various instruments and software, as discussed in §8.2.1. As an example of this process for English data, we can compare the location of stress in two related words, such as *hostile* and *hostility*, as shown in Fig. 12.1 (repeated from Fig. 8.14).

This representation provides a number of pieces of information concerning stress placement in English. Examining Fig. 12.1 starting from the top, the waveform provides information about intensity, in this case the greater intensity of the stressed syllable, which is the first syllable in *ˈhostile* and the second syllable in *hoˈstility.*

In the middle section of the graphic in Fig. 12.1, we can see the pitch track that indicates variation in pitch measured in cycles per second or Hz. In the case of *ˈhostile*, we can see that the first syllable shows the higher pitch, whereas in *hoˈstility*, it is the second syllable that exhibits the highest pitch in the pitch track.

Finally, at the bottom of Fig. 12.1, the spectrogram shows the greater length of the stressed syllable and the differences in vowel quality for stressed versus unstressed syllables. For *ˈhostile*, we can see that it is the first syllable that shows the greater vowel length, whereas in *hoˈstility* it is the second syllable that shows greater length.

Clearly, English exhibits all three acoustic properties discussed above as indicators of stress. In what follows, we will examine further cases of English stress assignment and the acoustic correlates that indicate it.

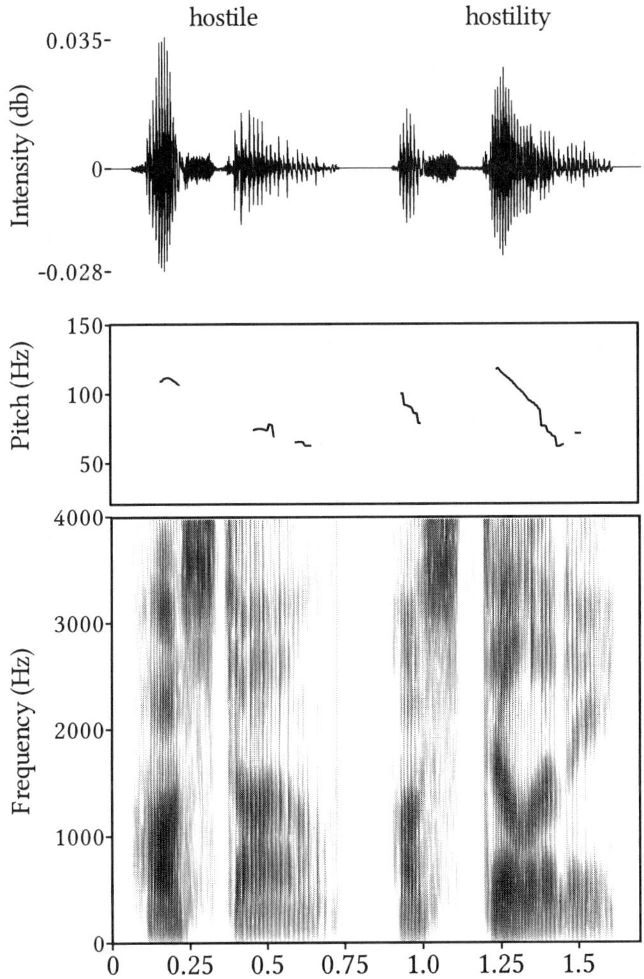

Figure 12.1 Acoustic correlates of stress

For the most part, we will focus on the waveform and pitch track, since information on vowel length from the spectrogram can also usually be extracted from the waveform.

12.2.1 Simple Words

We will begin our study of English stress by examining some of the simple words introduced in (12.1) to see how their stress patterns correlate with the acoustic properties discussed above.

We begin with ˈ*elephant*, a word with initial stress in English (Fig. 12.2). Since this word has three syllables, this is equivalent to antepenultimate stress in our terminology. Notice that the waveform shows the greatest intensity and longest vowel duration at the beginning of the word, i.e. on the initial syllable. Furthermore, the highest pitch is also located at the beginning of the word, as expected from a word with initial stress.

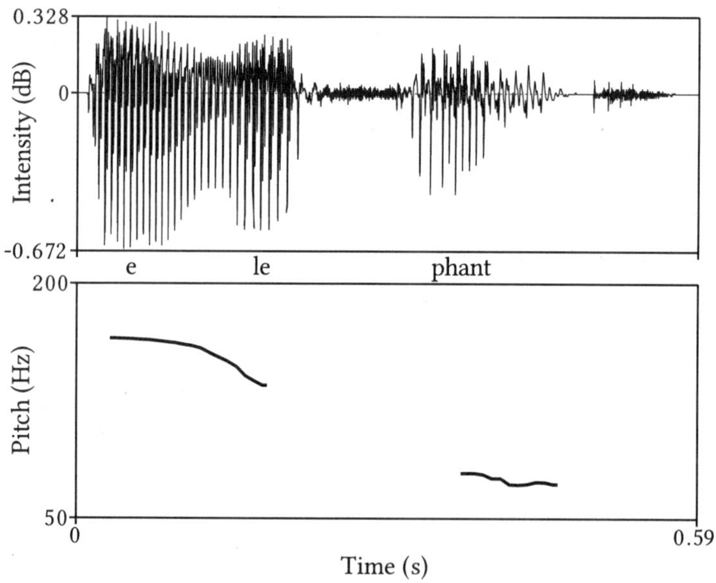

Figure 12.2 Stress in *elephant*

With *poˈtato*, we can see that stress is on the middle (penultimate) syllable, as shown by the greater intensity and vowel length of the middle syllable, as well as its higher pitch, as shown in Fig. 12.3.

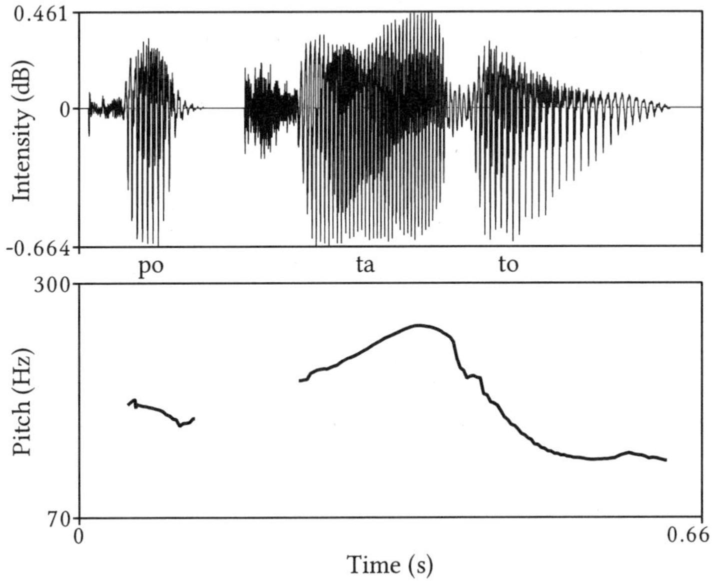

Figure 12.3 Stress in *potato*

ˌKangaˈroo has the primary stress on the final (ultimate) syllable, as indicated by the greater intensity and vowel length of the last syllable and the higher pitch at the end of the word, as is demonstrated in Fig. 12.4). These combined factors clearly correlate with the presence of final main stress on the last syllable of the word. This marks the word *kangaroo* as a somewhat exceptional noun in English, since it has final stress.

Note that in the case of *kangaroo*, there is also a secondary stress on the initial syllable, also clearly marked by the acoustic correlates in the waveform and pitchtrack, but slightly less prominently than the primary stress. This is often the case with longer words in English, where secondary stresses appear on alternating syllables from the main stress towards the beginning of the word.

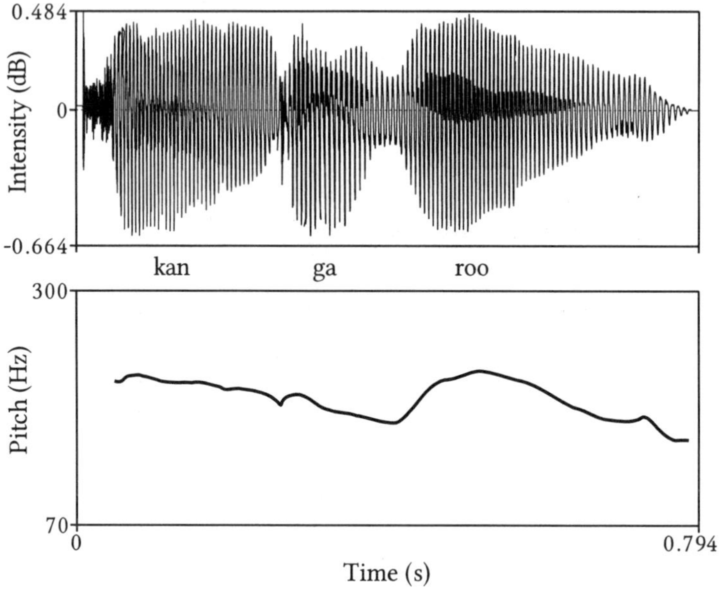

Figure 12.4 Stress in *kangaroo*

Examples of the effect of syllable weight may involve either long vowels, diphthongs or syllables closed by consonants. As an example, the word *Korea*, [kʰəˈriː.ə], shown in Fig. 12.5, has a second syllable long vowel, [iː], making the penultimate syllable strong, unlike the word *Kerala* [ˈkʰɛrələ], which has weak ultimate and penultimate syllables. Cases like the word *Korea* confirm the significance of syllable weight for stress assignment.

In the absence of any of the factors contributing to syllable weight, there must be some principle of default assignment of stress, since all content words must bear a primary stress in English. So, if a word has no heavy syllable, this default assignment of stress comes into play, as is demonstrated here by the case of the word *Canada*, shown in Fig. 12.6.

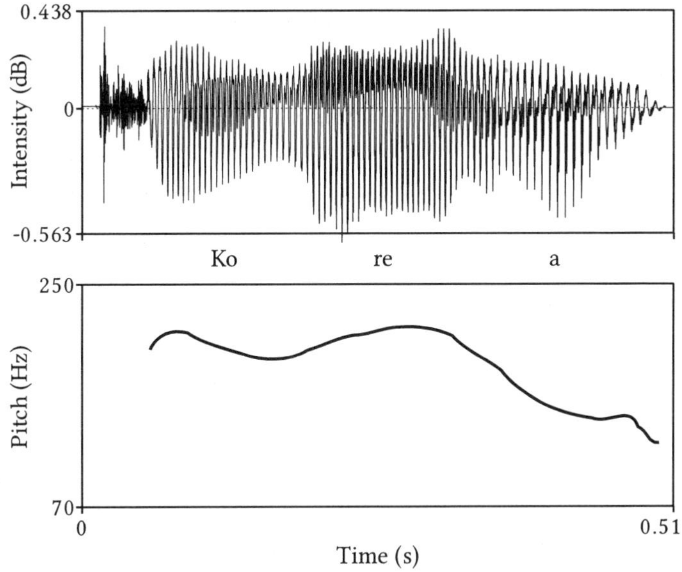

Figure 12.5 The word *Korea*

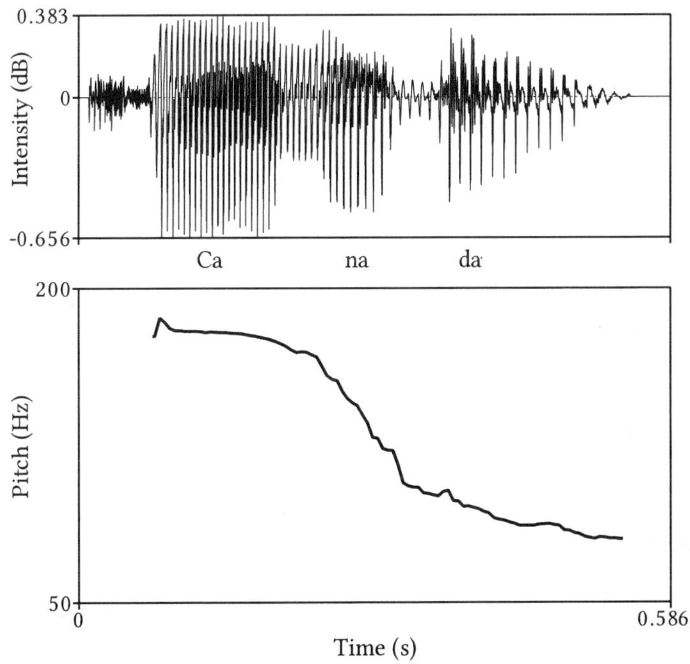

Figure 12.6 The word *Canada*

12.2.2 Non-phonetic Stress Assignment

As noted earlier, there are also non-phonetic factors influencing the placement of stress in English. Even though these conditioning factors are non-phonetic, the results are still reflected phonetically in the placement of stress in the word, and so they should be examined in any treatment of stress.

With respect to the syntactic category variation discussed earlier, the example of *transfer* provided in Fig. 12.7 demonstrates the stress differences between noun and verb. Such differences may only surface in the case where at least two syllables in a word are sufficiently heavy to bear the stress. Words such as *profit*, *butter*, or *whistle* are thus ineligible for syntactic category alternations, and have penultimate stress whether they represent the noun or the verb.

Morphological conditions on words and their parts are also an important factor in the determination of stress placement. This is clearly demonstrated by the stress differences between the related words *em'ploy* and *employ'ee*. Here, the attachment of an autostressing suffix necessitates the movement of the stress from the root onto the suffix, as shown in the illustration in Fig. 12.8

Such non-phonetic conditions on stress placement are an important aspect of any account of English stress assignment and must be carefully considered when describing the facts of English stress.

12.2.3 Stress in Compounds

Moving on to compounding in English, we can see that the nature of stress in compounds requires an adjustment to the stress of certain elements of the compound, typically a reduction in prominence for all but the first member of the compound. In the example of *greenhouse*, both *green* and *house* are independent words with their own main stresses, but when compounded to form the word *greenhouse*, only one member may bear the primary stress, and thus, there must be a reduction in prominence for the second member of the compound, as indicated in the waveform and pitch track in Fig. 12.9.

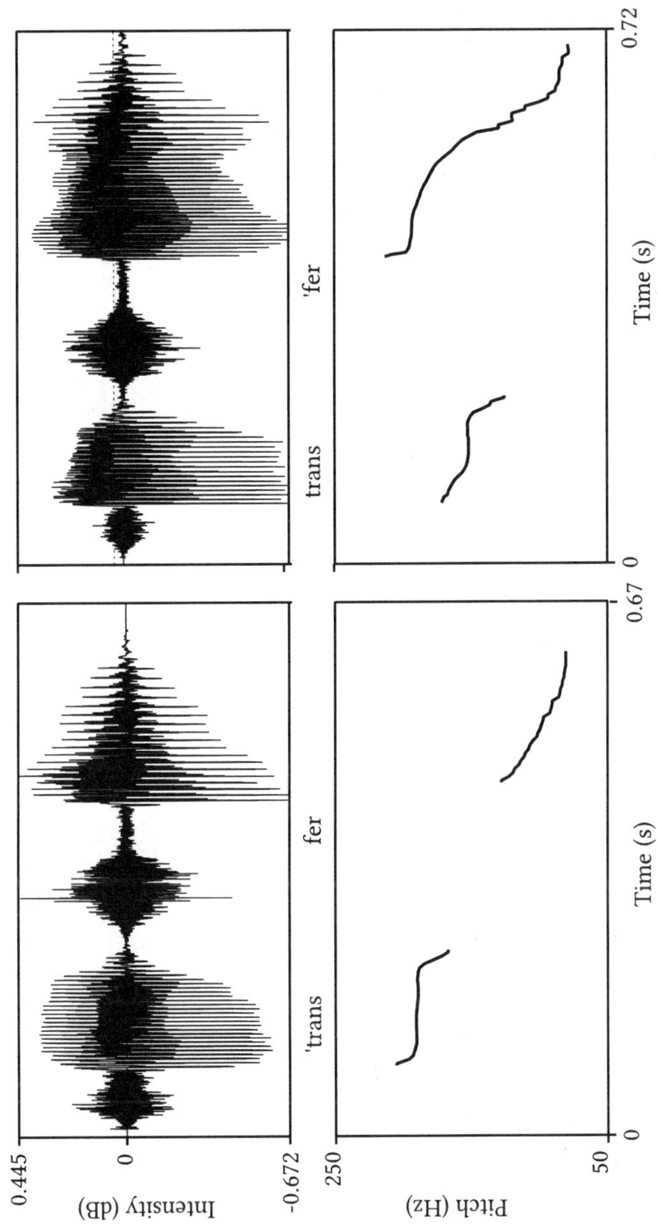

Figure 12.7 *transfer*$_N$ versus *transfer*$_V$

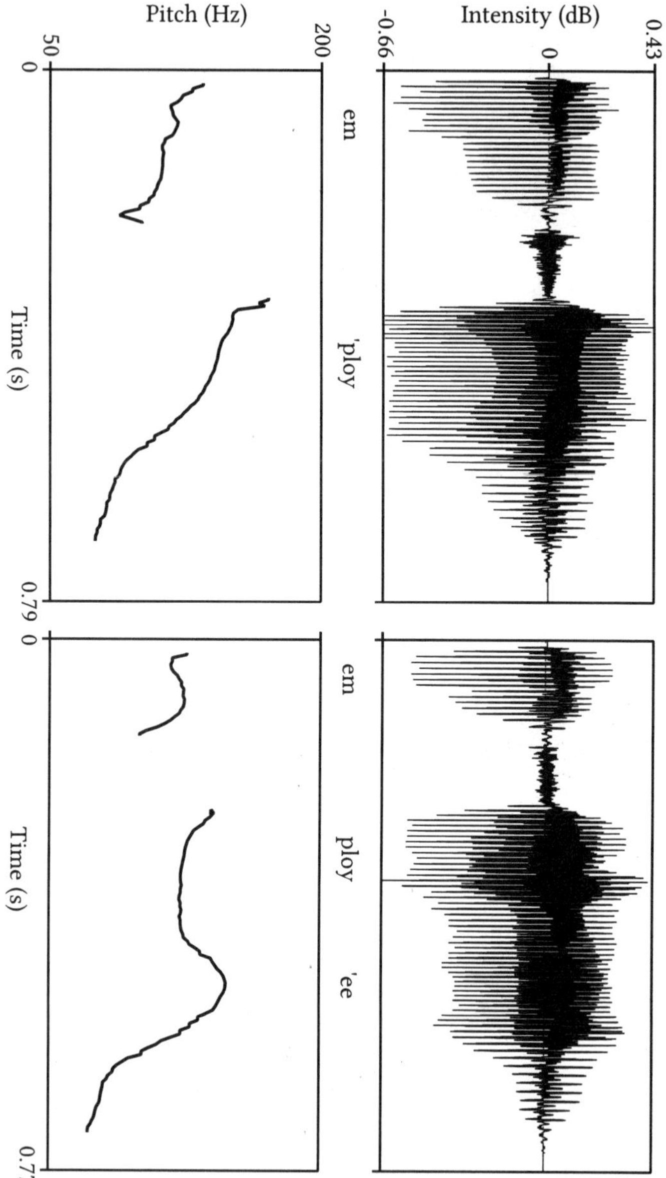

Figure 12.8 *employ* versus *employee*

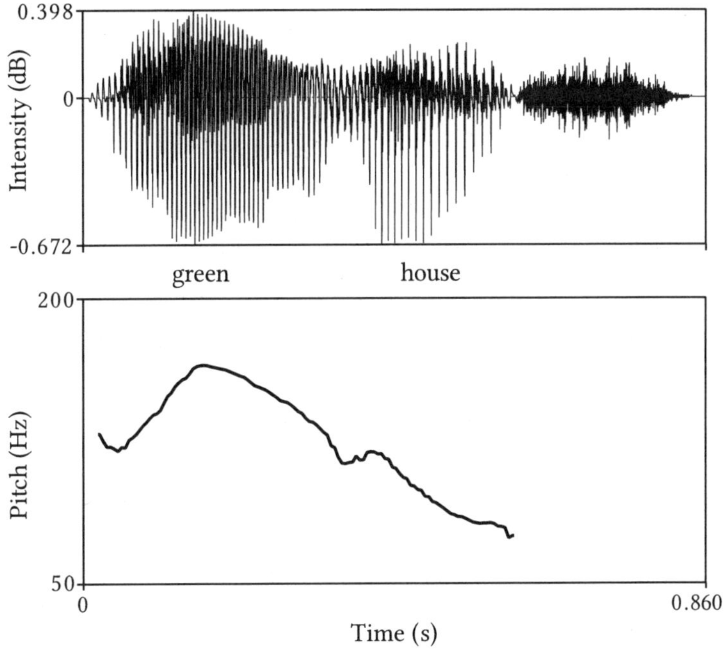

Figure 12.9 The compound *greenhouse*

As noted earlier, there are exceptions to the compound stress rule. One typical example of this is the form *apple pie*, which exhibits all the properties of a compound with the exception of its stress pattern. In this case, it is the final member of the compound that bears the strongest stress, as shown in Fig. 12.10. As such, *apple pie* would seem to be treated as more of a modifier-head construction than as a compound, with the word *apple* acting as a modifier of *pie*.

Cases such as *apple pie* are rare and serve as exceptions to a regular process of stress assignment in compounds.

12.2.4 Vowel Reduction

A prototypical property of English rhythm is its alternating pattern of strong and weak or stressed and unstressed syllables. A concomitant of

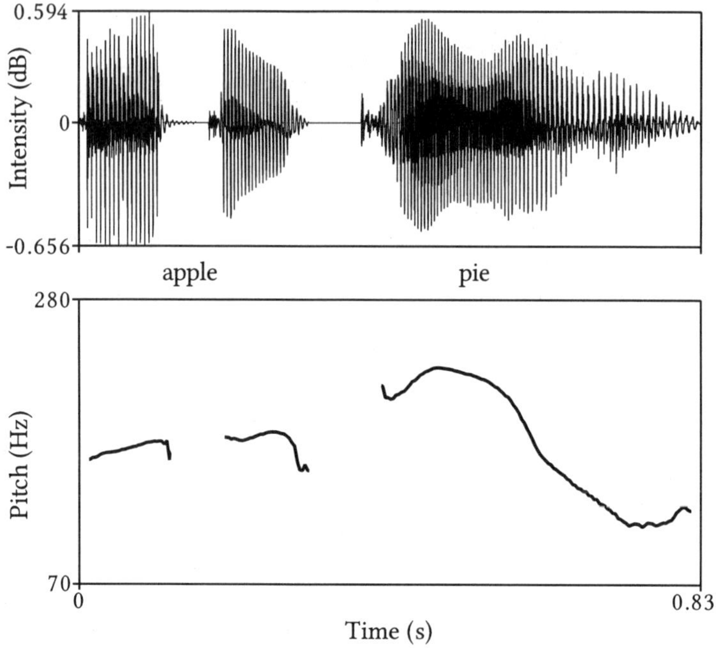

Figure 12.10 The compound *apple pie*

this alternation of strong and weak is a parallel alternation of full and reduced vowels. The most common reduced vowel in English is [ə], the mid central lax vowel, and so this vowel is often encountered in weak syllables that have no stress.

In order to examine the alternating stress pattern of English, it is necessary to select long, typically morphologically-complex words that exhibit the alternation clearly, such as the data in (12.14).

(12.14) **Stress Shift and Vowel Reduction**

national	nationality	nationalization
['næʃənəl]	[næʃə'nælər̥i]	[næʃənəlaɪ'zeɪʃən]

If we analyze these words acoustically, we can see that, not only does the stress move to a different syllable, but the quality of the vowels changes, according to the placement of the stress. We can see this clearly by examining the words from (12.14), analyzed as in Fig. 12.11.

If we compare the vowel of the same syllable position, for instance the /-al/ suffix, we can see that the first and second formant of this syllable in *national* are 400Hz and 986Hz, indicating a mid, back vowel, close to [ʌ]. Here, /-al/ is unstressed, as indicated by profile of the pitch track. In *nationality*, this syllable bears the main stress and its first and second formants are 657Hz and 1517Hz, approximately those of the vowel [æ]. Finally, the syllabic element of /-al/ in *nationalization* is very weak, but has formants similar to those of *national*, in the range of 382Hz and 968Hz. All of this shows that the shifting of stress results in quality and quantity effects on the vowels of a word.

12.3 Stress in British and American English

Many English loanwords that come from French differ in their stress patterns between American and British English. Typically, where American English has final-syllable stress, similar to the original French stress, British English places the stress on an earlier syllable. Examples of such differences appear in (12.15).

(12.15) **British and American stress patterns 1**

British	**American**	**British**	**American**	**British**	**American**
ˈadult	aˈdult	ˈcafé	caˈfé	ˈdebut	deˈbut
ˈballet	baˈllet	ˈchalet	chaˈlet	ˈgarage	gaˈrage
ˈbaton	baˈton	ˈchauffeur	chauˈffeur	ˈgourmet	gourˈmet
ˈberet	beˈret	ˈchiffon	chiˈffon	ˈparquet	parˈquet
ˈbidet	biˈdet	ˈcliché	cliˈché	ˈpastel	pasˈtel
ˈblasé	blaˈsé	ˈcroissant	croiˈssant	ˈpâté	pâˈté
ˈbrochure	broˈchure	ˈdebris	deˈbris	ˈsalon	saˈlon

An acoustic analysis of one pair of words from (12.15) clearly shows the variation in stress between British and American pronunciation. The

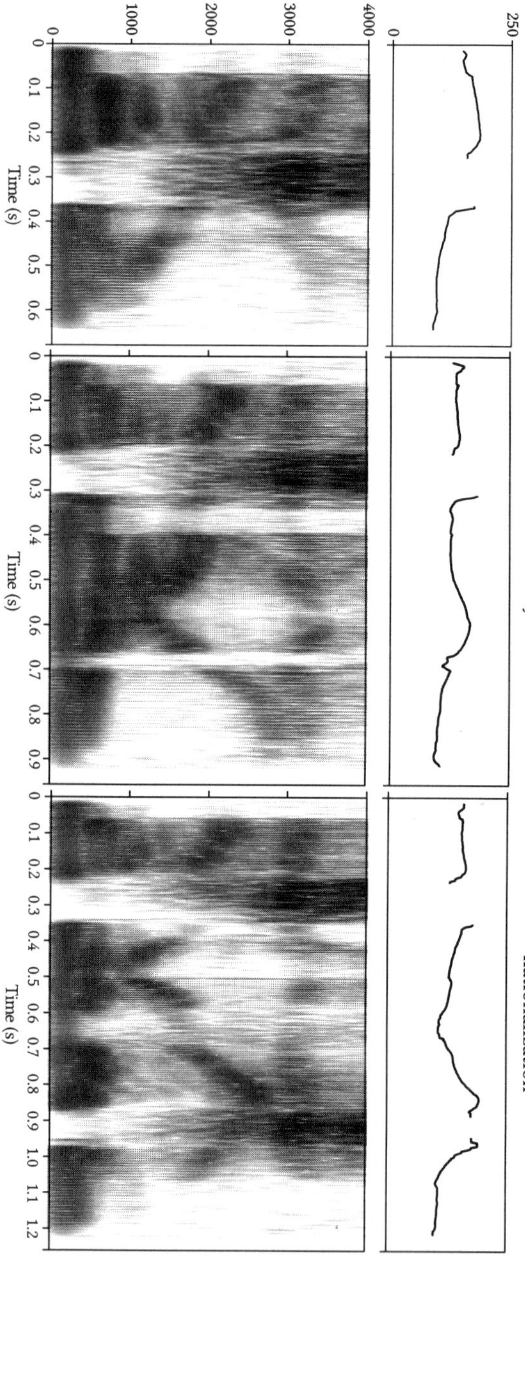

Figure 12.11 Stress shift and vowel reduction

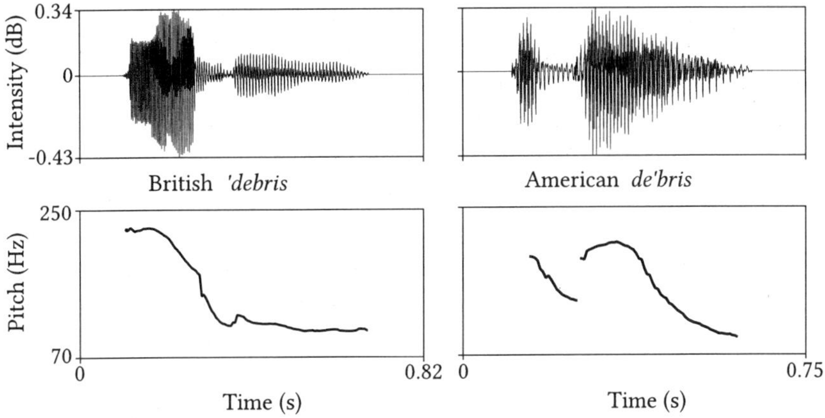

Figure 12.12 British and American variants of *debris*

word *debris* is typical of the stress differences between French borrowings in the two varieties of English, as indicated in Fig. 12.12.

Another area of variation of a similar type occurs in the pronunciation of names of French origin, such as those in (12.16).

(12.16) **British and American stress patterns 2**

British	American	British	American	British	American
ˈBernard	Berˈnard	ˈDegas	Deˈgas	ˈFrancois	Franˈcois
ˈManet	Maˈnet	ˈPauline	Pauˈline	ˈRené	Reˈné
ˈRenault	Reˈnault	ˈRenoir	Reˈnoir	ˈMichelle	Miˈchelle

Here again we can see that the American form of the word tends to have final stress, while the British form shows a penultimate pattern.

Similarly, with polysyllabic words, the American English form demonstrates final-syllable stress, following the original French stress, whereas British English places the stress on an earlier syllable, typically penultimate. Examples of such differences appear in (12.17).

(12.17) **British and American stress patterns 3**

British	American	British	American	British	American
atˈtaché	attaˈché	fiˈancé(e)	fianˈcé(e)	esˈcargot	escarˈgot

There are a few French words that have other stress differences. For example, *address*, *moustache*, *cigarette*, *limousine*, and *magazine* all have initial stress in American and final stress in British English. Words like *liaison*, *macramé*, and *Renaissance* all have initial stress in American English and second-syllable stress in British English.

The stress differences between British and American English may easily be extended to other varieties. Canadian English tends to follow American pronunciation, while Australian and New Zealand English tend to follow British English. For this reason, the discussion here may be used to understand any of the stress variations one may encounter.

Exercises

1. Explain the stress assignment, both primary and secondary, for each of the following words, referring to the conditions for stress assignment, the notion of neutral versus non-neutral, any changes in stress placement between forms and the reasons for the changes.

   a. employ_{V}
   b. $\text{employee}_{\text{N}}$
   c. $\text{employer}_{\text{N}}$
   d. $\text{employment}_{\text{N}}$
   e. $\text{employability}_{\text{N}}$

2. Show the stress assignment for the following words, including primary and secondary stress, where relevant.

   a. Canada
   b. satisfactory
   c. bandana
   d. Korea
   e. governmental

Further Readings

Much of the research on stress in English is phonological in nature. For an earlier but detailed description of the types of suffixes found in English, see Marchand (1960). SPE also discussed English stress assignment in detail, proposing very complex phonological rules to handle it. Allen (1978) discusses the different classes of suffix in terms of the notions of 'neutral' and 'non-neutral.' More recent studies of English stress assignment may be found in Kiparsky (1982) and Hammond (1999), among others.

More phonetically-oriented treatments may be found in Jones (1914, 1918) and Crystal (1969), among others.

Keywords: antepenultimate, auto-stressing suffix, Compound Stress rule, neutral/non-neutral, penultimate.

Glossary

This glossary is provided to help students find explanations for technical terms used frequently in the textbook. For abbreviations used in this book, readers should check the list of Abbreviations on page xxiii. For terms not included here, consult the Index for a reference to where the term is used.

abduction: 신체의 한 부분, 조음적 목적에서는 성대가 중심으로 부터 멀어 지는 것.

accent: 단어나 단어 결합체에서 가장 강한 운율적 에너지를 가진 지점.

adduction: 신체의 한 부분, 조음적 목적에서는 성대가 중심으로 가까워 지는 것.

Advanced Tongue Root (ATR): 인두(pharynx)영역이 넓어지도록 설근(tongue root)이 전방으로 이동되는 현상으로 소리의 특성을 기술하는 자질의 하나로 사용됨.

affricate: 폐찰음; 구강 내 공기가 차단된 뒤 점차 해제되면서 만들어지는 자음으로 폐지음(stop) 과 마찰음 (fricative) 이 연속되어 조음되는 것과 같음. [ʧ], [ʤ] 등.

airstream mechanism: 공기 흐름을 조절하는 방식.

antepenultimate: 어말에서 세 번째 음절에 속하는 (음절).

approximant: 접근음; 조음기관이 서로 접근해도 마찰이 생기지 않는 음; [w], [j], [ɹ], [l] 등.

articulator: 조음기관《혀·입술·성대 등》.

articulatory phonetics: 조음 음성학; 인간의 발화 음이 어떻게 만들어지는 지 연구하는 음성학의 한 분야.

aspiration: 기식(음); 발화 음에 수반된 강한 공기 에너지.

assimilation: 동화; 한 소리가 이웃한 또 다른 소리로 닮아가는 현상.

auto-stressing suffix: stress 를 유도하는 접미사.

binary features: 두 개의 값, + 또는 -, 으로 표현되는 자질.

breathy voice: 유성 기식음.

cardinal vowel: 기본 모음; 각 언어가 가지고 있는 모음을 기술하기 위해 기준이 되는 모음.

click: 흡기음, 혀차는 소리; 많은 아프리카 언어들은 이 소리들을 음소로 사용함.

closed syllable: 자음으로 끝나는 음절.

coda [ˈkʰoʊdə]: 음절의 종결부, 종성.

compounding: 복합어 blackboard, skyscraper 등과 같이 두 개의 단어가 결합하여 형성된 새로운 단어.

constraint: 특정 소리, 단어, 혹은 문장의 형태를 규정하는 제약.

content word: 내용어; 명사, 동사, 형용사, 부사 등 실질적 의미 내용을 가진 단어. Cf. function word.

contour tone: 내부적으로 상승, 하강 등 변화가 있는 성조.

contrastiveness: 발화 음 간의 기본적 대립성.

conversion: 형태의 변화 없이 단어의 품사를 전환하는 것.

creaky voice: 협착음.

deletion: 음운 탈락 현상.

demarcative stress: 단어나 상위 음성 결합체의 경계를 표시하는 스트레스.

devoicing: <유성음을> 무성음화.

diacritic [ˌdaɪ.əˈkʰɹɪtɪk]: 발음 구별 부호.

digraph [ˈdaɪˌɡɹæf]: 한 소리를 나타내는 두 글자, 이중음자 æ, œ, 등.

diphthong [ˈdɪfθɔŋ]: 이중 모음, 복모음 [aɪ, aʊ] 등.

dissimilation: 이화; 이웃한 소리와 달라지는 현상, 예를 들면 *sol-ar* vs. *flor-al.* Cf. assimilation.

egressive air [iˈɡɹɛsɪv ɛɹ]: 구강 밖으로 움직이는 공기의 흐름.

epenthesis [əˈpɛnθəsɪs]: 음운 삽입 현상, 예를 들면 English *spoon* vs. Korean 스푼.

falling tone: 하강 성조.

fortis: [ˈfɔrtəs]: 경음《ㄸ, ㅃ, ㄲ 등》. Cf. lenis.

fricative: 마찰음; 조음 기관의 거리가 좁아짐으로써 상당한 공기의 마찰을 통해 형성되는 자음.

function word: 기능어; 전치사, 관사, 대명사 등 문법적 관계를 나타내는 단어.

fundamental frequency: 기본 주파수; complex sound wave 의 최저 주파수.

gemination [ˌdʒɛmɪˈneɪʃən]: 쌍자음; 장자음.

glide: 전이음; 반모음 [j, w]. Cf. semivowel.

glottis: 성문; 폐에서 나온 공기가 통과하는 성대의 열린 공간.

hard palate: 경구개; 입천장의 딱딱한 부분.

heavy syllable: stress 를 유도하는 음절로서 장모음, 이중모음 또는 (언어에 따라서) 자음이 수반된 단모음이 이를 형성하는 데 기여함.

ingressive air: 구강 안으로 움직이는 공기의 흐름.

intonation: (소리의) 억양; 어조. Cf. stress.

labialization: 순음화; 일반적으로 이웃한 순음의 영향으로 조음시 입술의 움직임이 동반되는 현상.

language universals: 세계 언어들이 가지고 있는 보편적인 성질.

larynx [ˈlæɹɪŋks], **pl.** ***larynges*** [ləˈɹɪnˌʤiːz]: 후두, 소리상자라고도 불리며, 성대가 위치하고 있음.

lateral: 설측음, /l/ 과 같이 혀의 양쪽으로 공기가 지날 수 있는 공간을 만들며 형성되는 소리.

lax: 이완(음). Cf. tense.

lenis [ˈleɪnɪs]: 상대적으로 약한 구강 근육의 움직임과 공기의 저항으로 만들어지는 소리 (자음). Cf. fortis.

light syllable: 음절 말이 단모음으로 끝나는 음절로서 stress 를 유도하지 못함.

liquid: 유음; [l],[ɹ].

manner of articulation: 개개의 발화 음이 만들어지는 방식; 공기가 완전히 차단되어 저항을 받는 지 마찰을 받는 지 등.

metathesis [məˈtæθəsɪs]: 음위 전환; 단어 내 소리의 위치가 바뀌는 현상 [보기: aks > ask].

minimal word: 음운학적으로 가장 작은 단어.

monophthong [ˈmɑnəfˌθɔŋ]: 단모음. Cf. diphthong.

morpheme: 형태소; 뜻을 가진 최소의 언어단위.

morphophonemic: 두 형태소가 인접할 때 발생하는 음변화를 가리킴.

nasalization: 비음화; 음이 이웃한 비음과 닮아가는 현상.

naturalness: 유형학적으로 보편적인 성질.

neutral suffix: 단어 내 stress 위치 변화를 초래하지 않는 접미사.

neutral vowel: 모음 조화 제약을 받지 않는 모음.

non-neutral suffix: 단어 내 stress 위치 변화를 초래하는 접미사.

nucleus: 음절 핵; 음절의 중심을 이루는 음.

obstruent: 폐쇄성을 가진 소리의, 혹은 그 소리들.

off-glide: 이중모음의 두 번째 요소가 약한 경우.

on-glide: 이중모음의 첫 번째 요소가 약한 경우.

onset: 초성; 같은 음절 내 핵 앞에 나타나는 자음 혹은 자음 군.

palatalization: 구개음화; 음이 이웃한 구개음과 조음 위치상 닮아가는 현상.

palate [ˈpælət]: 경구개; 입천장의 딱딱한 부분.

peak: 음파의 정점.

penultimate: 어말로부터 두 번째의 (음절).

pharynx [ˈfæɹɪŋks], **pl.** ***pharynges*** [fəˈɹɪndʒiːz]: 인두.

phoneme: 음소; 대체되면 단어의 의미 변화를 일으키는 음성상의 최소 단위.

phonemic transcription: 대립을 일으키는 소리만을 표기.

phonetics: 음성학; 소리가 만들어지는 원리, 소리의 물리적 성질, 청자의 인지과정을 연구하는 학문.

pitch: 음조; 소리의 고저.

pitch accent: 일본어·중국어 등의 고저 악센트.

place of articulation: 성대부터 구, 비강에 이르기 까지 소리가 만들어지는 부분.

plosive: 파열음. [p], [t], [k], 등. Cf. stop.

prosody [ˈprɑsədi]: 운율학, 소리의 고저 (pitch), 조절 (timing), 리듬, 크기 등을 다루는 학문.

prothesis [ˈpʰɹɔθəsɪs], **pl.** ***protheses*** [ˈpʰɹɔθəˌsiːz]: 첨두음, splash, squeeze의 s등.

pulmonic airstream: 폐로부터의 공기 흐름.

resonant: 소리의 공명도가 높은, 공명성이 높은 소리.

rhotic [ˈɹoʊɾɪk]: 음절 끝이나 자음 앞에서 발음되는 r.

segment: 분절음.

semivowel: 반모음; 자음과 모음의 성질을 모두 가진 소리. [j], [w] 등.

soft palate/velum [ˈviːləm]: 입천장 뒷 부분의 부드러운 부분, 연구개.

sonorant: 공명음; 공기의 진동성이 높은 소리.

sonority: (소리의) 들림, 진동 (정도).

spectrogram: 소리의 물리적 성질을 나타낸 사진.

spirantization: 마찰음화.

stop: 폐지음; 구강 내 공기의 차단과 방출로 만들어지는 자음. Cf. plosive.

stress: 강세, 악센트. Cf. accent, intonation.

strident: 소리의 마찰성이 강한 (음).

suprasegmental features: 초분절음소, stress, pitch, tone 등.

syllabicity: 성절성; 음절핵을 형성할 수 있는 자질.

syllable: 음절; 필수적인 요소인 핵을 중심으로 전후에 자음이 올 수 있음.

syllable boundary: 음절간의 경계.

syntactic category: 통사적 범주, 품사.

tense: 경음; 조음 기관들의 상대적으로 더 강한 움직임이 수반되는 소리.

tensification: 경음화, 예를 들면 한국어 십구->십꾸.

tone: 음조; 성조; 음의 높고 낮음.

tone language: tone이 단어의 의미에 영향을 주는 언어들. 중국어, 아프리카 언어들.

trough: 음파의 가장 낮은 지점.

typology: 유형학; 언어의 음운적, 형태적, 통사적 유형에 따라 언어를 구분하는 학문.

underspecification: 잠재 표기; 예측 가능한 혹은 잉여적인 요소를 기저형에서 표기하지 않는 것.

velarization: 연구개음화; 조음되는 과정에서 혀의 뒷 부분이 연구개로 상승되는 현상.

vocal cords = vocal folds: 성대; 폐에서 나온 공기 에너지가 첫 번째로 변형되는 곳으로서 후두, 즉 소리 박스 내에 위치함.

vocal tract: 폐에서 나온 공기 에너지가 지나 가는 경로.

vowel harmony: 단어 내에서 같은 집단에 속하는 모음끼리 나타나는 현상, 모음조화.

vowel reduction: 모음 약화.

waveform: 음파; 파형; 소리를 형성하는 공기 에너지가 움직이는 양상을 나타낸 것으로서 파도의 형태를 이룸.

Bibliography

Abercrombie, D. (1967). *Elements of General Phonetics.* Edinburgh: Edinburgh University Press.

Allen, M. R. (1978). *Morphological Investigations.* PhD thesis, University of Connecticut.

Alwan, A. A.-H. (1986). Acoustic and perceptual correlates of pharyngeal and uvular consonants. Master's thesis, Massachusetts Institute of Technology.

Back, G., Nadig, S., Uppal, S., & Coatesworth, A. (2004). Why do we have a uvula? Literature review and a new theory. *Clinical Otolaryngology & Allied Sciences*, 29(6), 689–693.

Bagemihl, B. (1988). *Alternate Phonologies and Morphologies.* PhD thesis, University of British Columbia.

Baldwin, J. R. & French, P. (1990). *Forensic Phonetics.* London: Pinter Pub Ltd.

Bell, A. M. (1867). *Visible Speech: The science of universal alphabetics.* London: Simpkin, Marshall & Co.

Bell, A. M. (1882). *Sounds and their relations: A complete manual of universal alphabetics.* London: Trubner.

Bolinger, D. (1958). A theory of pitch accent in English. *Word*, 14, 109–149.

Bolinger, D. (1986). *Intonation and its Parts: Melody in spoken English.* Stanford, CA: Stanford University Press.

Butcher, A. (2004). 'fortis/lenis' revisited one more time: The aerodynamics of some oral stop contrasts in three continents. *Clinical Linguistics & Phonetics*, 18(6-8), 547–557.

Catford, J. C. (1988). *A Practical Introduction to Phonetics.* Oxford: Clarendon Press.

Catford, J. C. (1990). Glottal consonants ... another view. *Journal of the International Phonetic Association*, 20(02), 25–26.

Chiba, T. & Kajiyama, M. (1941). *The Vowel: Its nature and structure.* Tokyo: Tokyo-Kaiseikan Publishing Co.

Cho, T., Jun, S.-A., & Ladefoged, P. (2002). Acoustic and aerodynamic correlates of korean stops and fricatives. *Journal of Phonetics*, 30(2), 193–228.

Cho, T. & Ladefoged, P. (1999). Variation and universals in VOT: Evidence from 18 languages. *Journal of Phonetics*, 27(2), 207–229.

Chung, Y.-H. (2006). Loanword phonology and learnability: A case from North Kyungsang Korean. *Studies in Phonetics, Phonology and Morphology*, 3, 687–698.

Clark, J. E., Yallop, C., & Fletcher, J. (2007). *An introduction to phonetics and phonology.* Wiley-Blackwell.

Clements, G. N. & Osu, S. (2002). Explosives, implosives and nonexplosives: The linguistic function of air pressure differences in stops. *Laboratory Phonology* 7, 1.

Crystal, D. (1969). *Prosodic Systems and Intonation.* Cambridge, UK: Cambridgc Univerity Press.

Dalston, R. M. (1975). Acoustic characteristics of English /w, r, l/ spoken correctly by young children and adults. *The Journal of the Acoustical Society of America*, 57, 462–469.

Damico, J. S., Müller, N., & Ball, M. J. (2010). *The Handbook of Language and Speech Disorders.* Wiley-Blackwell, 1st edition.

Delattre, P. C., Liberman, A. M., & Cooper, F. (1962). Formant transitions and loci as acoustic correlates of place of articulation in american fricatives. *Studia Linguistica*, 16(1–2), 104–122.

Dell, F. & Elmedlaoui, M. (1985). Syllabic consonants and syllabification in Imdlawn Tashlhiyt Berber. *Journal of African Languages and Linguistics*, 7, 105–130.

Dell, F. & Elmedlaoui, M. (1988). Syllabic consonants in Berber: Some new evidence. *Journal of African Languages and Linguistics*, 10, 1–17.

Dutoit, T. (2001). *An Introduction to Text-to-Speech Synthesis*, volume 3. Dordrecht, Holland: Kluwer Academic Press.

Ewen, C. (1995). Dependency relations in phonology. In J. A. Goldsmith (Ed.), *The Handbook of Phonological Theory* (pp. 570–585). Cambridge, Mass., and Oxford, UK: Blackwell.

Firth, J. R. (1948). Sounds and prosodies. *Transactions of the Philological Society*, (pp. 127–152). Also in Prosodic Analysis (pp. 1-26), ed. F. R. Palmer. Oxford:

Oxford University Press, 1970.

Fromkin, V., Rodman, R., & Hyams, N. (2006). *An Introduction to Language.* Orlando, FL: Harcourt Brace, 8th edition.

Gavarret, J. (1877). *Acoustique biologique: Phénomènes physiques de la phonation et de l'audition.* Paris: G. Masson – Librairie de l'Académie de Médecine.

Gick, B. (1999). A gesture-based account of intrusive consonants in English. *Phonology,* 16(1), 29–54.

Gick, B. (2002a). The American intrusive l. *American Speech,* 77(2), 167.

Gick, B. (2002b). The use of ultrasound for linguistic phonetic fieldwork. *Journal of the International Phonetic Association,* 32(02), 113–121.

Gordon, M. (2003). Collecting phonetic data on endangered languages. In *Proceedings of the 15th International Congress of Phonetic Sciences* (pp. 207–210).

Gray, H. (1918). *Anatomy of the Human Body.* Philadelphia, PA & New York, NY: Lea & Febiger, 20th edition.

Hall, W. S. (1911). *Elementary Anatomy, Physiology and Hygiene.* New York: American Book Company.

Hammond, M. (1999). *The Phonology of English: A prosodic Optimality-Theoretic approach.* Oxford: Oxford University Press.

Haraguchi, S. (1988). Pitch accent and intonation in Japanese. In H. van der Hulst & N. Smith (Eds.), *Autosegmental Studies on Pitch Accent* (pp. 123–50). Dordrecht: Foris Publications.

Henton, C., Ladefoged, P., & Maddieson, I. (1992). Stops in the world's languages. *Phonetica,* 49(2), 65–101.

Himmelmann, N. P. (2006). Prosody in language documentation. In *Essentials of Language Documentation* (pp. 163–182). Berlin: Walter de Gruyter.

Hollien, H. (1990). *The Acoustics of Crime: The new science of forensic phonetics.* Springer, 1st edition.

Hollien, H. (2001). *Forensic Voice Identification.* Academic Press, 1st edition.

International Phonetic Association (1999). *Handbook of the International Phonetic Association: A guide to the use of the International Phonetic Alphabet.* Cambridge, UK: Cambridge University Press.

Johnson, K. (2003). *Acoustic and Auditory Phonetics.* Cambridge, MA: Wiley-Blackwell, 2nd edition.

Johnson, K., Ladefoged, P., & Lindau, M. (1993). Individual differences in vowel production. *The Journal of the Acoustical Society of America,* 94(2), 701–714.

Jones, D. (1914). *The Pronunciation of English.* Cambridge: Cambridge University

Press, 2nd edition.

Jones, D. (1917). *An English Pronouncing Dictionary.* London: Dent.

Jones, D. (1918). *An Outline of English Phonetics.* Cambridge: W. Heffer & Sons.

Jurafsky, D. & Martin, J. H. (2008). *Speech and Language Processing.* New Brunswick, NJ: Prentice Hall, 2nd edition.

Kaye, J. (1989). *Phonology: A cognitive view.* Hillsdale, NJ: Lawrence Erlbaum Associates.

Kean, M. L. (1972). *Are glottal stop and h sonorants?* Quarterly Progress Report 108, Massachusetts Institute of Technology, Boston, MA.

Kim, E.-S. (2003). *Theoretical issues in Nuu-chah-nulth phonology and morphology.* PhD thesis, University of British Columbia, Vancouver, BC.

Kim, M.-D. (2004). Correlation between VOT and F_0 in the perception of Korean stops and affricates. In *Eighth International Conference on Spoken Language Processing (INTERSPEECH 2004)* Jeju, Korea.

Kim, M.-R., Beddor, P. S., & Horrocks, J. (2002). The contribution of consonantal and vocalic information to the perception of Korean initial stops. *Journal of Phonetics*, 30(1), 77–100.

Kiparsky, P. (1982). Lexical phonology and morphology. In I.-S. Yang (Ed.), *Linguistics in the Morning Calm*, volume 2 (pp. 3–91). Seoul: Hanshin.

Koenig, W., Dunn, H., & Lacy, L. (1946). The sound spectrograph. *Acoustical Society of America Journal*, 18(1), 19–49.

Kurowski, K. & Blumstein, S. E. (1987). Acoustic properties for place of articulation in nasal consonants. *The Journal of the Acoustical Society of America*, 81(6), 1917–1927.

Labov, W., Ash, S., & Boberg, C. (2006). *The Atlas of North American English: Phonetics, phonology, and sound change: a multimedia reference tool.* Berlin: Walter De Gruyter, Inc.

Ladd, D. R. (1996). *Intonational Phonology.* Cambridge, UK: Cambridge University Press.

Ladd, D. R. & Himmelmann, N. P. (2008). Prosodic Description: An introduction for fieldworkers. *Language Documentatlon & Conservation*, 2(2), 244–274.

Ladefoged, P. (1996). *Elements of Acoustic Phonetics.* Chicago: University of Chicago Press, 2nd edition.

Ladefoged, P. (1997). Instrumental techniques for linguistic phonetic fieldwork. *The Handbook of Phonetic Sciences*, (pp. 137–166).

Ladefoged, P. (2003). *Phonetic Data Analysis: An introduction to fieldwork and instrumental techniques.* Oxford: Wiley-Blackwell.

Ladefoged, P. (2005). *Vowels and Consonants: An introduction to the sounds of languages.* Oxford: Blackwell Publishing.

Ladefoged, P. & Johnson, K. (2010). *A Course in Phonetics.* Belmont, CA: Wadsworth Publishing, 6th edition.

Ladefoged, P. & Maddieson, I. (1990). Vowels of the world's languages. *Journal of Phonetics*, 18, 93–122.

Ladefoged, P. & Maddieson, I. (1996). *The Sounds of the World's Languages.* Oxford: Blackwell.

Lieberman, P. & Blumstein, S. E. (1988). *Speech Physiology, Speech Perception, and Acoustic Phonetics.* Cambridge: University of Cambridge Press.

Lindau, M. (1978). Vowel features. *Language*, 54, 541–563.

Lindblom, B. (1986). Phonetic universals in vowel systems. In J. J. Ohala & J. J. Jaeger (Eds.), *Experimental Phonology* (pp. 13–44). Orlando, FL: Academic Press.

Lindblom, B. & Maddieson, I. (1988). Phonetic universals in consonant systems. In *Language, Speech and Mind: Studies in honour of Victoria A. Fromkin* (pp. 62–78). New York: Routledge.

Maddieson, I. (1984). *Patterns of Sounds.* Cambridge: Cambridge University Press.

Maddieson, I. (2001). Phonetic fieldwork. In *Linguistic Fieldwork* (pp. 211–229). Cambridge: Cambridge University Press.

Marchand, H. (1960). *The Categories and Types of Present-day English Word-formation: A Synchronic-diachronic Approach.* Wiesbaden: Otto Harrassowitz.

Mariotte, E. (1673). *Traité de la percussion ou chocq des corps dans lequel les principales regles du mouvement, contraires à celles que Mr. Descartes, & quelques autres modernes ont voulu establir, sont demonstrées par leurs veritables causes.* Paris: E. Michallet.

Minifie, F. D. (1994). *Introduction to Communication Science and Disorders.* Singular, 1st edition.

Minifie, F. D., Hixon, T. J., Williams, F., & Broad, D. J. (1973). *Normal Aspects of Speech, Hearing, and Language.* New York: Prentice-Hall.

Minkova, D. (2004). Philology, linguistics, and the history of [hw]~[w]. In A. Curzan & K. Emmons (Eds.), *Studies in the History of the English Language II: Unfolding conversations*, volume 2 (pp. 7–46). Berlin: Walter de Gruyter.

Nearey, T. M. (1977). *Phonetic feature systems for vowels.* PhD thesis, University of Connecticut.

Nolan, F. (1991). Forensic Phonetics. *Journal of Linguistics*, 27(02), 483–493.

Ogden, R. (2009). *An Introduction to English Phonetics.* Edinburgh Textbooks on the English Language. Edinburgh: Edinburgh University Press.

Passy, P. (1888). Our revised alphabet. *The Phonetic Teacher*, (pp. 57–60).

Perkins, W. H. & Kent, R. D. (1991). *Functional Anatomy of Speech, Language, and Hearing: A primer.* Boston: Allyn & Bacon.

Peterson, G. E. (1951). The phonetic value of vowels. *Language*, 27(4), 541–553.

Peterson, G. E. & Barney, H. L. (1952). Control methods used in a study of the vowels. *The Journal of the Acoustical Society of America*, 24, 175–184.

Pullum, G. K. & Ladusaw, W. A. (1986). *Phonetic Symbol Guide.* Chicago: University of Chicago Press.

Pullum, G. K. & Ladusaw, W. A. (1996). *Phonetic Symbol Guide.* Chicago: University Of Chicago Press, 2nd edition.

Påhlsson, C. (1972). *The Northumbrian Burr: A sociolinguistic study.* Lund: CWK Gleerup.

Rose, P. (2002). *Forensic Speaker Identification.* CRC Press, 1st edition.

Saeed, J. (1993). *Somali Reference Grammar.* Kensington, MD: Dunwoody Press, 2nd edition.

Schwartz, J.-L., Boë, L.-J., Vallée, N., & Abry, C. (1997). Major trends in vowel system inventories. *Journal of Phonetics*, 25(3), 233–253.

Seikel, J. A., King, D. W., & Drumright, D. G. (2009). *Anatomy and Physiology for Speech, Language, and Hearing.* Stamford, Conn.: Delmar Cengage Learning, 4th edition.

Shaw, G. B. (1914). *Pygmalion: A play in five acts.* London: Constable and Co. Ltd.

Shaw, G. B. (1962). *Androcles and the Lion [Printed in the Shaw Alphabet with a Parallel Transcription in Traditional Orthography].* Middlesex, England: Penguin Books.

Stevens, K. N. (1998). *Acoustic Phonetics.* Cambridge: MIT Press.

Stevens, K. N. & Blumstein, S. E. (1978). Invariant cues for place of articulation in stop consonants. *The Journal of the Acoustical Society of America*, 64(5), 1358–1368.

Stonham, J. (1999). *Aspects of Tsishaath Nootka Phonetics and Phonology.* Munich: Lincom Europa.

Sweet, H. (1880). Sound notation. *Transactions of the Philological Society*, (pp. 177–235).

Taylor, P. (2009). *Text-to-Speech Synthesis*. Cambridge: Cambridge University Press.

Van Riper, C. & Erickson, R. L. (1996). *Speech Correction: An introduction to speech pathology and audiology*. Boston: Allyn and Bacon.

von Helmholtz, H. & Ellis (tr.), A. J. (1912). *On the Sensations of Tone as a Physiological Basis for the Theory of Music*. London: Longmans, Green & Co., 4th edition.

Wells, J. C. (1982). *Accents of English: The British Isles*, volume 2. Cambridge: Cambridge University Press.

Whalen, D. H. & Levitt, A. G. (1995). The universality of intrinsic F_0 of vowels. *Journal of Phonetics*, 23(3), 349–366.

Wood, S. (1979). A radiographic analysis of constriction locations for vowels. *Journal of Phonetics*, 7(2), 25–43.

Yoshida, K. (2008). Phonetic implementation of Korean "denasalization" and its variation related to prosody. *Indiana University Linguistics Club Working Papers (IULCWP)*, 8, 1–23.

Zemlin, W. R. (1997). *Speech and Hearing Science: Anatomy and physiology*. Boston: Allyn & Bacon, 4th edition.

Zhou, X., Espy-Wilson, C. Y., Boyce, S., Tiede, M., Holland, C., & Choe, A. (2008). A magnetic resonance imaging-based articulatory and acoustic study of "retroflex" and "bunched" American English /r/. *The Journal of the Acoustical Society of America*, 123(6), 4466–4481.

Zhou, X., Espy-Wilson, C. Y., Tiede, M., & Boyce, S. (2007). An articulatory and acoustic study of "retroflex" and "bunched" American English rhotic sound based on MRI. In *INTERSPEECH 2007* (pp. 54–57). Antwerp, Belgium.

Zue, V. W. (1976). *Acoustic characteristics of stop consonants: A controlled study*. PhD thesis, Massachusetts Institute of Technology.

Index

Typos and other corrections

* The following list provides corrections to the text.

Page and Line/Ex. No.	Correction
56, 4 lines from bottom	Insert “that” between “Modern Korean” and “may be reintroduced”.
95, line 8	“kayageum” should be italicized.
105, line 3	Insert “indicated” between “turbulence” and “by”.
235, 7 lines from bottom	“penultimate” should be “antepenultimate”.